P9-DFC-910

SUSAN
SONTAG

SUSAN SONTAG

A BIOGRAPHY

DANIEL SCHREIBER

Translated from the German by
David Dollenmayer

NORTHWESTERN UNIVERSITY PRESS
EVANSTON, ILLINOIS

Northwestern University Press
www.nupress.northwestern.edu

English translation © 2014 by David Dollenmayer. Published 2014 by
Northwestern University Press. Originally published in German in 2007
under the title *Susan Sontag: Geist und Glamour*. Copyright © 2007 by
Aufbau-Verlagsgruppe GmbH, Berlin.

Printed in the United States of America

10 9 8 7 6 5 4 3 2 1

Library of Congress Cataloging-in-Publication Data

Schreiber, Daniel, 1977– author.
     [Susan Sontag. English]
     Susan Sontag : a biography / Daniel Schreiber ; translated from the
German by David Dollenmayer.
        pages cm
     "Originally published in German in 2007 under the title Susan Sontag:
Geist und Glamour."
     Includes bibliographical references.
     ISBN 978-0-8101-2583-4 (cloth : alk. paper)
     1. Sontag, Susan, 1933–2004. 2. Women authors, American—20th
century—Biography. 3. Authors, American—20th century—Biography.
4. Motion picture producers and directors—Biography. 5. Critics—
Biography. I. Title.
PS3569.O6547Z87913 2014
818.5409—dc23
                                                          2014001065

CONTENTS

Recently I spent an afternoon with a writer friend of mine who is working on his own biography of Susan Sontag. One of the first questions he asked me was whether I had had similarly ambivalent feelings about her when I started writing my book, in the wake of her death in December 2004. He was not the first person to ask me that.

On the contrary. To this day I hear from people who had met Sontag or knew her well about how difficult it was to get along with her. Few writers have commanded so much adoration for their work, and few have occasioned so much private disappointment and bitterness. She could be warm-hearted, crazy in a good way, and the best of confidantes. But she also had a tendency toward self-aggrandizement, and could be egomaniacal and at times downright cruel. Even if these qualities contributed to the brilliance and incisive clarity of her writing, they made for considerable misfortune in her personal life.

I began this book more or less by accident. I was living in Brooklyn at the time and had just decided to end my academic career, because to continue it would have meant returning to Germany, something I did not feel equipped to do. Sontag's essays had always been very important for me—a glimpse of hope, a life-line. Here was another model for writing, I had always felt. Here was another way to think about issues—intellectual but not academic. Even the essays I disagreed with I found inspiring. After the controversy triggered by her harsh words in the *New Yorker* regarding the 9/11 attacks, I saw her for the first time at a round-table at New York University. I could not help but be impressed by her, but I did not share her opinions; like everyone else I was too traumatized by the events that were overwhelming the city, where I had moved only a short while before. Yet, I valued the fact that she introduced a dissenting voice in a public discussion that was otherwise keyed to the inevitability of war. The uniformity of this discussion reminded me of nothing so much as the public debates in the East Germany of my childhood.

Sontag's death in December 2004 moved me quite deeply. I immersed myself in her fascinating life and wrote a long (and in Germany widely read) obituary for her. This was the starting point for my work on this biography. From the beginning I had intended it to be a small book, a portrait, one focused more on Susan Sontag the public figure. It was to be the history of an eminently intellectual life, a thoroughly cosmopolitan career, the story of someone who had singlehandedly imbued the American life of the mind with a certain kind of glamour. It would also be the first book to take account of Sontag's entire life. The only existing biography—Lisa Paddock's and Carl Rollyson's *Susan Sontag: The Making of an Icon*—had made an important contribution in research, but it was rather tendentious in places and left out the last decade of Sontag's life.

The three years during which I worked on this book were wonderful, but also difficult. Wonderful because I had the chance to immerse myself in almost everything Sontag had ever written or said. Wonderful, too, because I was able to meet and speak with some of the most fascinating people I have ever met. Lucinda Childs, for instance, or Marina Abramović, or Nadine Gordimer. Or the great Elizabeth Hardwick, who unfortunately has since passed away. Those years were difficult, too, however, because it quickly became clear that certain doors would not be opened to me. Some people important to Sontag, such as Annie Leibovitz, were not yet ready to talk. And David Rieff, Sontag's son and the executor of her estate, whom I was able to meet for an illuminating if slightly awkward afternoon, made clear that I would not have access to her diaries until they had been published. Difficult also because Sontag's character made it impossible for me to adopt the tone of unbridled admiration authors of literary biographies usually adopt. If I learned anything while writing this book, it was to accept ambivalence. To accept that every one of us has the potential to be both a bad and a good person at the same time, without even necessarily being aware of it.

My biography turned out to be a big success in Germany, by which I was happily surprised. Two volumes of Sontag's diaries have since been published, as well as two memoirs in which she plays a pivotal role: David Rieff's *Swimming in a Sea of Death* and Sigrid Nunez's *Sempre Susan*. I read these books with great fervor, naturally, though always wondering somewhere in the back of my mind whether I would have written my biography any differently had I read them before. And to my great surprise I discovered that I would not have. The Sontag in these private accounts was very consistent with the more public one I had gotten to know through my work. There might always have been a "good Susan" and a "bad Susan," as Salman Rushdie once put it, but the private and the public Susan Sontag were largely the same. The image she created of herself was too compelling. Even she succumbed to it. Of course, even Susan Sontag could not always be Susan Sontag. But she always felt the need to be.

No doubt I would have added more details to this or that passage, or put more emphasis on particular issues, clarified more dishonesties. We now know, for instance, that Sontag was a sixteen-year-old college student—in itself amazing enough—when she met the great hero of her youth, Thomas Mann, and not a fourteen-year-old high-school student, as she always claimed. Today I also would place more importance on the fact that she was addicted to amphetamines from 1964 to 1980. I would connect that fact with her mother's alcoholism and with the long catalog of her own often deeply unhappy relationships.

But mostly, this book and its themes would stay the same. I also suspect I would have no say in the matter. I didn't have when I wrote it. For this was one of those books that felt like it wrote itself. Or that it was written by life. By a life, to be precise—by one of the most gripping and inspiring lives one can imagine.

D.S.
Berlin, February 2014
Translated by Bill Martin

On January 17, 2005, a small group of artists, authors, and editors from around the world braved a fine drizzle to gather at the Montparnasse Cemetery in Paris and bury Susan Sontag. The writer Salman Rushdie was there, as was the actor Isabelle Huppert. So were the playwright and stage director Robert Wilson, the singer Patti Smith, Sontag's German publisher Michael Krüger, and the photographer Annie Leibovitz. David Rieff had chosen his mother's final resting place, and his Paris friends helped organize the funeral. Huppert recited "*Je t'aime, ô capitale infâme*!" (I love you, oh infamous capital!) from Charles Baudelaire's epilogue to *Les fleurs du mal*, a reference to Sontag's sometimes problematic relationship with the French capital that had become her second home, after New York. In place of eulogies, excerpts by Sontag's heroes Roland Barthes and Emil Cioran—their graves only a stone's throw away—were read. The participants also read passages from Sontag's own works, an oeuvre that at her death comprised nine celebrated collections of essays, four controversial novels, two largely unknown film scripts, and a relatively obscure play.[1] Translations of her works had appeared in thirty-two languages. The symbolic significance of this funeral seemed obvious. The author was being laid to rest in that world of the intellect she had longed to be a part of since her earliest childhood in the bleak desert landscape of Arizona. Not far from the graves of Samuel Beckett, Jean-Paul Sartre, and Simone de Beauvoir, Sontag was buried where devotees of postwar intellectual life could now also visit her grave.

Europeans will recall seeing footage of Sontag, the sage essayist and critic of America, receiving the Peace Prize of the German Book Trade in 2003. Eulogies from the German press,

such as those of Lothar Müller in the *Süddeutsche Zeitung* and
Henning Ritter in the *Frankfurter Allgemeine Zeitung,* recalled
Sontag's occasionally somewhat theatrical "aura of dissidence"[2]
and her role as "critical admonisher" and "moral authority."[3] In
the same vein, they also stressed Sontag's cultural criticism while
relegating her literary works and media stardom to the sidelines.

In America, however, the news of Sontag's death shared equal
billing in the headlines with reports of a disastrous tsunami in
Southeast Asia. Typical of American feelings toward Sontag was
the brilliant obituary in the *New York Times.* For four decades,
it said, Sontag's work had been ". . . part of the contemporary canon, discussed everywhere from graduate seminars to
the pages of popular magazines to the Hollywood movie 'Bull
Durham.' "[4] Superlatives abounded: not only was she "one of
the most lionized presences—and one of the most polarizing—in
20th-century letters," but "her image" had become "an instantly
recognizable artifact of 20th-century popular culture."[5] Another
indication that Sontag was mourned on a different scale in her
native land was the memorial held in New York City on March
30, 2005. Five hundred friends, companions, and acquaintances
gathered in Carnegie Hall to hear the Brentano String Quartet
play Ludwig van Beethoven's Quartet No. 15. The legendary
Mitsuko Uchida played Arnold Schoenberg's *Six Little Piano
Pieces* and Beethoven's Sonata No. 32. The attendees received
a memorial volume containing a collection of photographs of
Sontag, who remained strikingly beautiful into advanced age.
More than mere documents of an active life, the photos by Andy
Warhol, Henri Cartier-Bresson, Robert Mapplethorpe, Annie
Leibovitz, Peter Hujar, Jill Krementz, Richard Avedon, and
Thomas Victor illustrated the impressive bildungsroman that
constituted Sontag's biography and her various and passionately adopted roles in public life: avant-garde critic, arrestee at a
demonstration against the Vietnam War, political radical, earnest
filmmaker in Sweden, intellectual who looked youthful in defi-
ance of advancing age, and *engagée* novelist with a penchant for
romantic artists. In place of a gravestone, the assembled pictures

were the monument Susan Sontag had bequeathed to the media memory of Western culture, a culture of which she had become an indispensable part.

SUSAN
SONTAG

Memories of a
So-Called Childhood

(1933–1944)

*The distance from my origins
is exactly what I like. There is
nothing I could return to.*

Susan Sontag, in a 1987 interview

Memories are fragile things, especially memories of childhood.[1]
It is not just the lack of informative value in the bare facts of
who, what, when, and where that fade the further removed we
are from them. It is the essence of every childhood that early
life always exists as nothing but a collection of memories of
uncertain status. We live through the interval between the ages
of three and twelve without being particularly aware of it. Some
afternoons seem to stretch out forever. In times of great exuber-
ance, deep self-absorption, or abject humiliation, a day can seem
like an eternity. Every memory is only an approximation of the
actual event.

Each recollection is shaped by the stories of parents, siblings,
and relatives or takes the form of a photograph. Memories get
revalued in the light of present events or reinterpreted in psycho-
therapy. Sometimes we cannot even be sure we have not simply

invented them on impulse. Our memories are selective. We cut them to fit particular moments, messages, or images. And when we reveal them to others, we do it in the service of the deceptive process of self-fashioning—whether we mean to or not.

Surprisingly, the childhood memories of Sontag herself—who analyzed the mechanisms of memory with such rigorous acuity in *On Photography* (1977) and *Where the Stress Falls* (2001)—are a particularly tricky terrain. Certain scenes stand out in Sontag's remarks about her childhood, carefully illuminated vignettes that sometimes seem to be taken from the slightly yellowed photo album of a precocious young girl passionately in love with books.

Her whole life long, Sontag kept carefully guarded both her public image and her private sphere. It is difficult to see past the representations of her childhood that Sontag herself sketched out. Only the inconsistencies that crept into her statements about those early years and the episodes she later revealed to friends open up a wider view into the life of an isolated and exceptionally gifted girl neglected by a widowed and emotionally unapproachable mother with a drinking problem.

Not until Sontag was forty—and then at greater length after she turned sixty—did the writer make public carefully redacted portions of her childhood. At the center of her autobiographical story "Project for a Trip to China" (1973) is her search for the father who had died in that faraway place when Susan was only five and a fascination for the Far East, which remained indissolubly associated with him. "Pilgrimage" (1987), on the other hand, tells the story of her audience with the exiled Thomas Mann in Pacific Palisades and sounds like a confession. Sontag's son, David Rieff, a journalist who has reported on conflicts in the former Yugoslavia, Iraq, and South America, vouches for the authenticity of the details in both stories.[2]

Beginning in the 1990s, Sontag was more willing to expand upon the scattered remarks she had made about her childhood and family in the 1970s and 1980s. She welcomed interviewers into her sunny apartment in the Chelsea neighborhood of New

York City and seemed to feel comfortable in the role of sitter for a portrait. There she gave free rein to her recollections, even when she would occasionally tear up at unwelcome emotions.

Susan Lee Rosenblatt was born January 16, 1933, in Woman's Hospital in Manhattan because her mother, Mildred, feared giving birth in Asia. Sontag's father, Jack Rosenblatt, was the owner of the Kung Chen Fur Corporation in the Chinese city of Tianjin (then usually spelled Tientsin). Mildred seems to have been a typical colonial wife who would occasionally also work in the business. The Rosenblatts were a young and extremely prosperous couple possessed of a typical American entrepreneurial spirit. Mildred remained in New York for a brief time after Susan's birth, but she soon returned to Tianjin and left the baby (as she later also left Susan's younger sister Judith) in the care of an Irish-American nanny named Rose McNulty (or Rosie, as Susan would later call her). At first the improvised family of nanny and baby lived with Susan's paternal grandparents and later with other relatives until her parents finally purchased a house of their own in Great Neck, Long Island.

In "Project for a Trip to China," Susan recalled her parents' living room in Great Neck. It was decorated with Chinese elephants of ivory and rose quartz and with rice-paper scrolls. She also remembered a Chinese birthday present from those days: a bracelet of green jade so expensive she never dared to wear it.

But above all, the souvenir objects her parents brought back from China reminded Susan of their Chinese house, the house she would never see. As she grew up, this exclusion from the life of her father and mother was a deeply painful experience, as Sontag herself says in the retrospective story. Her parents would spend only a few months in New York before returning to China to resume "playing Great Gatsby and Daisy inside the British Concession," as she sarcastically put it.[3]

Traumatic experiences are typically suppressed for a long time, while their potential to cause psychic pain constantly increases. Often, the further back they lie, the stronger the urge to talk about them. Like the childhood memories of many older people, Susan Sontag's recollections are characterized not just by sentimental nostalgia, humorous reminiscences, and occasional mythic overtones. Often an unusually bitter tone creeps in, and sometimes real anger. And those are probably more appropriate emotions for the phase of her life she described as "my unconvincing childhood."[4] There are many indications that, for the highly sensitive child, the regularly recurring abandonment diminished her sense of self-worth. Some memories Sontag wrote down and talked about cast a melancholy light on these wounds. She told of the child's burning desire to travel to China with her parents. When she was still just a little girl, the assiduous Susan learned to eat with chopsticks to be more "Chinese" and thus earn the right to be taken along to the exotic land of China. Even in her fifties, she could still recall with a certain pride that foreign friends of her parents once praised the four-year-old for her "Chinese" appearance. Maybe the little girl thought herself was to blame for the inexplicable fact that her parents left her again and again, and she tried to erase her guilt by her eager adaptability. Mildred Rosenblatt seems to have encouraged and even, in a bored and somewhat heartless way, provoked her daughter's play with her identity. To get Susan to be quiet, she would tell her daughter that children in China did not talk. But as the observant girl soon noticed, such pedagogic fables followed no logical rules. Although her mother claimed that it was perfectly acceptable in China to belch after a meal, this behavior was of course forbidden at the Rosenblatts' dinner table.

Sontag's earliest memories were not connected to her mother but to her nanny Rosie. Although her family was Jewish, Susan received no religious instruction, and the Rosenblatts observed no Jewish holidays or rituals. Sontag did not even enter a synagogue until she was in her mid-twenties. Her Catholic nanny, however, sometimes took her along to Sunday Mass. One incident Sontag often related happened when she was four. Rosie would take her and her little sister to the park, and Susan once overheard Rosie telling another nanny (the two women in their starched white uniforms seemed like giants to the little girl), "Susan is very high-strung." The child was disconcerted and thought about what Rosie's words might mean and whether other people said the same thing about her.[5] As this episode, in which the gifted four-year-old tries to understand the difference between herself and other children, makes clear, many of Sontag's most important early impressions were connected to Rosie, who remained a maternal figure for her until she was fourteen. Later the nanny would reenter Sontag's life to care for Susan's own son, David.

The note of bitterness was especially audible when Susan spoke of Mildred, her beautiful, depressed, alcoholic, and unloved mother. Susan remembers her mother as positively obsessed with applying cosmetics to minimize the effects of aging. One absurd symptom of her obsession was that she forbade her daughter to address her as "Mother" in public. This prohibition must have affected the child all the more since her parents left her alone for such long stretches in any case. As long as she lived, Sontag referred to her mother only as "M," an abbreviation that stands as much for "Mildred" as for a secret "Mother" or "Mom" and expresses the melancholy anger Sontag always felt toward her mother. Some of Sontag's companions who were privy not just to her family memories but also to the relationship between the adult Susan and her mother—among them Sontag's later partner, the dancer and choreographer Lucinda Childs—shared the opinion that Mildred "wasn't the right mother for Susan."[6]

As late as 1992, Sontag became noticeably upset when telling a journalist from the *Los Angeles Times Magazine* about the huge emotional distance between herself and her mother. Mildred usually lay on her bed with the curtains drawn and a glass on the nightstand beside her, which the child thought was filled with water. Later, Sontag learned it was vodka. Whenever Susan came to her mother with a request, Mildred would say she was too tired and send the child away.[7]

When Susan was five, Mildred Rosenblatt returned alone from China and told her that her father would soon follow.

Four months went by before Mildred told her daughter what had happened. One day after lunch, the seemingly apathetic Mildred, probably still numb from the shock, took the little girl into the living room and told her that her father was dead. In October 1938, at the age of thirty-four, Jack Rosenblatt had died of tuberculosis in the German-American Hospital in Tianjin.[8] "I still weep in any movie with a scene in which a father returns home after a long, desperate absence at the moment when he hugs his child. Or children,"[9] Sontag could still declare forthrightly at the age of fifty-nine with the pathos of unresolved pain such memories entail.

Other indications of the traumatic effects of the experience are the irregularities in Sontag's memories. In both "Project for a Trip to China" and various interviews, she claimed she had already started school when she learned of her father's death. But a comparison of his death certificate and her report cards proves that recollection cannot have been accurate.[10] Susan did not begin school until September 1939. She also reported that, at the time, she barely understood what had happened and certainly was unable to come to grips with it. It is probable that the complete consciousness of her father's death only occurred later, after she had begun school.

A "ring, a white silk scarf with my father's initials embroidered in black silk thread, and a pigskin wallet with his name stamped in small gold letters on the inside are all I possess that belonged to him," Sontag wrote as a forty-year-old in "Project for a Trip to China."[11] She did not even know what his handwriting looked like. Beyond these things, she also had a few black-and-white photographs from before her birth of her father in a rickshaw and riding a camel. Even the specific memories of him that remained were like snapshots: "I remember him folding what seemed to be an enormous handkerchief, the size of a tablecloth, and putting it in his breast pocket. I can remember looking up at this giant and thinking it was the most amazing thing in the world to be able to fold that handkerchief, and make it do all those things, and it ended up this little, small thing, and you stuck it in your pocket!"[12] The nostalgic power of these memories and objects is intimately related to the tormenting ignorance Susan would always associate not only with her parents' trips to China but also with the irrevocable death of her father. She cannot even imagine the look of the country where her parents lived and her father died. The grief of the speechless child is manifest in the black-and-white photos. On the one hand, they conjure up the vivid presence of her father. On the other, they make it clearer with each passing year that he will never return. The part of her father that remains with Susan is her restlessness and powerful yearning for faraway places, her wish to travel to find explanations.

In a 1975 interview with Geoffrey Movius of the *New Boston Review*, Sontag described a scene in which this experience was repeated and again connected to a mixture of grief and wanderlust. They had been talking about her grandparents Samuel and Gussie Rosenblatt: "Most Americans are the children or grandchildren of immigrants, whose decision to come here had, to begin with, a great deal to do with cutting their losses. If immigrants retained a tie with their country or culture of origin, it was very selective. The main impulse was to forget. I once asked my father's mother, who died when I was seven, where she came from. She said, 'Europe.' Even at six I knew that wasn't a very good answer. I said, 'But where, Grandma?' She repeated, testily, 'Europe.' And so to this day, I don't know from what country my paternal grandparents came. But I have photographs of them, which I cherish, which are like mysterious tokens of all that I don't know about them."[13]

Europe suddenly seems to the girl just as distant, fantastic, glamorous, and mysterious as China and, moreover, similarly pregnant with significance through the death of her grandparents who had kept their country of origin a secret. The child was too young to be told about the antisemitic pogroms in late nineteenth- and early twentieth-century Poland that were likely the reason for their emigration. In 1975, Sontag facetiously declared her ignorance of what country the family was from although she knew very well that they came from Lodz, Galicia, and the area of Vilnius. Twenty-five years later, when she was working on her semi-biographical novel about the Polish-American actor Helena Modrzejewska, also known as Helena Modjeska, Sontag claimed with equal disingenuousness that she had been born in Poland. The poet Adam Zagajewski recalls that she did so either "to highlight her autodidactic achievements" or "to emphasize the intellectual potential slumbering in her Vilnius forebears."[14] Decades after the child was perplexed by the secrecy surrounding her family's origins, traces of the disturbance were still detectable in Sontag's willful play with her identity.

After Susan's father's death and the subsequent sale of the fur business, the Rosenblatt family suffered a social decline that was exacerbated by the Depression. Most of their domestic staff had to be let go. The rose quartz and ivory elephants were sold off. What is more, Susan began to develop such severe asthma that, at the suggestion of an obviously ill-informed doctor, her mother thought it necessary to move to a different climate. Accompanied by Rosie and a cook, Mildred and her two daughters moved to Miami for its sea air, and the life of the six-year-old was again turned upside down. Sontag told her son, David, that her memories of the year she spent in Florida as a child seemed as if they came from the nineteenth century, a series of "hazy images of white stucco houses with pseudo-Moorish detailing."[15] The contrast to New York could not have been greater. In this geographic confusion, the feeling of rootlessness Sontag later often spoke of could only have increased.

After a few months, during which Miami's damp subtropical climate only exacerbated the child's asthma, the family moved again, this time to Tucson, Arizona. Of all the places Sontag lived as a child, southern Arizona with its vast desert left the strongest impression on her. Tucson was the place she associated with her childhood "imaginatively" and called it the place where she grew up.[16] When the Rosenblatts arrived, Tucson was still a middling town of 30,000 inhabitants, many of them immigrants from Latin America. The city was famous for its therapeutic climate. In and around Tucson, there were about thirty hospitals and sanatoriums for patients with various respiratory ailments. The desert stretching away in all directions is one of the most beautiful landscapes in America.

Childhood in this vast desert landscape intensified Susan's solitariness. Although her nanny Rosie had moved to Arizona with them, Mildred still traveled frequently without telling Susan where and why she was going. Later, Sontag assumed that her mother had lovers. Moreover, the move meant even further social decline. It is not entirely clear how the Rosenblatts got by financially. Mildred apparently worked at least part-time as a teacher in the local high school. Their new house was on Drachman Street, an unpaved road at the edge of Tucson. When Sontag's literary agent and friend Andrew Wylie visited Arizona fifty years later, Larry McMurtry, another friend of Sontag's, showed him the house Susan had grown up in, a house trailer on a concrete foundation at the edge of the desert and the end of the world. "It was astonishing," Wylie recalled. "What I saw was the act of self-invention that constituted Susan. To have begun in this shabby little trailer on the edge of Tucson, one of the dreariest places in this country you can imagine living in, and to become such a commanding, deeply cultured and cosmopolitan intellectual—it was unbelievable."[17]

By the time she was three, Susan had already learned to read. As was typical at that time, she possessed an immense collection of comic books. At the age of six, she started to read "real books."[18] In Sontag's memories of her childhood literary expeditions, an evident need emerges to find an identity. Left to her own devices by her parents to find her own role models, she sought them in literature.

Sontag often identified Eve Curie's biography of her Nobel laureate mother, Marie,[19] as one of the most influential books of her childhood. In an era when intelligent girls had hardly any intellectual role models outside their family circle, the biography of a highly moral and brilliant Nobel laureate working in a masculine field of endeavor was a welcome object of identification for the child. Sontag would later recount that, like all ambitious girls of her age, she would have preferred to be a boy because it seemed so much simpler.[20]

Not incidentally, Marie Curie lived and worked in Poland and France—in a Europe that, in Susan's imagination, possessed a melancholy glamour. Curie became the unqualified heroine of Sontag's early childhood. From the moment she closed the book, she was determined to become a scientist. Even a Nobel Prize did not seem out of the question to her juvenile imagination.[21]

Susan Sontag later often painted a poignant picture of her childhood self as a solitary wanderer in the Arizona desert. Instead of going straight home after school, she liked to follow a stony trail through the desert, where she could take her time and admire the impressive saguaro cactus with their spiny, blood-red fruit. She collected pretty stones—it would be a lifelong habit—looked for snakes and arrowheads, and liked to imagine she had lost her way or was the sole survivor of a catastrophe. Although she played at being an Indian, she was a "Lone Ranger."[22]

"Of course I thought I was Jo from *Little Women*," Sontag recalled in a 1995 interview with Edward Hirsch. It is quite likely that she had both read Louisa May Alcott's novel and seen George Cukor's 1933 film version starring the brilliant and unconventional young Katharine Hepburn as Jo March. It was one of the most successful Hollywood films of the thirties and continued to be shown for years all over America, not least because of its optimistic view of family life during wartime. The plot of the novel contained some remarkable parallels to Sontag's life and presented her with another figure with whom she could identify. In *Little Women*, a mother, her daughters, and their nursemaid must cope with economic and emotional privations while their father is off fighting in the American Civil War. As is already clear from her masculinized nickname Jo, the protagonist Josephine is a tomboy: garrulous, cheeky, and interested in sword fights. She stages and acts in her own plays and loves to write. She is even talented enough as an author to sell a few ghost stories to a newspaper. Like Susan, Jo dreams of going to

Europe to study civilization at its source in the Old World. And like Susan, Jo ends up in New York and begins to write serious literature instead of sensational ghost stories.

The future author intuitively grasped this literary message. Always the serious, intense, thoughtful child whom Rosie had already recognized in her four-year-old charge, Susan wanted to write but said, "I didn't want to write what Jo wrote."[23] Katharine Hepburn must also have made a great impression on Susan. Off the screen as well as on, Hepburn had the reputation of being a devil-may-care tomboy. The contemporary press often made fun of her unladylike behavior, lack of make-up, and daring violations of Hollywood's stern code of conduct.

Susan Rosenblatt began first grade in September 1939, just as the Second World War was getting under way. As she told Ron Grossman of the *Chicago Tribune,* on the basis of her excellent reading skills she was promoted half a grade on the first day. She was promoted again on the second day, and by the end of the week, Susan found herself in third grade.[24] Sontag had few happy memories of school. In later life, she would often remark off handedly that she was the victim of a poor education in the disastrous American public school system but had been lucky enough to go to school before the era of school psychologists.[25] She told her fellow first-graders that she was born in China; she said it was her "first lie."[26]

Sontag recalled the fear she felt on December 7, 1941, the day the Japanese attacked Pearl Harbor. The Roosevelt administration portrayed America's subsequent entry into the Second World War as joining a "people's war" primarily to rescue European Jewry. During the next four years, Susan Rosenblatt, herself the descendant of European Jews, was deeply moved by news from the war. Reports of battles issued from staticky radios at home and at school. The sanatoriums in Tucson filled with soldiers. Groceries and consumer goods were rationed, and there were recurring power failures as well as Civil Air Patrols and sirens in the night, first-aid courses, and heart-rending newsreels of bombed cities, exploding buildings, and endless treks of refugees. Sontag said that she would never forget the ubiquitous phrase "for the duration"—as long as the war lasted. It suggested a certain optimism that allowed the girl both to see the current events of her childhood and at the same time to forget them for a while. "For the duration" meant that the present would be followed by a better future.[27]

Some of Susan's investments in that better future were the travel books of Richard Halliburton. With Halliburton, she could indulge her longing for travel to distant places—China and Europe—at least in her imagination. Even as a sixty-eight-year-old, Sontag waxed enthusiastic when talking about her collection of Halliburton first editions.[28] Sontag's partner Annie Leibovitz writes in her memoir that these were the books that ignited Susan's "lifelong ardor for travel."[29] Halliburton introduced Susan to the romance of travel. She read every one of the adventurer's books she could find, and they were a source of unadulterated pleasure and "successful volition."[30] They challenged her to take imaginary wing, and she happily accepted. And they were yet another connection to writing. Halliburton's example, she later said, gave her an idea of what it means to be a writer. It was "what I thought had to be the most privileged of lives . . . a life of endless curiosity and energy and countless enthusiasms. To be a traveler, to be a writer—in my child mind they started off as the same thing."[31]

And with the eagerness of a child, Susan set about realizing her dream. She assembled a four-page magazine containing her own summaries of recent battles and other articles she had written herself, and she planned to sell it in the neighborhood for five cents a copy. It was her first foray into writing.[32] In 1978, she told *Rolling Stone*, "I was a terribly restless child, and I was so irritated with being a child that I was just busy all the time. I was writing up a storm by the time I was eight or nine years old."[33] In a 1985 interview, she even dated her first attempts to write to her seventh or eighth year.[34] In 1987, she said she had begun to write at six or seven and added, "Plays, poems, stories."[35] Although in her later interviews Sontag seems to have often fallen prey to the seductions of self-dramatization, there is no doubt that she began to write at a very early age.

Sontag liked to paint this scene: the image of her childhood self, autonomous and independent of family and school and without any kind of encouragement, devouring and sometimes almost literally living inside the most challenging works of world literature. A chemistry set and a Madame Curie-style laboratory installed in the garage of the bungalow on Drachman Street had been only the beginning. Sontag nostalgically recalled her entire childhood as a journey full of intellectual and literary high points, a free fall into the paradise of world literature and philosophy. When she was ten years old, she discovered the Modern Library in a stationery store in Tucson. "And I sort of understood these were the classics. I used to like to read encyclopedias, so I had lots of names in my head. And here they were! Homer, Virgil, Dante, George Eliot, Thackeray, Dickens. I decided I would read them all."[36] She said that, to her, every book was a little kingdom.[37]

But in Sontag's romanticized version of her childhood reading, darker undertones occasionally intrude. Reading and listening to music represented triumphs for her, but "triumphs of being not myself."[38] Yes, the reading child was able to escape the strictures of her life. What also emerges, however, is the self-image of an insecure, highly intelligent child seeking to escape from her own skin as well, which she perceives as inadequate. And, finally, the self-image of an author emerges who succeeded in escaping from the confines of a provincial, solitary, and unappreciated childhood and precisely for that reason tends to exaggerate and idealize. It is difficult to imagine even a prodigy like Sontag voluntarily reading Arthur Schopenhauer and—as she often claimed—understanding him. If one takes at face value the statements she made in interviews through the years, the sheer volume of her childhood reading would be enough to overwhelm the time of even a highly gifted adult reader. Her descriptions of reading serve above all to promote the aura of genius in which Sontag consciously wrapped herself later in life. It is not a real child who emerges from these descriptions, but Sontag's idealization of the childhood she seemed to regard as merely a preliminary step toward her conception of what an intellectual should be.

Nadine Gordimer, the South African Nobel laureate and a close friend of Sontag's, reports frequent conversations about their "not particularly happy childhoods" in which, despite important differences, they recognized parallels such as the "autodidactic passion for reading and the literary life."[39] Nevertheless, both authors shared a deep antipathy for "the habit of many people to make their childhood responsible for their lives, which was in fashion for a long time."[40]

It is this idea of a duty to actively outgrow the circumstances one is born into that runs through all of Sontag's memories of her "so-called childhood." The adult summarily declares her early years to have been a series of events in which the entire spectrum of her later intellectual and literary pursuits was foreshadowed. On the one hand, she thereby retrospectively gives definite and predictive significance to a childhood that was by no means happy. On the other, her stake in this point of view is nothing less than the success she gained later in life, without which there would have been no possible justification for her childhood suffering. Sontag gave herself no other choice, so to speak, than to be successful. Anything else would have been to betray her lonely and literature-intoxicated childhood.

The Invention of Susan Sontag

(1945–1948)

We always believe in America:
We can start again, we can turn
the page, we can invent ourselves,
we can transform ourselves.

Susan Sontag, in a 2001 interview

Susan Sontag was twelve when her mother married Captain Nathan Sontag, a pilot in the Army Air Corps then recuperating in a Tucson sanatorium from wounds sustained in a plane crash five days after the Allied landing in Normandy.[1] Although Nathan did not adopt her two daughters, Mildred asked them to take his last name. Susan was only too happy to comply because she had been called a "dirty kike" several times in Tucson and hoped that the less Jewish-sounding "Sontag" would give her some protection.[2]

In addition, the name change gave the independent young girl the chance to try out a new identity based on the internalized fantasies she had spun from her intensive reading in Arizona. For Sontag, this turning point was nothing less than the beginning of her lifelong and deep-seated idea of self-invention. With the new, alliterative name that sounded like it belonged to a film star, Susan Sontag soon came to regard herself as a citizen of the intellectual and urbane world. From this point on and with childlike determination, she would expend great energy on the "Susan Sontag project," the multiplicity of ideas, interests, attitudes, and ambitions that would run through her entire life. While the lives of most pubescent teenagers revolve around romance and sexual experimentation, Susan Sontag tried to cut the umbilical cord to her parents mainly by way of entrance into high culture.

In 1946 Nathan, Mildred, Susan, and Susan's little sister Judith moved to Los Angeles along with Rosie the nanny and the family dog. The three years Susan spent in California would prove to be a defining experience for Sontag. Many of her friends remark how "Californian" she always was. Stephen Koch, author and professor of creative writing at Columbia University, smiles when recounting how Sontag often reminded him of a "California girl scout," and Steve Wasserman, former editor of the *Los Angeles Times Book Review,* recalls that "there was something about her openness to people and experiences that you could call Californian. She had none of the usual cynicism one usually associates with New Yorkers . . . Sontag understood California as the republic of self-invention, as America's America."[3]

California was the capital of self-made identities, where Greta Lovisa Gustafsson could become Greta Garbo, Archie Leach could turn into Cary Grant, Lucille Fay LeSueur into Joan Crawford, and Frances Gumm into Judy Garland. In the autobiographical story "Pilgrimage," Sontag recalls her enthusiasm at seeing glamorous film premieres in the newsreels. Limousines would pull up on Hollywood Boulevard and screen stars would emerge amid a storm of flashbulbs before the eyes of the thousands of autograph-seekers kept under control by mounted policemen.[4] But while the young Susan Sontag enjoyed spectacles like these, it was the cultural celebrities that made the strongest impression on her. She worshipped the famous exiles from Nazi Europe with an intensity equal to that of a film fan. In "Pilgrimage," Sontag describes details of her California youth and recalls her devotion to Igor Stravinsky and Arnold Schoenberg,

Thomas Mann and Bertolt Brecht, Christopher Isherwood and Aldous Huxley. These Europeans were for her "the gods of high culture" who seemed to be recovering from the experience of deracination incognito among the orange groves, palm-lined streets, movie theaters, surfers, neo-Bauhaus architecture, and hamburger joints.[5]

The euphoric postwar mood, the incipient economic upturn, and the middle-class suburbs springing up at the edge of cities all over America—all these had powerful effects on Susan. The family's new house was a somewhat run-down cottage amid rose bushes and birch trees on the edge of the San Fernando Valley in Los Angeles. Here Susan had her own room where she could spend all night reading by flashlight.

Nathan Sontag, especially, seemed swept up in American postwar optimism and his newly acquired family. Susan had memories of her almost frighteningly jolly stepfather hosting barbecues (at the time a brand-new form of entertaining) with steaks on the grill and buttered sweet corn. Her younger sister was also avid for their new life with its hit parades, radio comedians, quiz shows, and baseball games. To the thirteen-year-old Susan, however, the new scene seemed like a "facsimile of family life" in which she merely played a supporting role. In her mind, she was already long gone. "They couldn't start playing family now—too late!"[6]

While Mildred was usually apathetic and without appetite at family barbecues, Susan stuffed herself compulsively. Later she said that playing along and eating a lot seemed the best way to avoid conflict. The deep aversion to the customs and rituals of middle-class America that she developed at this time would remain burned into her psyche. She regarded herself as the "resident alien" in the family and could hardly wait to be released from the "long prison sentence" that constituted her childhood.[7]

Susan wrote that her stepfather often told her, "Sue, if you read so much you'll never find a husband," an admonition she responded to with teenage condescension: "I thought, 'This idiot doesn't know there are intelligent men out in the world. He thinks they're all like him.' Because isolated as I was, it never occurred to me that there weren't lots of people like me out there, somewhere."[8] Sontag felt great ambivalence toward her stepfather. Neither of the Sontags could understand the development of this daughter who was already showing signs of being emancipated and unconventional. Nor was Susan, with all her pent-up disappointments and aggression, able to adapt to the world of her parents. Rather, she soon learned to regard her interest in the realm of the intellect and high culture as a way to distinguish herself from her family, that is, as something that made her better than the "idiots" around her. What seems strange is how little she recognized that it was precisely these "idiots" who—whether out of tolerance or casual inattention and despite their completely different values—allowed her a surprising amount of freedom.

Susan entered North Hollywood High School early in 1947, a large, progressive school with about 2,000 students and a young faculty.[9] Sontag soon became the editor of *The Arcade*, the student newspaper, and continued to pursue her literary ambitions. Her contributions to the paper included film reviews, political opinion pieces, and occasional poems.[10] Sontag described herself as an uncomplicated student who did not appear to be two years younger than her classmates.

The lack of intellectual challenge, however, continued at North Hollywood High. For English class, Susan was supposed to write summaries of *Reader's Digest* articles; but every day after school, she visited the old established Pickwick Bookshop on Hollywood Boulevard to read her way through world literature.[11] It was not American authors whom she discovered there. In 1980 she told the Polish journalist Monika Beyer, "I found Europe when I was an adolescent, when . . . I began to read the writers that mattered to me, that I really cared about . . . The background that I invented, that I discovered, that mattered to me, was Kafka or Mann. These great discoveries that I made when I was about 14 changed my life. So was born my attachment for

European culture which I still think of as the source of culture. I still think of America as a colony of Europe."[12]

Susan's insatiable hunger for literature was not unlike her gorging at family barbecues. Her literary hunger was so great that, as she later reported, she even stole books despite the guilt and shame that tortured her for weeks afterward.[13]

Susan found another kind of fulfillment of her yearning for Europe in her friendship with Peter, a fellow student who had also lost his father. Half Hungarian and half French, Peter had fled with his mother from Paris to the South of France after his father had been arrested and murdered by the Gestapo. After a sojourn in Lisbon, the mother and son had come to America in 1941. Susan and Peter's friendship began in the school cafeteria with an exchange of stories about their dead fathers.[14] Later they frequented the movies together, usually at the Laurel Theatre, where they would hold hands and watch subtitled films such as Roberto Rossellini's *Open City* (1945), Jean Delannoy's *La symphonie pastorale* (*Pastoral Symphony,* 1946), Leontine Sagan's *Mädchen in Uniform* (1931), Marcel Pagnol's *La femme du boulanger* (*The Baker's Wife,* 1938), and Jean Cocteau's *Beauty and the Beast* (1946).[15] Although at the time movies were a more normal part of everyday life in America than in any other country, the children's choice of films is a testimony to their astonishing determination to be intellectual. Once again we see the beginning of a thread that would be woven in with others in Sontag's later life. She always remained an avid moviegoer with a special love for French and Japanese films.

Susan's determination to be an intellectual is also reflected in the magazines she found in the Pickwick Bookshop and read instead of the *Reader's Digest* stories assigned in school. In a 1981 interview with the British magazine *Commonweal,* she talked about the influence the intellectual periodicals of the late 1940s had on her, magazines such as *Partisan Review, Kenyon Review, Sewanee Review, Politics, Accent, Tiger's Eye,* and *Horizon:* "I'd never seen a literary magazine before; certainly I'd never seen anybody read one. I picked up *Partisan Review* and I started to read 'Art and Fortune' by Lionel Trilling; and I just began to tremble with excitement, and from then on, my dream was to grow up, move to New York and write for *Partisan Review.*"[16]

When Sontag read Lionel Trilling's essay in *Partisan Review* in 1948, the magazine was at the height of its influence and was nothing less than the house organ of the so-called New York Intellectuals, a coterie with Trilling as its unofficial leader. The artistic ideology celebrated in magazines such as *Partisan Review* was the totally new departure known as high modernism, a formalism so radical that it bordered on the metaphysical. Trilling's "Art and Fortune" argued that society needed novels to feel alive and that only through the literary dialectic of reality and illusion would the ideal reader find his or her own path to moral maturity. Susan Sontag proved to be precisely the kind of reader Trilling's essay hoped to win for the contemporary novel. The essay that she had stumbled upon could not have found a better audience than the girl obsessed with literature and with an intense desire to finally be an adult.

At night Susan read her novels and magazines until her eyes smarted, kept a journal, and wrote down lists of foreign words to increase her vocabulary enough to understand the jargon of the New York Intellectuals. Steve Wasserman remembers Susan telling him about this primal scene: "She told me she took an issue of the *Partisan Review* home and could not understand a word in it. But somehow she had the impression that what these people were talking about was enormously important to her and she was determined to crack the code."[17]

This resolution, carried out with great zeal and astonishing perseverance, seemed to occupy the same space in Sontag's life that other teenagers devoted to romantic encounters. Although she had some friendships with boys, her aesthetic interests were of more consequence to her. In "Pilgrimage," for example, she writes about Merrill, her best friend after Peter. She often went parking with him on upper Mulholland Drive, a famous lovers' lane with a great view out over the city. There beneath the starry sky and with a sea of lights spread out at their feet (a scene depicted in countless Hollywood films), the boy and girl confessed not their romantic passion for each other, but their love for contemporary chamber music. Chamber music was just then experiencing a renaissance thanks to European immigrants and the financial support of the film studios. According to Sontag, they would discuss the relative merits of the Busch and Budapest string quartets, of Schoenberg and Stravinsky, and then they would drive home.[18]

Besides reading challenging magazine articles and literary classics and listening to contemporary classical music, Sontag also devoted herself enthusiastically to visual art. When she was fourteen, she returned to New York for the first time since early childhood to spend the summer with her maternal grandparents. In an interview with museum director Philip Fisher fifty-five years later, she described her discovery of New York's museums. Every day she would spend several hours in the Museum of Modern Art, the Museum of Non-Objective Painting (the precursor of the Guggenheim Museum), or the Metropolitan Museum of Art, and she discovered an interesting phenomenon: although people would often stop and speak to her in bookstores or concerts because even at fourteen she still looked like a ten-year-old, in museums she was able to stroll around undisturbed.[19] The teenager soaked up everything she read, saw, and heard. As Sontag often said later, she had the feeling she could be all she wanted and achieve all her goals.[20]

But precisely because Sontag held herself to such high standards, she naturally was also in danger of suffering literary and intellectual embarrassment and humiliation, for instance, in her encounter with Thomas Mann, the German novelist who enjoyed enormous popularity in his American exile. Sontag's audience with the Nobel laureate took place after she had read *The Magic Mountain* in H. T. Lowe-Porter's 1927 translation. Reading that ironic bildungsroman was a decisive experience for the teenager. Sontag recalled being so excited while reading the book during the nights of early November 1947 that she could hardly breathe. There was so much she recognized as familiar, so much new to be discovered: her father had suffered from tuberculosis, as did the hero Hans Castorp, and had died from it. She knew tuberculosis patients from the sanatoriums of Tucson and had experienced similar symptoms during her own bout with asthma. How gratifying it must have been when Thomas Mann depicted the disease as "the very epitome of pathetic and spiritual interest."[21] Here began Sontag's intensive engagement with the metaphorical associations of disease, which ultimately resulted in *Illness as Metaphor* (1978), written during her first episode of cancer and probably her most influential work. Sontag mentions Mann's reflections on the psychopathological implications of tuberculosis as one of her main sources. One can also sense the influence of *The Magic Mountain* in her two last novels, *The Volcano Lover* (1992) and *In America* (2000).

It was Susan's friend Merrill who arranged the meeting with the German writer. According to her retelling in "Pilgrimage," it had been a simple matter of finding the great man's number in the Los Angeles telephone book and calling him up. And indeed, the presumptuous call met with success. Merrill and Susan were invited to tea and cake on the following Sunday in the Manns' house on San Remo Drive.

Sontag's description of the visit is both amusing and uncomfortable. It is an account of disproportionality in which probably the most famous novelist of the time meets a fourteen-year-old girl who cannot forgive herself for not coming up to the intellectual level of her hero. Mann seemed to find the two precocious young literature fans interesting, but "by real standards," thought Susan, "we hardly existed."[22] At the same time, Sontag depicts a certain disenchantment that began when she found herself actually sitting across from her idol as well as her realization that literary fiction seldom extends into real life. "Here I was in the very throne room of the world in which I aspired to live . . . The thought of saying that I wanted to be a writer would no more have occurred to me than to tell him I breathed . . . The man I met had only sententious formulas to deliver, though he was the man who wrote Thomas Mann's books. And I uttered nothing but tongue-tied simplicities, though I was full of complex feeling. We neither of us were at our best."[23]

Mann did not ask his young visitors what they thought of Franz Kafka or Leo Tolstoy but inquired instead about the high school curriculum and Ernest Hemingway. The bashful Susan was disappointed, embarrassed, and depressed. The great author did not recognize in her the nascent writer but saw only an interesting American high school girl. Even forty years later in her account for the *New Yorker,* Sontag was unable to laugh at the precocious earnestness of her teenage self. The meeting remained an embarrassment her whole life.

The experience, however, failed to deter Susan Sontag on her own path to literary fame. In December 1948, shortly before her sixteenth birthday, Sontag graduated a semester early from North Hollywood High School. She said later that the principal himself had advised her to do it; there was nothing more for her to learn there and she would just be wasting her time. At last she would be able to exchange her spiritual journeys with Halliburton and company for real travels.

Intellectual Delirium

(1949–1957)

*Returning at midnight from what
academics in that staid era were
pleased to call parties, more than
once we sat in the car until dawn
lightened the street, forgetting to go
into our own apartment, so absorbed
were we in our dissections of his
exasperating colleagues. So many
years of that, the delirious amity of
non-stop talking . . .*

Susan Sontag, "The Letter Scene"
(1986)

Susan Sontag began college when she was sixteen, got married
at seventeen, and became a mother at nineteen.[1] She entered
adulthood with such furious determination that her main goal
seemed to be to put adolescence behind her as quickly as possible. She appeared so sure of the standards she would use to
frame the project of her life that she did not need to waste time
asking questions or experimenting as most teenagers do. Much
of Sontag's concept of life during her college years was a product
of the era. The 1950s were, for women, a time of withdrawal into

27

private life. Many who had worked in offices or factories during the Second World War returned home and devoted themselves to a model of family life more traditional than the previous generation's. Any deviation from that model was generally viewed with suspicion.

Considering her later writings and political activism, it is surprising what conservative circles the young Susan Sontag moved in during these years. In the landscape of American academia at the time, it was difficult enough for an unmarried man to have a career. For an unmarried woman, it was well-nigh unthinkable. The student protests of the sixties were still a long way off. Most professors were venerable figures, many of them European Jews who had fled the Nazis and found an academic home at American colleges and universities.

Susan Sontag had read an article in *Collier's* about the University of Chicago and its undergraduate curriculum, which was based on the Great Books and had no electives. The Great Books were a list of approximately 100 classic works of literature, philosophy, history, and science compiled by early twentieth-century intellectuals who emphasized English, French, Latin, and Greek authors. In the early 1950s, the University of Chicago, still under the powerful influence of Robert Maynard Hutchins, was regarded as one of the most innovative and important academic institutions in the country. After a long tenure as president from 1929 until 1945, Hutchins stayed on as chancellor until 1951. With the financial support of the Rockefeller Foundation, he recruited some of the best minds of the United States and, during the Second World War, of Europe as well. Dozens of Nobel laureates are alumni of the university. Among other reforms, Hutchins eliminated varsity football and forbade the use of standardized textbooks on the grounds that, by presenting predigested facts, they inhibited free thought and debate. Instead, undergraduates read primary texts by Immanuel Kant, René Descartes, and other great thinkers and writers.[2] Hutchins's unconventional pedagogical reforms reestablished the classic liberal arts as the preferred curriculum for university students.[3]

It was a heady cocktail of canonical works that the University of Chicago served up to its undergraduates. In other words, it was precisely the course of uninterrupted study and discussion of the fundamental questions of intellect, society, and life that had quickened the imagination of the gifted teenager in the San Fernando Valley. Sontag thought that at "this eccentric place . . . they talked about Plato and Aristotle and Aquinas day and night."[4] She would not be disappointed. Years later, she declared that what Hutchins's University of Chicago offered was "the most successful authoritarian program of education ever devised in this country."[5]

Susan's mother was opposed to her daughter moving to the notorious capital city of the Midwest. "You'll only find Negroes and Communists there," Susan recalled her saying.[6] Mildred's reservations were typical of white middle class America's collective fear of nuclear war with the Soviet Union and of the anti-Communist hysteria that Senator Joseph McCarthy so skillfully stirred up in the media. Besides, the university was in Hyde Park, a neighborhood on the South Side of Chicago just then undergoing a spectacular decline into criminality and ghettoization as a result of white flight to suburbia.[7]

Since Susan would not be able to begin the University of Chicago until September in any case, Mildred Sontag suggested that her daughter register for the spring semester at the University of California at Berkeley. She hoped that Susan would like Berkeley enough to forget about moving to the cold and suspect Chicago. But Susan remained adamant. After a semester at Berkeley, she registered at the University of Chicago in September 1949. She passed the formidable entrance examination brilliantly, having already read most of the required writers and philosophers, so that in her case the usual four-year required curriculum was reduced to only two years.[8]

Sontag reminisced about her education at the University of Chicago as if it were a homecoming. The sixteen-year-old had left behind the suffocating atmosphere of her childhood and felt she was at last among her peers. In an interview with the

British *Independent,* she recalled standing in line on registration day and overhearing two upperclassmen talking about Marcel Proust. "I thought 'Oh shit, it's pronounced "Proost."' I had read *Remembrance of Things Past,* of course, but I had never used the name Proust to anyone except in my head and I had always thought it was pronounced 'Prowst.' It was actually a wonderful feeling—at last I was going to learn how to pronounce these names. At last, here were other people who read what I read. I felt I'd finally arrived and it was true, I had."[9] In a profile of Sontag at fifty-nine, the *Chicago Tribune* reported how emotionally attached Sontag still was to this idyll of uninterrupted learning. Her alma mater, she said, had been nothing less than "a magical place to be a 16-year-old."[10]

In addition to undergraduate courses, Sontag attended graduate seminars although she was not officially permitted to do so. She recalled the course offered by the natural scientist and philosopher of education Joseph Schwab, a powerful influence on the university's curriculum from 1934 to 1973, as "a new expedition into the world of ideas. I'd leave class tingling with a kind of ecstasy."[11] Schwab "was a genius teacher, the best embodiment of Chicago's Socratic method." His course Observation, Interpretation, Integration was like a master class for her, except that at first she seldom spoke. She was still too shy and lacking in confidence.[12]

Susan Sontag had worked her way through the lists of authors and philosophers she assembled in her bedroom in California and now made new lists, adding above all the philosophers of classical antiquity and German idealism to her personal intellectual pantheon. Intellectual activity continued even in the dormitory, for her dorm mates were mostly young people with similar interests who had chosen this relatively exotic college for the same reason. Mike Nichols, with whom Sontag acted in the college theater, would remain a lifelong friend. Other famous graduates of the University of Chicago include Saul Bellow; Philip Roth; Kurt Vonnegut; the journalist Seymour Hersch; Robert Silvers, cofounder and editor of the *New*

York Review of Books; and the Supreme Court judge John Paul Stevens.

Another of Sontag's professors at the university was Leo Strauss, a contemporary of Theodor Adorno, Herbert Marcuse, and Max Horkheimer. Strauss had studied under Edmund Husserl and Martin Heidegger before immigrating to the United States in 1938. Since 1949 he had held the chair for political philosophy at the University of Chicago and soon became one of the most influential figures in American academia. In sharp opposition to most modern philosophy, he founded the politico-philosophical neoconservative movement. Its adherents, such as Paul Wolfowitz, populated the innermost circles of power in Washington and became the godfathers of the second Bush administration. Strauss's seminars and lectures attained cult status among the Chicago intelligentsia. His extensive fan club included not just students but also other professors, intellectuals, and politicians.[13]

But the most important person for the young Susan Sontag was undoubtedly the author and literary scholar Kenneth Burke, one of the most renowned theorists of rhetoric in America. She often spoke warmly of Burke's fascinating way of approaching a text. In one seminar, he spent almost an entire year reading Joseph Conrad's novel *Victory,* word for word and image by image. Near the end of her life, Sontag declared emphatically, "I still read the way he taught me."[14] The goal of Burke's close reading was to understand the sources of human conflict with special attention to the dramatic and theatrical aspects of communication. His literary criticism was not formalistic; he understood the goal of literature as exerting a kind of influence on society, as a valuable aid to living and an introduction to action. Sontag herself would later prove to be a believer in the power of the word to effect change. Her approach in both essays and literary texts was always to think about and explain present phenomena in clear, unambiguous language.

Sontag was also fascinated by Burke's ties to the bohemian scene in Greenwich Village, where many authors, actors, directors, and free spirits were his friends. Burke gave Sontag a copy of his long-since-forgotten 1932 novel *Towards a Better Life* and told her he had shared an apartment in the Village with Djuna Barnes and Hart Crane. Sontag told an interviewer, "You can imagine what that did to me . . . Writers were as remote to me as movie stars."[15]

By this time, the imagination of the literature-obsessed young woman was focused on a new object: the life of the writers she idolized. In many respects, Greenwich Village was the birthplace of American modernism. Burke moved there in 1918 and had quickly become a leader and founding father of bohemianism in the Village. The American avant-garde between 1915 and 1930 included such visionaries as Eugene O'Neill, Marianne Moore, Marcel Duchamp, E. E. Cummings, Georgia O'Keeffe, Alfred Stieglitz, Edmund Wilson, and William Carlos Williams. Burke said that, for them, writing was a revolutionary act intended to shake up the reader and lead to reforms such as socialism, the emancipation of women and blacks, and the recognition of the alternative lifestyles of gays and lesbians.[16] Burke translated Thomas Mann's *Death in Venice* (1912), published musical and literary reviews, and wrote poetry and novels before opting for an academic career during the Depression.[17]

By the time Burke was reminiscing to his student Susan Sontag about his life with the flamboyant Hart Crane and the eccentric Djuna Barnes, the Village had already achieved mythic status in the American imagination as the manifestation of every imaginable form of rebellion, artistic lifestyle, sexual emancipation, and self-realization. Sontag eagerly absorbed his stories of life outside the mainstream, the life she wished for herself. Burke is, in fact, the only influence from Sontag's student days whom one can connect directly to her later essayistic, literary, and political work. While she learned rigorous philosophical argumentation from Strauss and Schwab, she inherited from Burke an avant-garde attitude that corresponded well to the personal and political stances that were clearly taking shape even before she turned twenty.

But the fantasy of the writer's life did not seem compatible with Sontag's academic trajectory. At the time, it would never have occurred to her to make that fantasy a reality. Instead, she was satisfied with the new role of "grateful, militant student."[18]

One of the rising stars at the University of Chicago was a sociology instructor named Philip Rieff, who was working on Sigmund Freud, Max Weber, and sociological theories of culture. Although Rieff was still writing his doctoral dissertation, he had already distanced himself from the then dominant empirical sociology and was on his way to becoming one of the most renowned and widely read sociologists in America. Friends suggested that Sontag go to one of his lectures on Freud. Fascinated by the silent, serious, and beautiful student in the first row, Rieff spoke to her after the lecture and invited her to dinner. That was followed by an invitation to breakfast the following morning, an invitation to lunch, and a proposal of marriage the following evening. He told her he knew she was the woman he wanted to marry the moment he first heard her voice. Fifty years later, Sontag told Suzie Mackenzie of *The Guardian*, "I'd never been called a woman before. I thought it was fantastic. I said yes. Isn't that crazy?" When she suggested they should sleep together, he said, "We'll marry first."[19]

Ten days later, they were married. Rieff was the son of a Jewish family from Lithuania and had grown up in Chicago. He seemed older than his twenty-eight years, and Susan, the Californian with long dark hair and a Mediterranean complexion, looked extremely young and exotic next to him. They made a strange pair and excited curiosity and gossip among students and professors. Soon after their wedding, Sontag attended one of Rieff's lectures and heard someone behind her whisper, "Oh, have you heard? Rieff married a 14-year-old Indian!"[20]

The young student heightened her striking appearance with an unconventional wardrobe. In a mixture of nonchalance and dramatic flair, she always wore jeans and dark, close-fitting sweaters. Considering that starched petticoats and constraining girdles were standard in the early fifties, it was an almost

scandalous outfit for a woman to wear.[21] Sontag's nonconfor-
mity anticipated the sartorial revolution her generation would
stage in the sixties.

Philip Rieff was Susan Sontag's first great love; with him she
fought the first emotional and intellectual battles of her struggle
to become an adult. When Suzie Mackenzie of *The Guardian*
asked if she had loved her husband, Sontag replied passionately,
"Oh yes . . . [I] loved him, it was a real marriage." But asked
if he had loved her, she was equivocal and somewhat bitter. "I
can't say that . . . I can't say that someone loved me. No. I just
can't."[22] On another occasion, she described Rieff as "passionate
. . . bookish . . . very, very unworldly. *I* was worldly, compared to
him."[23] Worldly enough that she made the extremely unconventional decision for that time to keep her own last name rather
than take his.

Sontag described the couple's relationship as a marriage of
Siamese twins. In "The Letter Scene," one of her rare autobiographical stories, she depicts the euphoria and the security she
felt in their early, happy years. The pair was never apart for longer than a few hours. This symbiosis provided Sontag with a
seemingly continuous intellectual and personal dialogue.[24]

In 1952, Philip Rieff got a teaching job at Brandeis University and the couple moved to Boston where, with Sontag's
active intellectual support, he continued to work on his dissertation, eventually published as *Freud: The Mind of the Moralist*
in 1959. Their son, David, was born in Cambridge, Massachusetts, in September 1952. Sontag's former nanny Rose McNulty
was brought there to care for the baby. Mildred Sontag did not
visit her grandson until he was eighteen months old. When she
finally came, she said something that would remain burned in
her daughter's memory: "Oh, he's charming. And you know I
don't like children, Susan."[25]

With Rose McNulty's help, Susan was able to continue her
education. In the fall of 1953, she enrolled as a graduate student
in English literature at the University of Connecticut in Storrs,
but she was dissatisfied with the program and left after a year

without a degree. In the fall of 1955, she entered the graduate program in philosophy at Harvard University. She continued to live, she said, "in an intellectual delirium." The couple's friends were mostly older academics, "German refugee intellectuals, largely Jewish."[26] Sontag and Rieff had long nighttime philosophical discussions with Herbert Marcuse, for instance, who also taught at Harvard and lived in the couple's apartment for a year.[27] At the time, Marcuse was developing his theory of "repressive tolerance," a central concept for leftist philosophers and the student revolts of the sixties and a strong influence on the young Sontag.

At Harvard Sontag also met Paul Tillich and Jacob Taubes, two of her greatest intellectual mentors and supporters. She was especially diligent in the courses she took from Taubes, an influential Austrian Jewish refugee who was teaching for two years at Harvard on a Rockefeller grant. Sontag would work with him for several more years until he returned to Germany to teach at the Free University in Berlin. But Sontag's graduate studies did not proceed as straightforwardly as one would expect of such a gifted student. She had left the University of Connecticut because she found the program unsatisfactory, and even at Harvard, where at first she registered as a graduate student in English literature, she missed the kind of intellectual guidance that had been so valuable at the University of Chicago. "Harvard was a superb university, but still, an ordinary university, with a big menu and no 'right way.' "[28] Nevertheless, she began to work as a teaching assistant in philosophy herself and was soon considered one of the brightest TAs in the department. At the time of her preliminary examinations for a master's degree, she was at the top of the rankings of Harvard graduate students in philosophy.[29]

The charismatic Jacob Taubes influenced an entire generation of intellectuals in America and Germany. As a teacher, he seems to have been talented and difficult in equal measure. Like Leo Strauss, he soon attracted a small circle of highly gifted students fascinated by his incisive ideas and affinity for

theories that encompassed the entire history of religion and culture. His patriarchal and authoritarian style could sometimes
express itself in bitter and wounding sarcasm. In short, like Rieff
and Strauss, he was the embodiment of the dominant, exotic,
European-Jewish father figure with intellectual and academic
allure to whom Sontag was attracted throughout her career.
Taubes's example undoubtedly also helped mold Sontag into a
fearless and disputatious debater. From Taubes she learned to see
paradox as intrinsic to thought and contradiction as a quality
that opened intellectual space rather than closing it. Like Taubes,
Sontag tended to make large cultural and historical connections
instead of spending her time minutely parsing isolated facets
of culture.

In Cambridge, Sontag also met Taubes's twenty-three-
year-old wife, Susan. Highly precocious like Sontag, Susan Taubes
also had a tendency to depression. At the time, she was studying
Simone Weil, the French-Jewish Christian mystic who attempted
to communicate an experience of grace above and beyond religion during the catastrophic years of the Second World War. The
two Susans soon became fast friends. Both had been relatively
solitary girls with little connection to the social ideal of American womanhood in the fifties. Both had married their academic
idols as young women. The friendship offered them a chance
to make tactical withdrawals from the increasingly conservative
dominance of husbands who were not enthusiastic about their
young wives' attempts to develop an identity of their own.

The intoxicating idyll of intellectual communion between
Sontag and Rieff was already beginning to show its first cracks.
Sontag later liked to relate an incident that marked a turning
point for her. At academic dinner parties there still existed a strict
separation between the professors and their wives. After dessert,
the men would withdraw to smoke cigars and discuss philosophy or university politics while their wives remained behind
in their own circle. The young Sontag did not know what to
talk about to the other wives and, after a number of unsuccessful evenings, she screwed up her courage and went over to the

professors. After some initial surprise, she was tolerated in their midst.[30] Through such emancipatory initiatives, the rift between Rieff and his unconventional young wife grew wider and wider, as he himself later admitted in an interview with *Esquire* magazine: "I was a traditional man. I thought marriage was for having children, a traditional family. I just couldn't adjust to the kind of family life she wanted. You see, there are families and anti-families. Ours was the latter, I suppose."[31]

The conflict between Philip's need to have a traditional family life and Susan's increasing desire to outgrow the role of student wife and mother was symptomatic of American family structure in the fifties. It was a conflict that remained unspoken in their otherwise highly verbal relationship, but it grew more and more serious. Sontag, who had read Simone de Beauvoir's *The Second Sex* in 1951, recalled that she became increasingly militant about putting de Beauvoir's ideas into practice for her own self-realization.[32] Philip Rieff, himself no mean polemicist, described his disagreements with his young wife in retrospect as a conflict of conceptions of life. His ideas involved a large family, hers a large library.[33]

As she had since childhood, Susan Sontag turned first to literature in search of a place to work out her conflicts. In the introductory chapter to her last novel, *In America,* she relates how she read George Eliot's *Middlemarch* when she had just turned eighteen, "and a third of the way through the book burst into tears because I realized not only that *I* was Dorothea but that, a few months earlier, I had married Mr. Casaubon."[34]

Sontag's reminiscence in the novel sums up her relationship with Rieff: on the one hand there is a young, precocious, but somewhat inexperienced woman who (like Dorothea) is sacrificing her own life and self-realization for the academic project of her older, conservative husband. On the other hand, there is Philip, working on his important dissertation on Freud and profiting greatly from discussions with Susan and her help with research and writing. In fact, many commentators and friends at the time described *Freud: The Mind of the Moralist* as the joint effort of both spouses. But Rieff was unwilling to share the academic credit with her.[35]

Sontag was feeling increasingly hemmed in by a life she had more or less stumbled into, and not just in her marriage but also in the academic social circles that were part of the bargain. She soon realized that she had no wish to be stuck in the academic world of Harvard and Brandeis, feeling more and more that "all the oxygen was going out of me."[36]

Another incident from that time is typical of the state of Sontag's feelings: "I remember once, I guess it was 1956 . . . I went into the movie theatre in Harvard Square. The movie that was playing was 'Rock Around the Clock.' And I sat there, I was twenty-three years old, and I thought, My God! This is great! This is absolutely fantastic! After the movie I walked home very slowly: I thought, Do I tell Philip that I've seen this movie—this sort of musical about kids dancing in the aisles? And I thought, No, I can't tell him that."[37]

Although today it is hard to imagine such a strict separation of lowbrow, middlebrow, and highbrow culture, in the fifties there was hardly any overlap between them. Academic culture had almost no contact with mass culture, and it was unheard of for a Harvard graduate student to go to a rock-and-roll film, much less find it exciting.[38] Bill Haley and the Comets' song "Rock Around the Clock" was the first big rock-and-roll hit to stay at the top of the charts for weeks on end. Hysterical teenagers gathered in hordes and sometimes actually rioted wherever Haley was due to perform. In 1955, after the song was used in the opening sequences of the film *Blackboard Jungle,* the sales figures exploded, paving the way for a whole series of rock-and-roll films that dominated popular theaters in the following years: *Rock Around the Clock* (1956), *Rock All Night* (1957), *Let's Rock* (1958), and *Go, Johnny, Go!* (1959).

Sontag, who in her essays would often compare pop music by the Supremes, the Beatles, or Patti Smith with Robert Rauschenberg's paintings or Friedrich Nietzsche's philosophy, had an instinctual, physical, almost erotic reaction to the new music, as she said in a 1975 interview with *Rolling Stone:* "Rock & roll really changed my life . . . It was Bill Haley and the Comets . . . And then I heard Johnnie Ray singing 'Cry.' I heard it on the jukebox and something happened to my skin . . . At that time, the late Fifties, I lived in a totally intellectual world. I didn't know one single person I could share this with."[39]

Sontag does not speculate as to what would have happened had she told her husband about the movie. Would he have laughed at her? Scolded her? Ignored or despised her? The more the young Sontag feared the judgment her husband would pass, the less she was able to define her own space within the marriage. Perhaps Philip Rieff would have liked Elvis Presley. Maybe he would have found it charming or courageous that his attractive, smart young wife was able to converse brilliantly with Marcuse one day and then try out some pop culture the next. It is possible he would have just dismissed it as an eccentricity. Or he would not have been pleased but would have accepted it. She foreclosed all these possibilities in the name of a false marital peace by valuing her husband's opinion above her own. Philip and Susan's marriage seemed now to be suspended halfway between the poles of erotic repression and intellectual openness, between a shared passion for philosophy and silence about passions they did not share.

In 1957, after Sontag had earned her MA in philosophy from Harvard, Paul Tillich recommended her for a fellowship from the American Association of University Women to go to the University of Oxford and work on her dissertation on the "metaphysical presuppositions of ethics."[40] At the same time, Rieff was offered a position at Stanford University. Their son, David, would stay with his paternal grandparents while Susan and Philip lived apart for the coming academic year. They promised to send each other airmail letters every day.[41]

Paris, a Romance

(1958–1959)

New York or Paris. Those were the two ideas of paradise for me. I luckily got to do both for large periods of my life. I do live in New York, but I certainly consider Paris my second city. I have spent a huge amount of my adult life there, and it's been my pleasure to think of France and French culture and . . . French cinema as central to my life.

Susan Sontag, from a speech in New York, 2003

Susan Sontag went abroad at a time when only four percent of Americans found it necessary to have a passport.[1] As she boarded the plane in September 1958 (a luxury in those days when crossing the Atlantic Ocean by ship was cheaper) on her way to St. Anne's College in Oxford, she was twenty-five years old. A brilliant academic career lay ahead. Yet Europe, the dream of her childhood and adolescence, held a number of surprises in store. For the first time, she was free of the demands and constraints of family life and the narrow, academic Harvard circle.

She justified her feeling of liberation by writing the promised daily letter to Philip. "One didn't think of using the transatlantic telephone merely to stay in touch in those days, so long ago. We were poor, he was stingy. I was drifting away, discovering life was actually possible without him. But I did write, every evening. During the day I'd be composing my letter to him in my head, I was always talking to him in my head."[2] Half joyfully and half guiltily, Susan Sontag was being swept out of the conventions of her marriage. She describes it as a situation she passively allowed to develop, as if it would have been a sacrilege to actively free herself from the structures of domesticity. Her own analysis of the nightly letter-writing ritual is symptomatic of this contradiction. The nearness she created by writing was simultaneously a way of keeping Philip at a distance, she explained: "If I write you, I don't have to see you. Touch you. Put my tongue on your skin."[3]

Sontag told Zoë Heller of *The Independent* how much she enjoyed her time in Europe and how much discovering her new freedom went hand in hand with bidding farewell to her life with Philip at Harvard. At Oxford and later in Paris, she explored a new and formerly suppressed facet of her personality and acted out the adolescence she had not experienced, with all the desires, possibilities, and pleasures she had denied herself in her eagerness to grow up. Sontag said she felt younger than she ever allowed herself to be before. "In fact that year in Oxford was the end of the marriage."[4] Provisionally, however, she kept this insight to herself, perhaps from shame and fear, but perhaps also from uncertainty and because she hoped this phase would pass: "I couldn't tell him I wanted a divorce, not by letter. My letters had to be loving. I had to wait till I returned."[5]

Not much is known about Sontag's time in Oxford. She always stated she had studied there in the brief biographical sketches that accompanied her later publications and magazine profiles, but it can be conjectured that, at that time, an American graduate student in philosophy would not have felt especially at home at the venerable institution, where even today graduation ceremonies are conducted in Latin. And she would have been made to feel uncomfortable not only because she was an American but also because she was a woman. In her 1988 autobiographical novel *Her Own Terms,* the British-American Judith Grossman wrote that, in the academic environment of Oxford in the late fifties, women were an even smaller minority than at elite American universities and were often patronized by their male classmates and professors. The curriculum and academic customs at Oxford also probably were not particularly to Sontag's taste. The English approach to philosophy was logical and analytic and had little in common with the wide-ranging and significantly less formal philosophic discussions Sontag was used to having with Strauss in Chicago and Taubes in Harvard. The academic milieu at Oxford had less to do with top-flight intellectual achievement and more with the formation of a social elite that could make conversation in the college halls and on the tennis courts.

After only four months at Oxford, Sontag moved on to Paris, the city of her childhood dreams, the city in which Jean-Paul Sartre and Maurice Merleau-Ponty had conducted a public debate about the problem of corporeality—a topic on which Sontag had considered writing her dissertation—and the city where legions of Americans were enjoying the glamorous life of bohemian exiles. At the very end of 1958, Sontag moved into a small mansard-roofed apartment in Saint-Germain-des-Prés.

The American journalist Stanley Karnow, son-in-law of the French lawyer and writer Nathalie Sarraute, recalls the fifties Saint-Germain-des-Prés as a fashionable part of town where well-off professionals gathered in chic galleries, bookstores, publishing houses, interior design shops, restaurants, bars, and cafés. Karnow, in those years the Paris correspondent for *Time* magazine, also remembers what a pervasive American atmosphere the cultural exiles lent to the city's image. Thousands of Americans went to Paris after the Second World War. The very name of the city held out a myriad of promises: "beauty, sophistication, culture, cuisine, sex, escape and that indefinable called ambience."[6]

Most of the Americans had fought in the war, and the G.I. Bill was paying for their education in Paris. They were studying art, literature, ballet, and even haute cuisine—or claimed to be. Among the Parisian exiles were beats, such as William S. Burroughs and Allen Ginsberg. Norman Mailer had written *The Naked and the Dead* (1948) in Montparnasse. As it had for the generation of American artists and intellectuals between the wars—John Dos Passos, Ernest Hemingway, Gertrude Stein, F. Scott Fitzgerald, and T. S. Eliot—Paris exercised immense cultural and social influence on the postwar generation as well.

It was not Sontag's first time in Paris. When she was eighteen, she and Philip Rieff had spent a month in France. Her decision to move to the center of the artistic scene in Paris rather than stay in Oxford probably had much to do with the favorable impressions it had left on the young couple as well as with the romantic dreams of European high culture of the well-read teenager. In the reminiscences she included in the foreword for the travel book *A Place in the World Called Paris* (1994), she describes how she was plagued by a yearning for the French capital like that of Masha for Moscow in Anton Chekhov's *The Seagull* (1896).

Although Susan Sontag obviously planned to do research for her dissertation in Paris libraries as well as attend lectures at the Sorbonne, the most important developments in her personal life did not take place in the academic environment. Sontag began to reorient herself fundamentally. The entries in her journals between 1958 and 1967 suggest that, for the first time in Paris, she was able to freely realize her sexual desires. They were closely connected to her conception of an alternative intellectual life outside the bounds of institutionalized universities, research papers, academic politics, petty positional debates, personal feuds, and the hierarchies she had experienced as a young student and professor's wife.

The intellectual world Sontag discovered in Paris centered on the cafés. Its protagonists were artists. Their motivation was their love for modern literature and film. This formative stay in

Paris would make her a Francophile for the rest of her life and lead her to return repeatedly to the metropolis on the Seine for extended periods. From there she brought back to America not just a series of new philosophical ideas but also the image of the independent Parisian intellectual. In Paris she learned that the formation of a set of personal convictions is nothing less than an existential drama that goes far beyond the forging of alliances within a university; even more, she learned that the adoption of an intellectual position can also be influenced by one's intuition, preferences, and idiosyncrasies, especially when it is not part of an academic discourse.

In a diary entry from December 29, 1957, Sontag compares her impressions of a visit to Greenwich Village with the bohemian life of Paris, where many Americans, Italians, English, South Americans, and Germans lived without being fractured by "national identification and mal-identification," without the "shared comedy of being Jewish." The biggest difference was the routines of café life she loved so much: "After work, or trying to write or paint, you come to a café looking for people you know. Preferably with someone, or at least with a definite rendezvous . . . One should go to several cafés—average: four in an evening."[7]

In another passage, she writes that although the city had long since ceased to be the Paris of her adolescent dreams—namely the "imaginary France in my head that consisted of Valéry and Flaubert and Baudelaire and Gide"[8]—it nevertheless still offered plenty of pleasurable opportunities to live the life of an outsider. Although she knew Los Angeles and New York, she had spent most of her life in provincial towns and now was enjoying her independence and a liberating sense of anonymity. Here is what her normal day in Paris looked like: "Awake in your *chambre de bonne* at eleven, lunch in a cheap bistro, afternoon at the Old Navy or some other not so modish café on the Boulevard St.-Germain, a baguette sandwich before adjourning to the first (or the second, or the third) film at the Cinémathèque, off with your friends to a bar with jazz or a bar that was simply,

properly, *louche*; then, not before three in the morning and, if
you were doing your job right, not alone, to bed."[9] Her time in
Paris coincided not only with her discovery of the bohemian life
but also with her realization that what she desired was the life
of a writer, a desire that had been buried in the shifting sands of
academia.

At first this ambition manifested itself as its opposite, as fear
of the consequences of this way of life. Sontag notes for example
that the *ratés*, the unsuccessful writers and artists who frequented
the cafés, terrified her. What she expected of herself as a writer
was decidedly different. Like many others before her, she kept
a journal to work out her first literary attempts: "Nothing pre-
vents me from being a writer except laziness . . . Why is writing
important? Mainly, out of egotism, I suppose. Because I want to
be that persona, a writer, and not because there is something I
must say. Yet why not that too? With a little ego-building—such
as the fait accompli this journal provides—I shall win through
to the confidence that I (I) have something to say, that should be
said."[10]

Sontag's formulation of her ambitions as a writer shows
her strong-willed motivation through self-doubt. Remarkably
absent, however, are ideas of inspiration, creativity, or sponta-
neity that dominate the self-image of most authors. Sontag is
most interested in the "role" of the artist, from which she hoped
for relief from her insecure and problematic self. Through writing, she intended to reach the self she dared not fully embrace
against the demands of her time, her family, and the academic
life. Unlike other authors who write *because* they have something to say, Sontag writes *in order* to have something to say.
What is impressive about these lines is the clarity with which
Sontag declares her intention, the honesty with which she admits
her vanity, and the unusually high demands she places on herself. Many of Sontag's journal entries move between the poles of
self-torment and ambition.

When Susan Sontag arrived in Paris, several acquaintances
were already there. She knew the author Harriet Sohmers, who

also worked as an artist's model, from Berkeley; the philosopher Allan Bloom from Chicago; and the future film theoretician Annette Michelson from Harvard. They were all part of the American exile scene into which Sontag would be absorbed during her sojourn in Paris. Sontag's friendship with Harriet Sohmers, with whom she began a love affair, was especially important for this phase of her life. Her diaries portray their fraught relationship in minute detail. It bewildered her and drove her to attacks of self-loathing and effusive declarations of love. The relationship with Sohmers especially upset Sontag when Harriet discussed her requirements concerning the form and limits of an "affair." Like Susan, Sohmers also had a heterosexual relationship; she lived with a Swedish painter in an apartment on Boulevard Saint-Germain. Sohmers seemed mainly to project her romantic dissatisfaction onto the affair with Sontag, while Susan's yearnings and needs went much further.

The two women participated in café society, went to movies and museums, and took trips to Italy, Spain, and Greece together. Their relationship was always marked by great, tumultuous drama. Once when they were giving a party, Harriet slapped Susan hard in the face. Allen Ginsberg was in attendance and asked why she had done it. After all, Susan was younger and prettier than Harriet, and Harriet answered, "That's why!"[11]

The stormy relationship of the two ended in disappointment. By accident, Sontag ran across Harriet's diary and read that her lover was especially interested in her erotic passion but otherwise did not like her very much. Sontag portrays this discovery in her journal in a particularly strange way. Instead of being hurt or disappointed, she displays an artificial indifference. She admits to being indignant but above all takes this episode as a reason to analyze the various facets of her friend's personality.[12] Not until two days later can she admit to herself that she feels hurt and even traumatized. The intellectual control she desperately attempts to maintain completely slips from her grasp. Although she had had no illusions, she writes, she assumed that Harriet at least liked her.[13] Nevertheless, in Sontag's perception for the next few years, Harriet continued to be the "finest flower of American bohemia,"[14] an endlessly glamorous promise of another way of life free of traditional constraints, that Sontag would now try to make her own.

At a cocktail party in February 1958, the twenty-six-year-old Sontag met three icons of the life of the intellect she imagined for herself. The party took place in the apartment of the philosopher Jean Wahl, who seemed to care little about his outward appearance. Sontag counted three holes in his pants through which his underpants were visible. The historian of science Giorgio de Santillana was present, as well as an older man who looked like Jean-Paul Sartre.[15] The description of this party is one of her longest diary entries and betrays the sometimes naive fascination Sontag brought to the event. Every detail of Wahl's chaotic apartment in the Rue Le Peletier is noted with painterly precision: the North African furniture, his thousands of books, the flowers, the pictures, the children's toys, the heavy tablecloths, and Wahl's beautiful Tunisian wife, thirty years his junior. As Sontag's commentary on Wahl shows, her fascination sometimes slides into mordant flippancy.[16]

Sontag's writings from the sixties show how much she profited from and was shaped by her ambivalent attitude toward French intellectual life and its stars. Especially significant was her friendship with Annette Michelson, later a professor of film and one of the founders of the journal *October*. Sontag's friend Stephen Koch describes it as "an important intellectual event in Susan's life."[17] The world of postwar art and culture was territory more or less unfamiliar to the PhD student from Harvard, and Michelson helped her to explore it, drew her attention to interesting authors, talked to her about artists and directors, and introduced her to the cultural scene in Paris.

Sontag arrived in Paris at a time of new beginnings that heralded the sixties in both Europe and America. Paris at the end of the fifties was the nucleus for the most important developments in literature, film, and political theory during the decade to come. On May 22, 1957, the critic Émile Henriot coined the phrase *nouveau roman* in *Le Monde* to describe the new development in French literature led by the authors Nathalie Sarraute, Alain Robbe-Grillet, Marguerite Duras, and Michel Butor. The books of this new generation shared a stern intellectual opposition to the narrative forms of the traditional novel. According to these authors, psychological character development, narrative continuity, and the omniscient narrator—that is, all the traditional conventions—were unsuited to describe the recently concluded world war and the incipient Cold War. The "new novels" experimented with narrative perspective and narrated time. They aimed to eliminate traces of the author as much as possible from the text and make literature into a linguistic event whose meaning lies more in the interpretive power of the reader than in the intention of the author. Sontag, like them a zealous reader of Beckett and Kafka and also of her revered teacher Kenneth Burke, derived inspiration from the intellectual implications of these novels. Although she would later deny that the *nouveau roman* had influenced her own fiction, many of its hallmarks were to be found in her first two novels, *The Benefactor* (1963) and *Death Kit* (1967).

Another facet of Paris life would also have a liberating and influential effect on Sontag's life. Whereas in Cambridge she felt constrained to watch popular movies clandestinely, now she was able to indulge this pleasure to her heart's content and often watched several films a day. Unlike the United States, where films were generally consigned to the realm of popular culture and shunned by most intellectuals, Parisians were almost religiously devoted to films by such great directors as Jean Cocteau and Jacques Tati. The American film critic Elliott Stein, who also lived in Paris at the time, reports that he introduced Sontag to the art film scene, especially the legendary Cinémathèque Française, a renowned motion-picture archive that offered daily film screenings. Stein also introduced her to such French directors as François Truffaut and Jean-Luc Godard.[18]

It was customary in the movie houses in the Latin Quarter to organize public discussions after the showings, and literary journals featured serious film critiques. Hollywood movies (forbidden during the German occupation) were also the subject of detailed reviews and often supplied with pompous labels such as "retro-surrealist" at a time when hardly any American critic took movies seriously. Sontag, a lifelong film devotee, brought her passion with her when she returned to the United States and always considered the discussion of movies a serious intellectual undertaking.

Contemporary French political discussion would prove no less decisive for Susan Sontag's life. It was pursued with a passion and radicalness unthinkable in the America of the fifties, especially in academia. In the United States, Communism was characterized as the archenemy and even the slightest sign of sympathy for the Soviet Union was unmercifully attacked. In the French cafés, however, an intense discussion was under way about the social alternatives offered by the Eastern Bloc countries, even to the point of open sympathy for them. Only three years previously, during the McCarthy era, Americans were being imprisoned for such views.

Even after Nikita Khrushchev's February 1956 speech, in which he revealed Joseph Stalin's crimes, the topic lost little of its currency. Instead, the repression and persecution of dissidents in Warsaw, East Berlin, Budapest, and Prague were debated as moral dilemmas for the Western Left. This resulted in a curious double strategy that would remain in place for decades: on the one hand, hesitant condemnation of the crimes of Communism—crushing of workers' rebellions in the German Democratic Republic, Hungary, and Czechoslovakia—on the other, hesitant sympathy for the goals of Communism and its philosophical and ethical foundations.[19] It was a double strategy that Sontag herself would follow until the end of the seventies. What she brought back to the America of the sixties was, first, the unheard-of radicalism of her leftist position—a radicalism she would maintain heedless of scandals it caused—and second, the general conviction that partisanship was an existential duty in Western democracies.

Sontag's unconditional choice of an existence as a writer and oppositional intellectual necessarily went hand in hand with the gradual abandonment of her life as an academic and the immediate end of her marriage to Philip Rieff. Asked in 1975 why she had divorced him, Sontag said she intended to "have several lives" and that seemed impossible in her symbiotic relationship with her husband. She had to decide "between the Life and the Project"[20]—the Susan Sontag project. With impressive consistency, Sontag accepted the consequences of her decision. She would later describe her separation from Rieff as extremely sad. She portrayed the decision that turned her life completely upside-down with a dramatic flair but with little empathy for the dilemma confronted by her husband. As Sontag recalled it, when she flew back to Boston from Paris, the overjoyed and unsuspecting Rieff broke out of the waiting area at the airport to give her a welcoming embrace. After retrieving her luggage and before he had even put his key in the ignition, Sontag told him she wanted a divorce. A few days later, she picked up her son, David, from Rieff's parents and moved to New York.[21]

The New York Nexus

(1959–1963)

It never occurred to me that I couldn't live the life I wanted to lead ... I had this very simple view: that the reason people who start out with ideals or aspirations don't do what they dream of doing when they're young is because they quit. I thought, well, I won't quit.

Susan Sontag, in a 1992 interview

The American poet and Pulitzer Prize winner Richard Howard, translator of Michel Foucault, Roland Barthes, and Michel Leiris and one of Sontag's lifelong friends, recalls how often Sontag talked about the drama of her divorce and how important it was for her.[1] According to Howard, Susan was quite open with her husband about her reasons for wanting the separation.[2]

In March 1959, Susan and her son, David, moved to New York. With her typical flair for self-dramatization, Sontag told interviewers that she arrived in the metropolis with only two suitcases and thirty dollars. Later it was seventy dollars,[3] a somewhat more realistic amount that would be about $450 in today's dollars. Because of the low rents in New York at the time, it would have been enough to make a start.

As Sontag told it, it sounds like a version of the American dream: a twenty-three-year-old single mother without resources moves to a huge and hostile city intending to live there as an author, filmmaker, and intellectual. And on her own and against all odds, she realizes her dream. There could not have been a better place than New York for Sontag to convert her fantasy of the bohemian life into reality. In this city, everything seemed possible for a young, ambitious woman. In those years, the metropolis attracted artists who created subcultures unimaginable anywhere else in the United States. Especially for young writers, the combination of myth, raw material, and talent was irresistible. The metropolis was just then enjoying an economic boom. Skyscrapers sprouted in midtown Manhattan and on Wall Street at the same time that a bohemian scene took shape in older buildings on the Upper West Side. The media industry was booming, not only because of the rapid development of television. New York also had the greatest concentration of publishers, magazines, and newspapers in the country plus a concentration of literary, artistic, and musical talent probably unrivaled by any other city in the world. The American art world was just beginning to cut the umbilical cord to its European models and assert its independence. Norman Mailer, Gore Vidal, and Philip Roth defined the literary scene. John Cage, Ned Rorem, and Philip Glass were composing works that would revolutionize modern music.

David Rieff recounts that at first, the little family lived in relative poverty.[4] Out of pride and—as she suggested in several interviews—an early feminist consciousness, Sontag refused to accept alimony from her husband. She also indignantly refused her lawyer's application for child support for David even though she was unemployed.[5] The divorce agreement also stipulated that Rieff could claim sole authorship of *Freud: The Mind of the Moralist,* a book on which Sontag had worked tirelessly, side-by-side with him.

Still working on her dissertation and uncertain about her academic career, Sontag found a temporary job, probably with the help of Jacob Taubes, as an editor at the prestigious but stolid journal *Commentary*. But instead of serving as a jumping-off point for Sontag's career as a writer, the daily grind of editorial work proved to be exhausting. Annette Michelson remembers how often Sontag complained to her about the dull lives of the editors and the monotonous office work.[6] But for six months, the full-time position ensured support for her and David. Mother and son moved into a small, inexpensive two-room apartment on West End Avenue between 74th and 75th Street on the Upper West Side.

In the fall of 1959, Sontag left *Commentary* to teach one course at the City College of New York and another at Sarah Lawrence College, leaving more free time for her own work. Then in 1960 Jacob Taubes took a professorship in the religion department of Columbia University and offered Sontag a full-time position as lecturer in the philosophy of religion. The idea was to make it possible for her to finish her dissertation. Sontag taught seminars on such topics as the sociology of religion and began to write book reviews for the *Columbia Daily Spectator,* the student newspaper.[7]

There was a price to pay for taking an academic job. "I didn't cook for David . . . I warmed for him,"[8] Sontag once said facetiously. But even if David had to eat too many prepackaged frozen dinners, he grew up in an exciting artistic and political atmosphere. Sontag once told the *New Yorker*'s Joan Acocella that "David grew up on coats," that is, the coats on the bed at the countless parties she took him along to.[9]

Two weeks after arriving in New York, Sontag began to explore the art scene, where she soon made a number of important acquaintances, including Claes Oldenburg. She also began to attend happenings, off-off-Broadway plays, experimental films by Jonas Mekas, and for the first time in her life, she danced.[10] "My mother was a person with truly boundless energy," her son recalls. "It was her single most distinguishing characteristic. I used to joke that she had a 24-hour day folded up inside the first one. She just wanted to have every experience: go to every movie, every dance performance, every club."[11]

Indeed the boundless energy with which Sontag managed to juggle several jobs, an active cultural life, numerous romances, raising a child, and building a career as a writer is the most astonishing thing about her. Her journals from these early New York years seldom mention depressive moods, but they are full of eloquent records of her restlessness. On a single Saturday, for instance, she visits a museum in the morning, rushes in a taxi to lunch with friends, then to a theater in the afternoon to see Ernst Lubitsch's 1932 classic *Trouble in Paradise*. Reading and maternal tasks occupy the early evening, after which she goes to the movies again to see a Kenneth Anger film and then to a party. Finally, she goes to a midnight showing of a Brigitte Bardot film.[12] Richard Howard recalls that, despite her limited financial resources, Sontag never took the bus or subway. It would have seemed absurd to her not to pay for a taxi to bring her exactly where she wanted to go exactly when she wanted to get there.[13]

Sontag's rapidly expanding circle of friends began as a colorful assortment of people, most of whom she had met through her Paris lover Harriet Sohmers. The latter had also moved to New York, and she and Sontag remained friends despite their break-up. Sohmers introduced her to the Cuban-American artist María Irene Fornés and the writer Alfred Chester. While the beautiful Fornés, later to become a well-known feminist playwright, at the time was mainly a painter and devotee of the bohemian scene, Chester was an ambitious writer who had just begun to earn a reputation as a talented literary critic. The four friends became an inseparable quartet at parties and other events. The writer Edward Field, a close friend of Chester and Sohmers, recalled encountering the three women all together for the first time at a poetry reading in a bar on the Bowery. They surrounded Alfred Chester, a small, unattractive man with a disheveled toupee (he had lost all his body hair as a result of a childhood illness and suffered from the stigma all his life), like "a trio of vivid young goddesses . . . or a phalanx of protective amazons."[14]

The quartet was bound together not only by their Francophilia (María Irene Fornés and Alfred Chester had also lived in

Paris), their literary ambition, and their attraction to bohemian culture, but also by their predilection for erotic experimentation. They were among the avant-garde of the sexual revolution that would slowly spread throughout the country, beginning in New York, Los Angeles, and other American metropolises. Not only did Sontag, Sohmers, and Fornés have affairs with each other, but Susan also had one with Alfred Chester although he was a homosexual. He even wanted to marry her. Three years later, he became seriously psychotic, broke with his three friends, denounced Sontag in letters to Edward Field and Paul Bowles as a hated literary rival, and moved to Tangiers. Shortly thereafter, totally isolated by his growing paranoia, he committed suicide in Israel.[15]

Alfred Chester had a considerable influence on Sontag's early career as a writer. Stephen Koch says that it was primarily Chester who showed Sontag the way out of academia and into freelance writing. He was especially popular with the editors of *Partisan Review,* the magazine Sontag had admired since her girlhood. He had a good instinct for the personal power games and intrigues of the New York Intellectuals and not only provided Sontag with valuable contacts but also gave her a feeling for what went on behind the scenes.

But the complicated triangular relationship among Sohmers, Fornés, and Sontag was very difficult to negotiate. Elliott Stein describes it as "this crazy lesbian thing, where they would throw beer bottles at each other's heads and accuse each other of not loving them anymore."[16] Even if these memories of Field and Stein seem to be rather subjective (in the spirit of the time), there is evidence that they contain more than a grain of truth. Sontag's long pent-up emotional energies were now released in all their strength. She seemed to enjoy her newly acquired freedom to the full, especially since the cultural climate in New York made this radically possible for the first time. Sontag later recalled that, in those years, she simultaneously lost her mind and had it firmly under control. She thought of herself as "slumming" in the bohemian scene, ready and willing to explore what it had to offer, but at the same time it was always obvious that "I was going to take [it] back to whatever I thought my real life was."[17]

At length, Sontag and Fornés began a serious love affair, for which Sohmers never forgave them.[18] Richard Howard reports how devoted to Fornés Sontag remained even later in life. Sontag had unusually complicated relationships with all her lovers. When an affair was over, her emotional enthusiasm usually turned into uncontrolled aversion, which she never tried to hide. Under the influence of deep disappointment, Sontag loved to supply her friends with hard-edged, mordant assessments of ex-lovers, male and female. Fornés, however, was an exception. Susan seldom said anything negative about her, regularly attended the openings of her new plays, and remained in loose contact with her for many years.[19]

María Irene Fornés soon moved into Susan and David's West End Avenue apartment, and a two-year relationship began that would be one of the happiest in Sontag's life. With her Cuban roots, Fornés expanded Sontag's bohemian and academic experience with a large measure of Latin American influences that harked back to Susan's childhood in Tucson, where she had grown up with Cuban immigrants. She began to learn Spanish and developed a long-lasting fascination for Cuba and Fidel Castro, who had seized power two years earlier. Sontag, David, and Fornés ended up spending the summer of 1960 in Cuba.[20]

The published excerpts from Sontag's journals make clear how close and fulfilling the relationship between her and Fornés was. In them, the extremely vulnerable Sontag sketches the petty jealousies and disappointments she suffered and her own, often exaggerated, demands on her partner. A few years later, the relationship would founder on such demands. But the greatest discovery in this relationship was Sontag's unconditional acceptance of the fact that her erotic needs included sexual relations with women. In Paris, she had told Annette Michelson that she was not a lesbian and Harriet Sohmers represented only a temporary "vice" for her. By the end of 1959, she had admitted to herself that she desired women as well as men. With Fornés, she experienced erotic fulfillment such as she had not known before, and she associated it with the renewal of her writing: "I lust to write."[21]

And in fact, the relationship would be marked by great productivity for both women. Fornés liked to recount in later interviews what the two of them considered the initial spark that ignited their writing: "We were in a cafe in Greenwich Village, hoping we would see a friend or someone who would know of a party and invite us ... In the meantime Susan starts talking about how she is not too happy because she wants to start writing and doesn't seem to find the time or the way to start. I ... said, 'Start right now?' And she said, 'I know, I keep postponing it.' And I said, 'Do. Start right now. I'll write too!' "[22]

Both authors saw in this incident the birth of their existence as writers. Fornés began her career as a playwright, and Sontag began to write her first work of fiction, the difficult but stylistically sure-handed high-modernist novel *The Benefactor*. In gratitude, she dedicated it to Fornés although their relationship was over by the time it was published.

Fornés also looked back on this time with nostalgia. She repeatedly remarked facetiously that she only began to write plays because she wanted to help Sontag at the beginning of her career. For weeks, the two of them would sit across from each other at the big table in their apartment, each at a typewriter, and stop only to read each other passages from their work in progress.[23]

Moreover, Fornés and Sontag founded a women's writing group that lasted barely a year and included mostly their friends, such as Susan Taubes, the young wife of Jacob Taubes whom Sontag had befriended at Harvard. Alfred Chester dubbed the group wickedly "La Societé Anonyme des Lesbiennes," which both suggests the incipient rivalry between him and Sontag and touches a sore point. For Sontag, it was in fact becoming more and more clear that her writing was closely connected to her sexual needs. Her relationship to the latter was complicated and the source of considerable feelings of guilt. She wrote in her journal, "My desire to write is connected with my homosexuality. I need the identity as a weapon, to match the weapon that society has against me. It doesn't justify my homosexuality. But it would give me—I feel—a license."[24]

Philip Rieff, who in the meantime had accepted a position at the University of Pennsylvania, was furious at the reports of his ex-wife's new life, news he probably learned when his son, David, visited him. The first edition of his book *Freud: The Mind of a Moralist* had included an acknowledgment to "my wife, Susan Rieff"—in and of itself a paternalistic affront to Susan, who had never taken her husband's name—but the acknowledgment was deleted in the second edition. The struggle between the two former spouses continued to escalate, with Rieff attempting to gain custody of David with the argument that Sontag was an unfit mother because of her lesbian relationships. This attempt was a shock to Susan who—herself fatherless as a child—had always strongly insisted that David have a good relationship with his father and had sent him on visits to Rieff in California and Pennsylvania as often as possible.[25]

There ensued a custody battle that was grist for the gossip columns of several New York dailies. The *New York Daily News* headlined its courtroom commentary "Lesbian Religion Professor Gets Custody." With his nose for a good story, Alfred Chester reported that Sontag and Fornés appeared in the courtroom, "stunning" in dresses, heels, and makeup. The judge was so smitten by the glamorous duo that he could not believe they were lesbians.[26]

Despite winning the case and retaining custody of David, Sontag was shocked by the trial. Although from the beginning it was unlikely that a court of the time would grant custody to the father rather than the mother, the Stonewall Uprising and the birth of the gay and lesbian civil rights movement lay far in the future. Homosexuality was still a punishable offense in New York, even if it was seldom prosecuted if practiced behind closed doors and by women. According to Richard Howard, the mud-slinging campaign in the press left deep wounds. He thinks that it was a factor in Sontag never openly admitting to having lesbian lovers. Philip Rieff later regretted having sued Sontag for custody "for the effect the divorce had on his son."[27]

While Sontag was still dealing with the consequences of her divorce, she continued to work on her novel, especially on weekends and during the summer months of 1962 and 1963, when she did not have to teach at Columbia. She said she literally wrote *The Benefactor* with David sitting on her lap. Sometimes he would wake up in the morning to find his mother asleep at the typewriter.[28] But despite the enormous stress inherent in her life as a single mother, the work seemed like a high that happened "almost effortlessly."[29]

The protagonist of the novel, a sixty-year-old reclusive Frenchman named Hippolyte, could not have been further from the twenty-nine-year-old author and her life in New York. Sontag has Hippolyte narrate his bizarre life in the salons of interwar Paris in the first person. The novel's central device is the reversal of the normal hierarchy between reality and a dream world. Hippolyte rigorously transforms reality according to the model of his own, often bizarre, dreams. His life becomes a shadow of his egotistical, eroticized, and unconscious imagination.

Hippolyte can hardly be called a "hero," and the novel hardly has a "plot." Instead, experiences are loosely narrated as a string of often-unconnected events. Hippolyte has an affair with his patroness Frau Anders; has bit parts in various films; flirts with experimental religion; socializes with his friend Jean-Jacques, a promiscuous homosexual hustler; and finally goes on a trip with Frau Anders to an Arab country where he sells her into slavery. The dream sequences gradually reveal themselves as grotesque caricatures of contemporary aesthetic debates, which makes the novel a sort of meta-essay—larded with philosophical and religious theories—on the systematic investigation of one's own imagination.

Thus at a time in her life when Sontag herself was beginning to consistently act out her conception of life, she writes a novel about the dangers of just such consistency: Hippolyte is gradually revealed to be a deeply immoral, apolitical man without a conscience. While Sontag realizes her aesthetic goals, she is negotiating their moral limits in the novel. *The Benefactor* is a rigorously modernist text that basically must be read more than once to catch the numerous ironic references to Descartes's *Meditations,* Voltaire's *Candide,* and the Greek myths of Hippolytus. In its cool austerity, however, it displays a sure feeling for literary presentation even if the text can hardly be evaluated using traditional narrative and psychological categories. The plot leads nowhere; its incomprehensible aimlessness intentionally probes the limits of novelistic form. The influences of French modernism and the *nouveau roman* are unmistakable in its unusual refusal to narrate realistically, even if Sontag heatedly denied them in several interviews.[30] She herself said she had unconsciously used her teacher Kenneth Burke's 1932 novel *Towards a Better Life,* the work he had given her when she was sixteen, as a model. With its collection of artificial vignettes, negotiation of a radical egoism, and rejection of classic narrative conventions, Burke's novel is not unlike the *nouveau roman* and can easily be understood as a model for Sontag.

It is unimaginable in today's media landscape in either America or Europe that an original and stylistically ambitious novel with abstruse content would be successful. But with her unerring feeling for new artistic and social movements, Sontag had found a niche. The American literary world was ripe for trends that had already been in existence in France for five years. Having written eighty pages of the novel, Sontag began looking for a publisher for the manuscript and did not have to look very long.

Robert Giroux, chief editor for Farrar, Straus and Giroux (FSG), tells how the young Sontag showed up in his office with her manuscript. She said that Jason Epstein, the influential Random House editor, had turned down her book (whose working title was *The Striking Man: Dreams of Hippolyte*) but had suggested that Giroux at FSG was the only editor in New York who would understand her novel.[31] Giroux was known for his readiness to take a risk on a new work that might sell badly but was of great literary importance.

Sontag herself recalled the meeting in a much different and more romantic version than Giroux. FSG was housed on Union Square in notoriously shabby offices with ancient linoleum floors. The neighborhood was at that time better known for its drug dealers, homeless people, and pickpockets, who every morning would make way for the gleaming Mercedes of the publisher Roger Straus. Sontag said FSG had always been her first choice. After all, it had published her heroes of 1930s Greenwich Village modernism. At the time, in her "infinite naïveté," she did not know what an agent was and thought every publisher had just one editor for fiction, so she put her manuscript into a carton, addressed it "To the Fiction Editor," and dropped it off with a secretary.[32]

FSG was already one of the most interesting publishers in America and combined high literary standards—represented by its chief editor Giroux—with the specific glamour of the New York intelligentsia—represented by the publisher Roger Straus, a member of the metropolis's high society. Straus was the son of the society matron Gladys Guggenheim and the husband of Dorothea Liebmann, heiress to the Rheingold beer fortune. Since its founding in 1946, FSG had published twenty Nobel Prize winners, including T. S. Eliot, Czesław Miłosz, Nadine Gordimer, Joseph Brodsky, and Seamus Heaney; seventeen National Book Award winners; and seven Pulitzer Prize winners. At the beginning of the sixties, Straus's stable of authors included names that were synonymous with literary prestige, such as Marguerite Yourcenar and Isaac Bashevis Singer.

In May 1961, less than two weeks after submitting her manuscript, Sontag signed a contract with FSG. Her advance was a mere $500. But Roger Straus was known for tirelessly promoting his authors and making sure their books, even if not initially very successful, remained in print for the long term, got translated and published in other countries, and were reviewed in magazines and newspapers, with which Straus had excellent contacts.[33] Sontag could not have found a better publisher.

Thus began a lifelong, intimate friendship between author and publisher that was closely bound up with Sontag's career as a writer and intellectual. Her German publisher Michael Krüger calls their friendship "as pure and beautiful and intense a father-daughter relationship as one could imagine."[34] This aspect of their relationship is also emphasized by Jonathan Galassi, FSG's current chief editor: "He was sort of half father, half comrade . . . They often quarreled, but they also phoned each other all the time. There was a paternalistic aspect to Roger's relationship with Susan, which Susan found pleasant but also patronizing . . . She had never had a real father and I think she found a lot of comfort in the relationship. He was her protector."[35]

Even though the records in the FSG archive in the New York Public Library suggest that Straus treated most of his authors at the beginning with the same solicitous care, his relationship with Sontag was special. He admired her and often said how nervous he would be every time he met her for lunch, a nervousness that was mutual, as he would learn later. Sontag felt herself required to drink cocktails at these business lunches because she thought it was standard procedure. Unfortunately, alcohol did not agree with her and she would always spend the rest of the day in bed.[36]

Straus was very enthusiastic about Sontag's manuscript, as his letters to her show. He wrote that *The Benefactor* was "wonderfully inventive" and "original, powerful, compelling."[37] Straus thought he had discovered in Sontag one of the most important writers of the new generation. He put the novel at the top of his list for the fall of 1963 and within a few months of receiving the completed manuscript had sold the foreign rights for *The Benefactor* to publishers in England, France, and Italy.[38]

Sontag was now also invited to the soirees the Strauses held in their townhouse on the Upper East Side, some of the most important social events of the city. Here Straus brought together publishers and journalists and introduced them to his authors. One could encounter the critic Edmund Wilson feeding canapés to the Strauses' poodle and meet Philip Rahv, chief editor of the *Partisan Review,* as well as Robert Silvers, who would soon cofound the *New York Review of Books.* According to Adam Zagajewski, Straus loved to talk about his famous authors. He did it "in a way a prestigious coach would discuss virtues and weaknesses of his athletes—with a touch of loving superiority . . . affectionately and yet somehow aristocratically. He was like a prince who adores his writers and yet savors the fact that his own fingers are not ink-stained."[39]

Stephen Koch says that Sontag very much enjoyed these glamorous parties. "You went into the Straus' townhouse and it was wall to wall with Nobel laureates." One would encounter Mikhail Baryshnikov, George Balanchine, or Richard Avedon as if stepping into a caricature by Al Hirschfeld.[40]

Richard Howard remembers what a natural Sontag was at making new contacts, striking up friendships, and meeting influential people. "She could be very, very nice—even seductive—to people she wanted something from. She just could not talk to stupid people."[41]

Thus Sontag quickly gained entrance into other circles closely connected to Straus's. She met Random House's publisher Jason Epstein and his wife, Barbara, and the legendary patroness of the arts and dramatic coach Stella Adler, whose circle included popular actors and singers such as Marlon Brando and Frank Sinatra but also high culture figures such as John Cage, Merce Cunningham, and Martha Graham.

Sontag understood instinctively how to move among these groups. The American composer Ned Rorem met her at a party during those years and recalls what an extraordinary impression she would make upon entering a room.[42] "She possessed obvious star quality," says Stephen Koch. "When she arrived at a party, people turned around to look. She was a dramatically beautiful presence who naturally commanded attention."[43]

Sontag's natural and self-confident contact with this exclusive society is all the more remarkable when one recalls how difficult it was to gain admittance. The gathering of New York's high society of writers, artists, and intellectuals was an almost hermetically sealed world with strict criteria for admission. Ned Rorem describes how, during a party at Stella Adler's, Andy Warhol showed up at the front door. Although they were relatively close friends, Rorem had to send him away because he would have made a bad impression with his flippant behavior.[44] Sontag seemed to exude an irresistible mixture of intelligence, hipness, sex, and beauty, so that, as she herself once said, she had Jasper Johns, Bobby Kennedy, and Warren Beatty all at her feet.[45]

At one of Roger Straus's parties in the spring of 1962, Sontag also met William Phillips, the editor in chief of the *Partisan Review*, the very magazine she had read and excerpted in her bedroom at night as a fourteen-year-old, and the one she considered the best magazine in America. Phillips offered to publish one of her essays.[46] Her first work for the *Partisan Review* appeared in the summer 1962 issue, a critique of Isaac Bashevis Singer's novel *The Slave*. She explored the possibilities of a modern, antipsychological and antirealistic novel that would differentiate itself—like her own still unfinished manuscript—from traditional narrative forms. Already in evidence is the remarkable lucidity with which Sontag is able to deploy the tools of an academic to analyze new aesthetic developments and then explain them in a comprehensible way. She would further refine her thoughts about a new vision of the possibilities of the novel form in her essay on the French *nouveau roman* author Nathalie Sarraute. In its reflections on the didactic function of literature, it almost reads like a programmatic argument for Sontag's own literary work of that time. Despite her critique of the *nouveau roman,* she is strongly in favor of the attempt to rescue literature from the bourgeois values of the nineteenth century and raise it to the level of new, radically modern movements in twentieth-century art, music, theater, and architecture.

In quick succession, a series of Sontag's essays appeared in the *Partisan Review* and also in smaller periodicals such as *The Moviegoer, Book Week, The Nation,* and the *Evergreen Review.* She wrote on topics as varied as the happenings that were revolutionizing the New York art scene, the novels of the Italian modernist Cesare Pavese, and the films of Alain Resnais. She seems to understand her writing primarily as documenting the avant-garde transformations shaking the contemporary literary, artistic, and cinematic world. Everything new, unknown, even obscure awakened her interest. With great acuity, she analyzed phenomena that most members of the intellectual establishment hardly took seriously and teased out what were in her eyes their immense social significance.

In December 1962, the printers of the *New York Times* went on strike. The strike would last almost two months, and during that time, Robert Silvers, Elizabeth Hardwick, Robert Lowell, and Jason and Barbara Epstein met and discussed how they could replace the *New York Times Book Review,* the flagship newspaper's Sunday literary supplement, with a new review. They believed that the quality of the reviews in the supplement had already fallen considerably. The *Book Review* seemed to favor commercial trade book titles, and it often dispatched challenging books in ignorant and smug critiques. This strike seemed a once-in-a-lifetime opportunity to launch an independent review that would provide a platform for serious literary journalism. Jason Epstein contacted publishers unable to promote their spring lists in the *Times* on account of the strike. Silvers, Hardwick, and Lowell exploited their contacts to find authors and financing for the undertaking. In February 1963, the first issue of the *New York Review of Books* appeared. During the subsequent decade, it would became the central organ for American intellectuals because of the quality of its articles and its nose for important political issues, a position it continues to occupy today.

The first issue contained articles by Norman Mailer, Gore Vidal, W. H. Auden, Mary McCarthy, Elizabeth Hardwick, and the young Susan Sontag who, according to Hardwick, "simply belonged" when they were mulling over possible contributors to the magazine.[47] Sontag reviewed the collected essays of Simone Weil, the object of her friend Susan Taubes's research. Although Sontag's academic specialty was the philosophy of religion, her discussion of the implications of Weil's essays for that field is subordinate to her description of her own ambivalent relationship to the French philosopher's Gnostic theories, fatalistic attraction to asceticism, and intellectual martyrdom, topics she feels simultaneously drawn to and repelled by.

Sontag's essay on Weil was the beginning of a lifelong if not uncomplicated loyalty to the *New York Review,* for which she wrote up to the end of her life and where her best-known essays first appeared. Her characteristic combination of high serious-ness and hipness, her understanding of the sensibility of the established New York Intellectuals, and her unquenchable curi-osity about subcultures with special attention to contemporary developments and moods exactly suited the spirit of the times.

As the journalist David Denby and the historian Arthur Mar-wick have both suggested, the early sixties were the last truly "serious" moment in U.S. culture. America's cultural landscape was undergoing radical change with the beginnings of global cultural exchange—especially with Europe—and the emergence of subcultures in New York and elsewhere. The signs of cul-tural change ranged from revolutionary developments in art to experimental theater groups to architectural think tanks and the beginning of the civil rights and feminist movements. While the circulation of ideas was radically accelerating, and thus also the media's demand for the new and the spectacular, popular culture had not yet become the exclusive force, television did not yet dominate the everyday life of American households, and society was not yet collectively preoccupied with the effects of the Viet-nam War. Entertainment conglomerates did not yet control mass culture. Irony was still a mode of aggression that separated those in the know from the rest of society, not yet simply the back-ground noise to a flood of images.[48]

When *The Benefactor* appeared in the fall of 1963, its author had already made a name for herself in New York. In addition, Roger Straus secured glowing blurbs from influential New York critics and writers for the dust jacket. Hannah Arendt, for exam-ple, praised Sontag as a great writer and especially admired her ability to knit together a real story from dreams and thoughts. Kenneth Burke praised *The Benefactor* as an extraordinarily good fantasy, intelligent and deep. Robert Flint, Sontag's former boss at *Commentary*, was captivated by the themes derived from European modernism and recognized in the novel a sober, imaginative exploration of every imaginable root cause for refusing to construct a plot.[49] Roger Straus even sent a copy to his friend Arthur M. Schlesinger Jr., then special assistant to John F. Kennedy, recommending it to him as one of the best books of the last fifteen years.

Despite this publicity campaign, Sontag's first novel met with only a lukewarm reception outside New York, which was also reflected in the sales figures. Although no records of the sales can be found in the FSG archive in the New York Public Library, the statements of Sontag's royalties for the novel suggest that, while not a complete economic disaster, it cannot be called a success either. Typical of its reception outside the world of the *Partisan Review* and the *New York Review of Books* was the piece in the *New York Times Book Review*. Here the novel was branded an "anti-novel" and invidiously criticized for its "fashionable imports of neoexistentialist philosophy and tricky contemporary techniques" in which "the characters do not lead lives, they assume postures."[50]

It is evident that Sontag's publisher from the beginning was also speculating on the glamorous aura of its author. In a change from the original plan, the book did not appear with the fulsome blurbs by Burke and Arendt on the back of the dust jacket, but instead with a full-page photo of the twenty-nine-year-old author. Harry Hess's black-and-white image shows a young woman of positively profligate beauty. She could just as well have been a model for a glossy fashion magazine in her contemporary designer outfit with her deep black hair fashionably cut to mid-length. Her expression is one of grave seriousness. This symbiosis of an intellectual subject and the objectified image of a beautiful woman found here for the first time its classic expression. Thus the publication of *The Benefactor*, while not a smashing success, laid the essential cornerstone for its author's future career as well as establishing her signature image that remains in force to the present day. With playful ease and—as many of her friends testify—with her own mixture of innocence and calculation, Sontag was able to cultivate this image that brought the idea of glamour and romance into the dry, masculine intellectual world. And it was precisely this image that made Sontag, the difficult avant-garde author, interesting for other media. For *The Benefactor,* she received in the winter of 1963 the Merit Award from the Condé Nast magazine *Mademoiselle,* known for publishing serious short fiction in addition to its stock-in-trade cosmetic tips, horoscopes, fashion advice, and entertaining articles. Cowinners were Barbra Streisand and the Russian cosmonaut Valentina Tereshkova. Leo Lerman, the editor in chief of *Mademoiselle,* would later become Sontag's friend. The magazine praised her as "the most interesting young writer of the year" and reproduced the Harry Hess photo from the dust jacket. Writing in the *New York Times,* the critic Carolyn Heilbrun gave trenchant expression to the new liaison between glamour and intellect: "Barbra Streisand appeared no more exemplary as Singing Comedienne, or Valentina Tereshkova as Cosmonaut than Susan Sontag as Writer."[51]

Thus began the iconization of Sontag's image that would play a continuing role in her career. No one was more responsible for that than Joseph Cornell, one of the few American masters of surrealism. For his famous collage-box *The Ellipsian,* he used a copy of Harry Hess's photo, tattered at the corners, as if to illustrate the elapse of time. The art critic Deborah Solomon described the effect as follows: "In Cornell's collage, the photo of Sontag—torn at the edges to suggest the passage of time— occupies the upper right corner of the page, from whose heights she stares into space with cool self-possession. A scrap from a chart of the solar system and penciled circles endow her with an otherworldly dimension."[52]

Camp

(1964)

*If I had to choose between the
Doors and Dostoyevsky, then—of
course—I'd choose Dostoyevsky.
But do I have to choose?*

Susan Sontag, *Where the Stress
Falls* (2001)

The year 1964 is generally regarded as the beginning of the "sixties" in America—not the actual decade but the mythical era of rebellion and social upheaval.[1] The year 1964 was the point at which various threads from the late fifties and early sixties—social criticism, subcultures, pop culture, and political liberalism—seemed to weave together into various radical movements that fought their battles in the arenas of politics, the press, art, theater, and especially in the typically American arena of lifestyles. 1964 was the year Martin Luther King Jr. was awarded the Nobel Prize and Congress passed the Civil Rights Act. It was the year the peace movement and the New Left began to form; the year a pop group from Liverpool crossed the Atlantic and Beatles hysteria reached the United States; and the year when acts of rebellion, recreational drugs, Eastern religion, and sexual liberation broke out of their bohemian ghetto. Even middle-class kids suddenly began to read Allen Ginsberg, study Zen Buddhism, and smoke marijuana. It was the year Andy Warhol's muse Edie Sedgwick moved to New York and Warhol himself moved into a new studio on 47th Street in midtown Manhattan, covered it completely with aluminum foil, and thus founded the legend of the Silver Factory. It was also the year Susan Sontag became famous.[2]

Sontag continued to juggle various demands on her time: her son, David; the New York avant-garde scene with its underground movies and experimental theaters; her university teaching post; and finally her career as writer and essayist. This fast life inevitably led to decisions of lasting consequence. María Irene Fornés became more and more estranged from her sometimes difficult partner, and the couple finally split up completely.[3] After *The Benefactor* was published, the contradiction between Sontag's academic career and her literary ambitions became more acute. The fact that she had not completed her dissertation, instead becoming more and more involved with the literary world, led to difficulties with Columbia University. Roger Straus, who had recommended his author for fellowships from the Rockefeller and Merrill foundations, discreetly but urgently told his friend Harry Ford at the latter foundation, "As you may know, she is a member of the Philosophy faculty at Columbia, where her writing efforts have been greeted most unphilosophically by her senior colleagues. As a result of this stupid attitude, she is now in financial need."[4]

Sontag's academic mentor and promoter Jacob Taubes was at this time negotiating his return to Germany to take up a post at the Free University in Berlin, so she could expect no more support from him. Her job would be at risk once he was gone. Finally, however, her publisher's efforts on her behalf bore fruit. On the basis of her literary and critical publications, the Rockefeller Foundation awarded her a post as writer in residence at Rutgers University during the academic year 1964–1965, and for 1965, she also received a fellowship from the Merrill Foundation. These awards put her in a position to leave her unloved instructorship in Columbia's Department of Philosophy.

Sontag's friend Annette Michelson seemed very surprised by this turn of events. The art historian was pursuing an academic career in film studies, at the time still a completely obscure discipline, and could not understand why Sontag would so cavalierly abandon her university career in favor of a highly insecure existence as a freelance writer, apparently without a backward glance.[5] But Sontag's departure from academia was not quite as straightforward as that. Three years later, she still regretted not having finished her dissertation and even planned to complete it after all—probably on recent French philosophy—and earn her PhD from Harvard.[6] But she never carried out this plan. The numerous teaching positions, honorary doctorates, and professorships that were later offered to her she mostly also turned down, often with the flippant justification that she had too much respect for a real PhD to accept an honorary one. Although she kept abreast of scholarly publications in the areas of literature, film studies, and cultural history, her essayistic approach remained basically antiacademic. She repeatedly stressed that the life of a writer and that of an academic were mutually exclusive. She had, after all, seen "academic life destroy the best writers of my generation."[7] It is not difficult to discern behind this remark a pose of wounded vanity. Herself one of the best authors of her generation, Sontag's failure in academia was due not only to her wish for an antiacademic life but also to the fact that she was a woman in the still strongly patriarchal world of the universities.[8]

At the end of the spring semester in 1964, Sontag left her teaching position at Columbia and began life as a freelance author and essayist. After early difficulties earning enough to get by, she increasingly was able to support herself with her writing.

In the few published journal entries from that year, Sontag's personal problems sometimes shade into self-loathing. With great clarity she mounts attacks against herself, criticizing her tendency "to censor [*sic*] others for my own vices, to make my friendships into love affairs, to ask that love include (and exclude) all."[9] What fell victim to her new notoriety was her literary output. After finishing *The Benefactor* in 1962, Sontag wrote

essays almost exclusively. A second novel she had already begun
proved too short of breath and appeared as a short story titled
"The Dummy" in the September 1963 issue of *Harper's Bazaar.*
Otherwise, journalism and essays predominated until the fall of
1965, and for good reasons. For one thing, the intense life Sontag led in New York was expensive and her essays, reviews, and
articles paid much more than novels or short stories. The *Atlantic Monthly,* for example, paid $500 for a 3,000–3,500 word
article, as much as FSG paid her for the completed manuscript
of her entire novel. For another thing, her extraordinary articles
appeared to gain her more—and more immediate—recognition
from colleagues and friends than her fiction.

Yet as her journal shows, writing at this time became a real
challenge and even a torture for Sontag. "A freshly typed manuscript, the moment it's completed, begins to stink. It's a dead
body—it must be buried—embalmed, in print," she said.[10] By
her own admission, she needed to build up pressure to write.
Her work got done in intense bursts: "I write when I have to
because the pressure builds up and I feel enough confidence that
something has matured in my head and I can write it down."[11]
Moreover, she tended to revise again and again for as many as
ten drafts.[12] Sontag's friend Judith Thurman, the biographer of
Isak Dinesen, recalls how moved she was by the way Sontag confronted her writing difficulties. She repeatedly told Thurman in
great upset how "impossible, impossible in a stupid way" writing was for her.[13] Other friends of Sontag's tell how dramatically
every writing block would be overcome—by writing through the
night without eating or sleeping, so that she would lose a lot
of weight. Not until she was completely drained would she lie
down on the floor next to her desk and sleep for two hours.[14]

Moreover, this way of writing, a way Sontag herself described
as "undisciplined," not only made it difficult to work continuously on a novel but also made it hard to meet the demands
of journalism. Deadlines and precise descriptions of content to
come were anathema to her. When William Phillips of the *Partisan Review* offered her the prestigious post of theater critic

previously held by Mary McCarthy (at the time the most prominent intellectual in New York), Sontag accepted, although she did not want to write theater reviews. She recalled self-ironically what happened: "After the second round I told Phillips I couldn't go on."[15] Although the two reviews (republished in her 1966 collection *Against Interpretation*) sound like typical Sontag texts of the time—that is, intelligent, polished, and original—she keeps veering off from her actual assignment of writing about a theater production. Instead, she writes at length about films that occur to her as associations but otherwise have nothing to do with the play under review. While in other essays from this time her deep-seated enthusiasm motivates her writing, she had none for the staid, naturalistic plays prevalent in New York theaters. They had little or nothing to offer to the radical aesthetic sensibility that fired her thinking and writing and probed all aspects of culture. Sontag wanted to choose her own topics: artistic work she admired and relatively unknown authors, artists, and films. She understood her essays as "cultural work." She wrote them, as she would later stress, above all from a feeling for their relevance, with a view to "what *needed* to be written."[16]

"Art," Sontag wrote in her journal in July 1964, is "a way of getting in touch with one's own insanity."[17] And so by choice she involved herself in controversies that included the areas of art that brought her into contact with her own "dark side," the part of her personality that was the object of social discrimination and against which she felt she needed to mobilize her writing as a "weapon." For example, she found that writing about contemporary underground films that challenged strict American censorship and sometimes had to be screened illegally gave her an opportunity to give these feelings space to express themselves. Richard Howard tells how Sontag called him up in excitement one day, saying there were rumors that somewhere in New York they were going to show Jean Genet's 1950 *Un chant d'amour* (*A Song of Love*), a scandalous art film—banned in the United States—that contains explicit images of gay masturbation in a French prison. Howard and Sontag immediately set out and went from one underground cinema to the next—from the Gramercy Arts Theatre of Jonas Mekas to the New Yorker Theater, a revival house owned and operated by Daniel Talbot—until they finally discovered where the film was playing.[18] Sontag referred to herself as "film crazy." She indulged the passion for movies she had contracted in France with unusual fanaticism. Whenever her crowded schedule allowed, she still went to the movies several times a day. She wrote essays and reviews of what she had seen and participated in symposia on avant-garde film.[19]

On March 3, 1964, the New York Police Department raided one of the centers of underground films, Diane di Prima's New Bowery Theater, during a showing of Jack Smith's semipornographic film *Flaming Creatures* (1963), which includes an orgy participated in by heterosexuals, gays, lesbians, and drag queens. It was not just a question of enforcing censorship laws. Instead, it was an out-and-out purge because that summer New York was hosting the World's Fair, a gigantic international consumer event. The police arrested both the organizers and audience members, confiscated copies of the film and also of Andy Warhol's early documentary *Jack Smith Filming "Normal Love"* (which has been lost ever since), and obtained an injunction to close the theater. This police action unleashed a wave of protests and demonstrations against censorship in which Sontag participated.[20] Her passionate defense of the film appeared in *The Nation* on April 13, 1964, under the title "A Feast for Open Eyes" and was republished in *Against Interpretation*. She compares Jack Smith to Luis Buñuel and Sergei Eisenstein and places him in the tradition of abstract expressionism and pop art. She vehemently defends the film against the official accusations of pornography that led a month later to a widely reported trial. On the basis of her article, Sontag was asked to testify as an expert witness, but the director lost the trial nevertheless.

In Sontag's essay as well as in her testimony before the court, she countered the accusation of pornography with the pathos and innocence of the sexually deviant images. She interpreted them not as pornographic lust but rather as visual play that also manifested itself in the exaggeratedly amateurish use of a handheld camera and overexposed film. Sontag closes her essay with the emphatic declaration, reminiscent of Herbert Marcuse's theory of repressive tolerance, that *Flaming Creatures* is "a triumphant example of an aesthetic vision of the world" and represents a type of art that "has yet to be understood in this country," whose critics have traditionally located art in "the space of moral ideas."[21]

The remarkable thing about this essay is its development of an individual voice with a precise intellectual vocabulary that takes on supposedly scandalous topics and addresses fundamental questions of cultural politics and criticism. With this combination, Sontag hit precisely on the disruptive atmosphere of those years and at the same time understood that with her essay she could have a much greater influence on contemporary social debates than with her literary texts. In a radical tone, she proclaims in her essays the gospel of a new era and the arrival of a new generation.

"It wasn't a great period for fiction," Sontag told the journalist Ellen Hopkins. "People were more interested in talking about ideas."[22] Even Dwight Macdonald, part of the bedrock of the New York intelligentsia, recommended that his young colleague pursue a career as literary critic.[23] He had met her through Roger Straus, and she had accused Macdonald of not understanding her generation at a symposium on contemporary literary criticism in the fall of 1963. "No one's interested in fiction, Susan," he said. "Naaaahhh. Write essays!"[24] Sontag's publisher Roger Straus and her editor Robert Giroux were of the same opinion. Both of them suggested that Sontag's next book should be nonfiction.[25]

Among New York's writers and journalists, Susan Sontag had acquired the reputation of an "intellectual It-Girl." It was a title she seemed both to seek and to disdain, especially after the *New York Times* repeatedly used the phrase to refer to her.[26] As contemporaries report, the publication of a new Sontag essay in the *Partisan Review* or the *New York Review of Books* was always an event, so unique and fresh was her style, so unexpected and exciting her topics.[27] A volume of essays seemed to Roger Straus the next logical step to build the reputation of his protégé and make Susan Sontag into a brand name closely associated with his publishing house.

In early April 1964, at Straus's request, Sontag drew up a list of essays she had already published and a synopsis of articles still in the planning stages. The list included her essays on Albert Camus, Claude Lévi-Strauss, Michelangelo Antonioni, Cesare Pavese, and Jean-Luc Godard and ideas for texts on interpretation, camp, style, the new sensibility, and science-fiction films, as well as sketches of essays on the aesthetic of stillness and pornographic literature. These writings were to form "the backbone of her next book or two,"[28] the famous essay collections *Against Interpretation* (1966) and *Styles of Radical Will* (1969).

The publication of those two volumes was preceded by a carefully planned marketing campaign. Straus acted as Sontag's agent for magazines and journals and saw to it that her writings appeared in well-respected publications. FSG staff member Lila Karpf wrote to the publisher's British, French, and Dutch outlets that "Roger was in many cases instrumental in getting Susan the assignments for some of these essays and reviews" and that she hoped "a similar campaign" in those countries would "produce similar results." Karpf would understand, she continued, that "there is not much money in this kind of effort" but rather that it was a "literary chore which will only pay off in the long run."[29]

But Straus's real stroke of genius consisted in offering Sontag's writings not just to the highbrow journals that had already published her pieces but also to such magazines as *Vogue, Mademoiselle, Harper's Bazaar, Life,* and *Time.* Although these publications had no real connection to high culture, they had significantly larger circulations and paid more for articles. This was a positively unheard-of thing for serious writers to do. In a witty 1966 essay for the *New York Times* titled "Notes on Cult; or, How to Join the Intellectual Establishment," Victor S. Navasky wrote that, in addition to publishing articles in the *New York*

Review, Commentary, and *Partisan Review,* one might also write for the *New Yorker* from time to time, but anything below that would be a sacrilege for a New York intellectual.[30]

At the end of her essay on Jack Smith's *Flaming Creatures,* Sontag introduces the concept of camp into her description of the film as a "way of relishing mass culture."[31] At the time, "camp" was mostly a code word in the gay subcultures of New York and London. It designated an ironic attitude that derived sophisticated, knowing amusement from such things as kitschy films, novels, and mass-produced decorative objects. As an attitude, camp (a concept that never really made it into the cultural discourse of the Continent but always remained a specifically Anglo-Saxon phenomenon) was the epitome of a reception that allowed one to enjoy cultural products that did not fit into the traditional patterns of high bourgeois culture. One could enjoy and, at the same time, stand knowingly above camp objects, amused at the aestheticization of the trivial. The idea of camp was a notion of dissident taste, a sensibility that acknowledges high culture while undermining it at the same time.

Sontag had long been planning to write about the concept of camp, not necessarily because she shared this sensibility (as she would write, she was equally attracted to and repulsed by it), but because she was fascinated by how her gay friends, such as Alfred Chester, Richard Howard, Elliott Stein, and the artist Paul Thek, had adopted the camp attitude and turned it into a mark of distinction.

Sontag was aware that her essay on this subject would be controversial. She had offered it to the *Partisan Review,* where it had unleashed a furious editorial debate. Sontag's partisan William Phillips was just barely able to get it accepted over the objections of Philip Rahv, the second editor of the magazine, who vigorously objected to Sontag's unconventional style.[32] For one thing, the topic of homosexuality was taboo. For another—and this weighed more heavily on the scale for the intellectual circles in which Sontag moved, where gays and lesbians were at least tolerated—any engagement with mass culture was scorned.

"She knew," says Richard Howard, "that she was writing the Camp article more or less for the public."[33]

The 1964 essay "Notes on 'Camp,'" written mostly during a visit to Paris in the summer of that year and published in the fall issue of *Partisan Review*, was Sontag's big breakthrough and is still considered her most famous essay, especially in the United States. Sontag's friend Elliott Stein served as her inspiration for the camp sensibility. He rented a room in the Hôtel Verneuil where she often visited him, a room that had also been the model for James Baldwin's 1956 novel *Giovanni's Room*. Stein's room was like a catalog of camp taste: kitschy lamps hung from gilded plaster walls, and a photo of Jean-Paul Sartre stood in a place of honor next to one of a gay street walker.[34] Sontag's essay exploits this random juxtaposition of kitschy artifacts not just in the content but also in the form of her essay. Instead of structuring the piece in the traditional way, Sontag divides her essay into fifty-eight numbered paragraphs, each having the character of a philosophical aphorism and describing one facet of the camp phenomenon. The aphoristic quality is underscored by witty quotes from Oscar Wilde scattered throughout the essay; Sontag considered Wilde's dandyism to be the original model for the camp sensibility.

But Sontag's key move consists in raising camp from the status of a subculture and declaring it to be a third path of aesthetic experience, the equal of serious high culture and avant-garde extremes of feeling and consciousness. Accordingly, she capitalizes the word "Camp" throughout the essay as if it were a proper noun like Dadaism or Renaissance, formally elevating a subversive sensibility to the status of a style: "And third among the great creative sensibilities is Camp: the sensibility of failed seriousness, of the theatricalization of experience. Camp refuses both the harmonies of traditional seriousness, and the risks of fully identifying with extreme states of feeling."[35]

Sontag inventories this style or "creative sensibility" and records a veritable catalog of camp artifacts: from Tiffany lamps, Vincenzo Bellini operas, *Der Rosenkavalier*, Gina Lollobrigida, and Greta Garbo to the novels of Ronald Firbank, *Swan Lake*, and Josef von Sternberg's Marlene Dietrich films. The result is an essay scandalous and serious in equal measure that threatened "the pantheon of high culture: truth, beauty, and seriousness"[36] with a love of ironic pathos, exaggerated stylizations and "flamboyant mannerisms susceptible of a double interpretation."[37] In an American culture saturated by consumer culture and entertainment products, camp represents for Sontag survival by style. Despite its apparent acceptance of mass culture, camp taste is for her not an affirmation of the entertainment industry. Rather it functions as an aesthetic filter that makes it possible to live in that culture. If there was a user's manual for lifestyle in those years, then it was Susan Sontag's "Notes on 'Camp.'"

Reactions to the essay were many and varied. On the one hand, copies of it were distributed free to enthusiastic patrons of Daniel Talbot's New Yorker film house, where Sontag had researched camp taste watching countless movies.[38] On the other hand, *Partisan Review* received a flood of letters from readers upset by the homosexual themes and the serious treatment of pop culture.[39] But the fame that the concept "camp" would achieve in the following years far overshadowed these complaints. Suddenly Sontag's camp concept was being used as a label for more and more new cultural phenomena. Frequently camp was misunderstood and used as a synonym for "pop" or "ironic." A long-lived and widely circulated variation of this misunderstanding in the visual arts was to equate camp with the experimental films, silk-screen prints, and Brillo-box sculptures of Andy Warhol or with the pop art paintings of Roy Lichtenstein, Robert Rauschenberg, and Claes Oldenburg. While the pop art movement that began in New York and conquered the world during those years had very little to do with Sontag's concept of camp, it resisted traditional aesthetic categories in the same way. Both explicitly referred to mass culture and ironized the accepted categories of art and entertainment. But while camp taste retrospectively availed itself of a plethora of the kitschy products of mass culture, pop art proclaimed the arrival of a new and much more anonymous media era. Thus, more or less unwillingly, Sontag lent apparent intellectual respectability to an ultrafashionable phenomenon that found expression, for example, in Andy Warhol signing cans of Campbell's soup that cost twelve cents and reselling them in his gallery on the Upper East Side for six dollars.

As Thomas Meehan reported in a 1965 *New York Times* article in which he duplicitously dubbed Sontag both the "Sir Isaac Newton of Camp" and "Miss Camp," within a few months of the publication of her essay the concept of camp had become a catchphrase on everyone's lips. For a brief time, whether something was camp or not replaced the question of what was "in" and what was "out." People in the know made a game of speculating about whether something was "real" or "fake," "conscious" or "unintended," "high" or "low" camp.[40]

As strange as it seems today that one critical essay could catapult a thirty-one-year-old woman into intellectual stardom, it was possible on the East Coast of America in 1964. Sontag's reputation achieved a decisive breakthrough with a report about her essay in *Time* magazine on December 10, 1964.[41] The most important magazine of its time for the American middle class, with a circulation twenty times larger than the *Partisan Review, Time* called Sontag "one of Manhattan's most talented young intellectuals." Other newspaper and magazine articles followed suit. "Suddenly," summarized the *New York Times* critic Eliot Fremont-Smith, "Susan Sontag was there—instead of being announced, she had been proclaimed." As Fremont-Smith described it, "She did not creep modestly and hesitantly onto the intellectual scene. Instead, she burst from nowhere amid something like a ticker tape parade."[42]

The visual proof of Sontag's fame are the "Screen Tests," the three-minute 16-millimeter portrait films of Andy Warhol that are a Who's Who of the sixties New York avant-garde from Allen Ginsberg and Dennis Hopper to Bob Dylan. Sontag, too, embodied Warhol's inimitable sense of glamour and pop culture. Warhol was so inspired by Sontag's essay (and probably even more by the attention it received in the press, as Warhol specialist Callie Angell says) that a year later he would shoot a film titled *Camp* in which Jack Smith, the director of *Flaming Creatures*, also makes an appearance.[43] Although Warhol knew that Sontag did not have a very high opinion of him, he was so impressed by her charisma that he made seven "Screen Tests" of her, an honor otherwise accorded only to Edie Sedgwick, Lou Reed, Nico, and Baby Jane Holzer, all members of Warhol's New York studio the Factory.[44] In the "Screen Tests" now in the collection of the Museum of Modern Art in New York, one sees an attractive young woman whose serious and sometimes arrogant aura also conceals great insecurity—at times smiling, at others bored, pouting, smoking, grinning a grin that does not seem to fit her face, and hiding behind dark sixties sunglasses. Warhol planned to include her in two compilations of the Screen Tests, *13 Most Beautiful Women* and *50 Fantastics and 50 Personalities,* but he never completed them.

Styles of the Avant-Garde

(1965–1967)

> *The real life of the mind is always*
> *at the frontiers of "what is already*
> *known."* . . . *The most interesting*
> *ideas, after all, are heresies.*

Susan Sontag, in a 1975 interview

After the success of the camp essay, Susan Sontag's reputation as a critic of the new cultural sensibility was firmly established.[1] Her essays stood out from the journalistic landscape of the day, as many contemporaries recall. They had a fresh voice and at the same time conveyed a sense of daring.[2] Her status as an experimental novelist and young intellectual was so extraordinary that, at the suggestion of her publisher Roger Straus, the Merrill Foundation awarded her a year's fellowship in 1965. In March 1966, there followed the George Polk Award for Cultural Criticism and a Guggenheim Fellowship. Sontag was increasingly invited to congresses, readings, and other events that gave her, a passionate traveler, opportunities to visit places she had dreamed of as a child. During these years, she spent summers in Paris and also traveled to Czechoslovakia, Yugoslavia, Germany, Morocco, Italy, Cuba, Vietnam, Laos, Sweden, and England, a list that would be extended over time. Besides honors, these invitations also entailed obligations, for instance, serving on the jury of the Venice Film Festival in 1967; appearing at conferences of PEN International, a worldwide association of writers; giving readings on tours for her European publishers; and researching her essays. These travels allowed her to keep up with the newest international developments in literature, film, and art. Supported by the fellowships, which finally enabled her to concentrate completely on her writing career, Sontag completed her first collection of essays, *Against Interpretation,* a work that still influences debate and provokes academic discussion.

The title essay, in particular, provided a slogan for literature, art, and film criticism in the years that followed. First published in the *Evergreen Review* in late 1964, "Against Interpretation" heralded the end of the old-fashioned art criticism long the rule in most of the highbrow magazines for which Sontag wrote. Sontag draws a line from the Platonic and Aristotelian theory of art as an imitation of nature to the most influential Marxist and Freudian theories of interpretation. She formulates a brilliant and biting polemic against the contemporary interpretive practice of excavating a subtext of "real" meaning underlying the actual text.

In this sense, according to Sontag, interpretation is simply reactionary and betrays a bourgeois refusal to allow art to stand on its own. When criticism reduces a work of art to its "meaning," criticism tames it, makes it into a compliant and manageable commodity, and robs it of its ability to unsettle. Seen in this way, interpretation represents nothing but the contamination of individual emotional experience: "Today is such a time, when the project of interpretation is largely reactionary, stifling. Like the fumes of the automobile and of heavy industry which befoul the urban atmosphere, the effusion of interpretations of art today poisons our sensibilities."[3]

Sontag's declared intention is not to return to some sort of imagined age of innocence, an age prior to any theory of art. Instead, her goal is to defend art against its critics, since current interpretation is nothing less than—as she formulates it in one of her typically insightful phrases—"the revenge of the intellect upon art."[4] She develops the rudiments of adequate critical practice using the example of film. For her, film represents a form of aesthetic perception that places the "pure, untranslatable, sensuous immediacy"[5] of its images at the center of attention. The job of the critic is to describe this "sensuous surface"[6] and analyze its stylistic form, not to concentrate on its meaning. In a television interview twenty-eight years later, Susan Sontag said that, in the sixties, she did not understand why literature and theater could not be as modern as the contemporary cinema and its pantheon of great directors—Godard, Resnais, Antonioni, and Ingmar Bergman.[7] The film critic Elliott Stein says the fact that Sontag as an American intellectual placed film (still suspect as a form of popular culture) above the traditional high cultural forms of literature and fine art was as scandalous for most of her contemporaries as it was liberating for the new generation of artists and academics.[8] Equally liberating for the younger generation was Sontag's open call for a cultural revolution. In a culture "based on excess, on overproduction," whose result is "a steady loss of sharpness in our sensory experience,"[9] the critic has above all a crucial political function. And so Sontag closes her essay with a stirring and cryptic call to arms that would become one of her most quoted sentences: "In place of a hermeneutics we need an erotics of art."[10]

The collection *Against Interpretation* was a sensation because—in the words of the literary critic Eliot Weinberger—"cloaked in a familiar and unthreatening critical discourse, it finally brought the tenets of Dadaism and Futurism and Surrealism to Riverside Drive, where the modern had been Joycean and Eliotic, a territory patrolled by New Critical, Freudian, and Marxist exegetes."[11] What Sontag had to say was not necessarily new. It was rather a clarion call that needed repeating every few years in any case, a call that, at that moment, shook the New York intellectual scene out of its drowsiness.

The collection closed with an equally brilliant essayistic piece of cultural revolution that started an even bigger stone rolling and described even more aptly the utopian sensibility of the sixties. The essay "One Culture and the New Sensibility" (in 1965, Straus had a shorter version of it published in *Mademoiselle*) took aim at the distinction between high and popular culture and became a foundational text for pop criticism. With her characteristic talent for igniting controversy, Sontag proclaimed a new understanding of culture no longer primarily based on a literary model but rather including all areas of art under the aspect of sensuous experience.

It is difficult to imagine today how radical this view was and what a scandal it provoked at a time when the distinction between high culture and mass culture was not only precisely delineated but also formed the basis for the self-definition of intellectuals and academics. To many intellectuals, Sontag's polemic and programmatic turn to pop seemed like high treason. What turned the sacrilege into a scandal was the fact that Sontag cited as the visionaries of this modern understanding of culture such philosophers as Friedrich Nietzsche and Ludwig Wittgenstein as well as Antonin Artaud, John Cage, and the French theorists Claude Lévi-Strauss and Roland Barthes. Sontag's essay is a declaration of war against the ignorance of her colleagues. She firmly declares that "the feeling (or sensation) given off by a Rauschenberg painting might be like that of a song by the Supremes."[12] A painting by Jasper Johns or a film of Jean-Luc Godard's could be as accessible as the music of the Beatles and enjoyed without condescension as complex and sensual aesthetic experiences. Contemporary avant-garde trends in painting, film, and music that reflected this "new sensibility" represent for Sontag "a more open way of looking at the world and at things in the world, our world."[13] They map out new standards of beauty, style, and taste.

Like "Notes on 'Camp,'" the essay "One Culture and the New Sensibility" broke a taboo by taking popular culture seriously and submitting it to intellectual analysis. It was this violation of a taboo more than anything else that made Sontag famous. When *Against Interpretation* appeared in January 1966, it was celebrated by critics as "a vivid bit of living history here and now, and at the end of the sixties it may well rank among the invaluable cultural chronicles of these years,"[14] as Benjamin DeMott put it in the *New York Times Book Review.* The fact that Sontag's attachment to popular culture was somewhat suspect (as DeMott hints in his ironic headline "Lady on the Scene") only contributed to the book's success. As Sontag's friend Robert Mazzocco wrote in the *New York Review of Books,* her style was "brilliant, punchy, brisk, and, in a characteristically contemporary way, a little perverse."[15]

Against Interpretation was more than just an extensive compendium of sixties culture. Sontag knew how to combine her interest in radical avant-garde aesthetics with her interest in equally radical political change, in the service of which she first of all threw overboard traditional notions of morality. Her conception of the role of the intellectual included work toward real social progress. *Against Interpretation* calls for a new form of criticism not just to make the avant-garde aesthetic more comprehensible but also, with the help of that aesthetic, to sensitize all of society and expose it to new possibilities of experience. What is evident here is a positively youthful belief in the power of art and the superiority of the critical intellect. The culture had to change so that individuals could become new and better human beings.[16]

It is particularly striking that no review of *Against Interpretation* failed to mention Sontag as a public persona who seemed to enact herself in her writings. For example, Norman Podhoretz, the publisher of *Commentary,* remarked cynically that the New York Intellectuals were united in casting Sontag as the new "Dark Lady of American Letters," a role formerly assigned to Mary McCarthy, who in turn had been promoted to grande dame since Sontag's appearance on the scene.[17] Comments like this make clear that, at the time, a woman possessing superior intelligence was still regarded as an exception, especially since Sontag was not afraid to challenge her male colleagues. In their letters and diaries, the women associated with the New York intellectual scene—Elizabeth Hardwick, Diana Trilling, and Hannah Arendt among others—often comment mordantly on the misogyny prevalent among their male counterparts.[18] But this latent misogyny set its sights on the figure of Sontag, in particular, because her incipient fame outstripped anything women normally achieved in the male intellectuals' narrowly circumscribed world. What the macho sensibility accepted in a man like Podhoretz was impermissible for a woman if she did not want to end up in a niche. Today it would be unthinkable to call a writer (or at least, a serious writer) a "literary pin-up" or as good as call her a dominatrix by speaking of her "intellectual riding-crop."[19] Such low blows had the obvious subtext that a woman, especially an attractive woman, cannot be intelligent too.

Although Sontag had already established herself in New York with her editorial work at *Commentary* and the publication of her essays in *Partisan Review* and the *New York Review of Books,* with the appearance of *Against Interpretation* she became a thorn in the side of many long-established New York Intellectuals. She represented a new generation that no longer observed the rules of the literary game. Her revolutionary cultural proclamations caused great unease in men like Dwight Macdonald, Edmund Wilson, Irving Howe, and Robert Lowell. All of them had been convinced Marxists in the thirties and forties but after their rejection of Stalinism had reached a liberal-bourgeois consensus in the fifties that had no room for revolutionary ideas.[20] But it was also the popularity Sontag enjoyed in mass-circulation magazines that was anathema to them. At New York parties and soirees, she was a celebrity. She moderated readings by Nathalie Sarraute and Vladimir Nabokov at the 92nd Street Y on the Upper East Side. She was a star participant in the symposia that structured the intellectual life of New York and enjoyed locking polemical horns with the elders whose critical practice she regarded as simply irrelevant.

With her focused attacks on "critics" in general and "literary sensibility" in particular, Sontag did not make herself popular. She liked to lard her writings with deliberate and often-exaggerated provocations against the supposed provincialism of American criticism, which she sweepingly condemned, often in spite of knowing better, to launch her own polemical theses.[21] On the one hand, this was accepted practice in New York intellectual circles, as Victor Navasky points out in his essay on the establishment of the time: "If you want to join the New York intellectual establishment . . . all you've got to do is make the right friends and then attack them."[22] On the other hand, Sontag always overdid her attacks. A further provocation was her enthusiastic Francophilia. The engagement with French authors and filmmakers that runs through the pages of *Against Interpretation* was dismissed by many of her American colleagues as a trendy pose. But the affront was deeper than that. Most American writers and critics were deeply sympathetic to European authors and cultural models. The difference in Sontag's Francophilia, however, was how partisan it was. Her friend Stephen Koch says that Sontag believed implicitly "that Europe was a place where culture had made people better than in America. She was convinced that it was extremely important to combat provincialism in oneself, one's environment, and in all of America."[23] Her enthusiasm for continental culture was a counterpart to her sweeping criticism of her own society.

Partisan Review editor Philip Rahv, for example, positively despised Sontag for the Francophile positions she adopted.[24] As his diaries reveal, Edmund Wilson (in those days the unofficial chairman of the New York Intellectuals) thought just as little of Sontag.[25] It is also well known that Mary McCarthy could not stand Sontag, an opinion she offered freely in numerous interviews. Her antipathy was so great that she could hardly keep it in check. She attacked Sontag at public events and in one unrestrained outburst called her "the imitation me."[26] Irving Howe, who wrote for *Commentary, Partisan Review,* and the *New York Review of Books* as well as cofounding *Dissent,* passed a judgment on Sontag that was as devastating as it was unjust. He called her a public relations woman who constructs "skillfully rebuilt versions of aesthetic notions long familiar and discarded" and who was a "highly literate spokesman" for those "who have discarded or not acquired intellectual literacy."[27]

Sontag had influential defenders and patrons in Roger Straus and Elizabeth Hardwick—Hardwick always rode to the counter-attack when people started talking about unfavorable reactions to Sontag: "Oh well, Mary—Mary couldn't stand anyone!"[28] With Sontag's growing fame and her image as a radical, Francophile, and cosmopolitan aesthete with a special taste for pop culture, it became increasingly clear that her positions were too extreme for most of her colleagues. Even the *New York Review of Books,* for which Sontag had written since it was founded, dropped her as one of its writers in the year after *Against Interpretation* was published. Sontag complained bitterly about it to her friends Richard Howard and Roger Straus as well as to William Phillips, the editor of *Partisan Review.*[29]

Sontag's letters to Roger Straus show that, with the exception of the *New York Review of Books,* she took all this antipathy in stride. She either ignored it or expressed her respect for her "honorable" opponents with a slightly ironic undertone. Straus was closely connected to almost everyone of consequence on the New York scene, often because he was their publisher and sometimes via his famous parties. In this regard, it would have been undiplomatic for Sontag to speak unfavorably about her rivals. But friends, including Richard Howard and Stephen Koch, report that she sometimes adopted an impatient and somewhat snooty manner in her swift, sharp counter-offensives whenever she felt herself under attack.[30]

On the larger media stage, however, the situation looked different. The political and cultural movements of the sixties were no longer confined to the major cities and the universities and colleges. They had instead become a current running through the entire society. The emerging movement needed a theoretician, and its opponents needed a figurehead at whom to take aim. Susan Sontag seemed the ideal person to fill this double role, for her essays provided not just arguments but also a mood, a tone, and an atmosphere that reflected the new developments as few other contemporary texts did. Sontag projected the image of an authority on the contemporary scene and was identified by the media and students all over America as a trend scout who knew what was new and could make underground culture comprehensible for the mainstream. At the same time, her personality offered itself as a model for the new sensibility. Sontag seemed especially appropriate for all these roles because she was able to project her star quality onto the media stage as well. Her first magazine interviews from those years were, like her writings, controversial and accompanied by photographs of a tomboyish young woman—often in pensive, elegant poses—barefoot and in jeans, smiling enigmatically, and leaning against a doorjamb. She was the subject of radio portraits—one of them on WNYC's series *People and Ideas*—and made TV appearances, for example in November 1964 on the BBC program *Monitor,* where Jonathan Miller interviewed her.[31] The *Monitor* interview was discussed and parodied for months in the British press and elicited thousands of letters from viewers accusing both of them of pretentiousness and pseudo-intellectualism.[32]

While Sontag's brand of intellectualism violated the British ideal of understatement and self-irony, that lack of modesty was not a problem in America, where people have always understood the need for self-promotion. What distinguished Sontag's public relations from those of other members of the intelligentsia was that she could bridge the gap between egghead and middle-class culture. Unlike in Europe, it was unusual in America for popular magazines and daily papers to ask intellectuals their opinion about public affairs. Sontag succeeded in winning the respect of the middlebrow media while many of her colleagues shied away from association with such publications. Photos of Sontag, often with her son, David, were soon gracing the pages of *Vogue* and *Mademoiselle.* For many young women, she became a role model and example long before feminism was a real movement. Lesbians recognized themselves in Sontag's writings with their frequent, more or less encrypted allusions to homosexuality, as Sontag's later lover the Stanford professor Terry Castle recalls.[33] Sontag's writings were read by an entire generation of post-beatniks according to Wendy Lesser, the editor of the

Threepenny Review. Everyone who considered himself or herself culturally literate read the essays of Susan Sontag, at the latest once *Against Interpretation* had appeared.[34]

Many of Sontag's friends and associates report that, in those years, she was magically attracted to fame—its financial advantages, the possibilities for travel it provided, and the interesting and enjoyable personal contacts it facilitated. Sontag's closest friends, such as Stephen Koch, Richard Howard, and Annette Michelson, trace this seducibility—sometimes with an amused smile, sometimes with a certain undertone, sometimes with admiring pride—above all to her California youth. Everyone from the East Coast immediately recognized Sontag's social style as Californian. She was a self-confident, loud, sun-kissed, and exotic creature in the canyons of Manhattan, a creature as keen on art films by Godard, Resnais, and Bergman as she was fascinated by such contemporary stars as Henry Fonda, Warren Beatty, and Brigitte Bardot; as knowledgeable about Nietzsche, Hegel, and Herbert Marcuse as about pop stars like the Beatles, Dionne Warwick, and the Supremes.[35]

The special accent Sontag added to the somewhat dry West Coast intellectual style was the insight that even writers and thinkers could be stars. In her journals, Sontag records the almost erotic relationship to fame in her reaction to a Greta Garbo film: "I wanted to *be* Garbo (I studied her; I wanted to assimilate her, learn her gestures, feel as she felt)."[36] During Sontag's attendance at the PEN International Congress in Bled, Yugoslavia, she notes in laconic admiration that Norman Mailer, at the time the enfant terrible of American literature, was an example of "how to be pure and be a movie star."[37] In a letter to Roger Straus, she describes Sartre, de Beauvoir, Camus, and Merleau-Ponty as "literary movie stars."[38] For Sontag, fame and brainwork were not mutually exclusive but closely connected. In her eyes, it was precisely the intellectual writer who was predestined to achieve a special sort of fame. It was a fame that went hand in hand with her often-expressed desire to write texts that criticized a cultural community, offered it guidance, and moved it forward.

Sontag's model in this endeavor was without a doubt the French intelligentsia. With her talent as a writer and thinker and her flair for public relations, Sontag created a niche for this kind of writing in her native land. She went so far as to tell Jean-Louis Servan-Schreiber in an interview for the French television station TF1 that "the idea of the intellectual is an idea more or less created in France." For her, Voltaire represented the first intellectual with "this vocation of being at the same time an artist, a creator, or writer, a person of conscience who gets involved in moral and political questions."[39] Of course, Sontag laid claim to this description for her own work. And in fact, she succeeded in establishing it in the American media and creating for herself the role of representative intellectual. Her editor William Phillips called her a "premature legend."[40] In the mass-circulation media, her aura of an egghead film star was taken literally. In portraits like Carolyn Heilbrun's August 1967 article in the *New York Times*, bizarre comparisons with Marilyn Monroe would appear, probably suggested by her alliterative name.[41]

Roger Straus was euphoric about the critical success of *Against Interpretation,* and Sontag proudly noted the sales figures in her diary. The first edition of 8,000 copies quickly sold out, an impressive figure for a work of highbrow nonfiction.[42] Straus and Lila Karpf quickly realized that Sontag could achieve similar fame abroad and strove to market her there as they had in the United States. They planned to turn Sontag into an international brand name. Personally or with the help of literary agents, and frequently for laughable honorariums that did not even cover their time or copying and postage costs, they placed Sontag's essays in such publications as *Akzente* and *Die Zeit* in Germany; *Der Monat* in Switzerland; *Bonniers Litterära Magasin* and *Ord och Bild* in Sweden; *Revista de Occidente* in Spain; *La Fiera Letteraria, Epoca,* and *L'Espresso* in Italy; *Art and Artists* in England; *Nagyvilág* in Hungary; *Vindrosen* in Denmark; and *Paideia* in Japan.

The publishers' main goal was a long-term investment in Sontag's international image that would yield profits in later editions.

Lila Karpf summarized the success of this strategy in euphoric terms after receiving an issue of the Swedish *Bonniers* containing a translation of "One Culture and the New Sensibility," writing to Sontag that her worldwide fame was flourishing.[43] Sontag found a loyal international readership, especially in Germany, Italy, France, and Sweden, where she was taken much more seriously as a thinker than she sometimes was in America. Even before *Against Interpretation* was published in those countries—for each of which Sontag herself made a separate selection of the essays she considered particularly relevant and sometimes also wrote a new foreword—she became one of the most important American authors. She was so revered in Europe as a representative voice of her era that even three and a half decades later in *The Dreamers* (2003), his nostalgic, kitschy film set in 1968, Bernardo Bertolucci features a close-up of a bookshelf filled with Sontag's books.

Fame, however, did little to change Susan Sontag's basic way of life. She never lost sight of her real work. She still "watched twenty Japanese films and read five French novels a week," says Richard Howard.[44] And it was precisely this insistence on intellectual standards that led her to reject the media-assigned role as "Miss Camp," defender of pop culture, and the "Natalie Wood of the Avant-Garde." After the publication of *Against Interpretation*, this image seemed to be firmly established, and Sontag remarked that she had been partly misunderstood and exploited for an aesthetic agenda she did not agree with. She was especially offended by the attribute "Miss Camp." At several public events in 1966, she made it clear that she had heard enough about camp, it did not interest her anymore, and she would simply like to retire the concept.[45] Her letters to Roger Straus often deal with the shaping of her image and organizing her publicity. Thus, against Straus's advice, she turned down an offer to take over the movie column in *Esquire* from Dwight Macdonald. Sontag based her decision on the fact that the magazine represented "that kind of pop-celebrity fame one should run in the opposite direction from."[46] A few days earlier, in another letter to Straus, she had turned down an extremely lucrative offer from the art book editor Marion Javits to cooperate on a limited edition of one of her texts to be accompanied by Robert Rauschenberg prints. Sontag was in London at the time and under the pressure of a deadline for her next novel, *Death Kit* (1967). She turned down the offer and added, "Isn't this the kind of ultra-chic occasion—me and Rauschenberg—that's bound to be written up in LIFE and TIME + will confirm that image of me as the 'with it' girl, new Mary McCarthy, queen of McLuhanism + camp, that I'm trying to kill?"[47]

But Sontag's relationship to her fame was less straightforward than she lets on in her letter to Straus. Instead, she became increasingly entangled in a simultaneous search for, and rejection of, popularity. Nowhere was this conflict more apparent than in the social circles in which she combined Hollywood glamour with the underground scene. Thus, she had a long if intermittent affair with Warren Beatty, who was at the zenith of his career with the release of *Bonnie and Clyde* in 1967.[48] Sontag was distantly amused that the two of them appeared in the gossip columns of the tabloids and that crowds would gather around them when they went walking in New York and had to stop for a red light.[49] Like most of Sontag's relationships, this one was difficult. Sontag loved to relate how, in a reversal of the classic gender roles, she sometimes had to wait forty minutes for Beatty, killing time leafing through magazines while he was in the bathroom getting ready to go out.[50]

Sontag spent a lot of time with the circle around Jasper Johns—her other important romantic involvement at the time—to which the choreographer Merce Cunningham and the composer and performance artist John Cage also belonged. Like other artists who were intimate friends of hers in those years, such as the photographer Peter Hujar and his partner Paul Thek, Johns was part of a New York art scene where it was almost an aristocratic badge of honor to be gay, lesbian, or bisexual. It was understood as part of an avant-garde self-conception whose unconventionality was a conscious affront to American mainstream culture. Sontag was part of this game of sexual identities. In her journal, there are numerous expressions of admiration for Johns. In an undated entry from late 1965, she cites him as one of the main influences on her intellectual development along with John Cage, her teachers at the University of Chicago, the *Partisan Review,* and the French philosophers Artaud, Barthes, Cioran, and Sartre.[51]

In an ideal way, Johns combined two personality traits that fascinated Sontag at the time: fame and madness. Moreover, he had what she described as a certain "authority and elegance. He is never flustered, apologetic, guilty, ashamed. Perfect certitude."[52] She wrote, "Jasper is good for me. (but only for a while.) He makes it feel natural + good + right to be crazy . . . to question everything."[53] In the end, Johns passed on to her his sunny penthouse on the 27th floor of 340 Riverside Drive, one of the apartments Sontag loved the most.

"Like all of us in those days," reports Stephen Koch, "Susan was fatally attracted to crazy people." For example, one of Sontag's best friends, the artist Paul Thek, was charming, brilliant, and handsome, but also totally psychotic. He phoned Sontag ten times a day and wrote her eighty-page letters. Sontag pretended "she was teaching him about Nietzsche's philosophy," and Thek pretended "he understood what she was saying," Koch recalls with amusement.[54]

Paul Thek had many friends, including Andy Warhol. Thek was also the inspiration for the title of Susan Sontag's first volume of essays. Ned Rorem, another of Thek's friends, recalls how much Thek liked to end discussions of art with an arrogant, nasal, and wonderfully absurd, "Oh, I'm against interpretation, I'm against interpretation."[55] In gratitude, Sontag dedicated the first edition to him.

Susan Sontag also became an obsession for the artist Joseph Cornell. It was a part of Cornell's artistic practice to celebrate divas in quirky and intrusive ways. He wrote a letter to Sontag after seeing her in a PBS discussion of American public education. Sontag was already a fan of his surrealistic works, and she replied to his letter. For two years, Cornell would visit his idol, and he gave her several collages, which he later asked her to return. He constructed fantastic and absurd stories about Sontag, claiming she was related to the nineteenth-century German soprano Henriette Sontag but also that she was the great-great-grandmother of Jean-Paul Belmondo, that she enjoyed eternal youth and had lived through the centuries in New York, wearing various disguises.[56]

Another important friendship that began in those years was with the young Robert Wilson, who was just taking his first steps into the world of experimental theater after graduating from the Pratt Institute. Wilson was so enraptured with Sontag that he even sneaked into a lecture she gave to the American Association of University Women in the Waldorf Astoria. Only women were admitted, but he watched secretly from the balcony. Her androgynous and glamorous allure, her dark, sonorous voice, and the distanced way she read her text all reminded him of Marlene Dietrich.[57] Shortly thereafter, he met her at the home of mutual friends, and they remained devoted for the rest of Susan Sontag's life.

Partly through the influence of María Irene Fornés, Sontag was close to the avant-garde theater scene and an avid theatergoer. A good friend was Joseph Chaikin, founder of the legendary Living Theatre. Through these contacts, she also met the directors Peter Brook and Jerzy Grotowski in London in the summer of 1966, encounters she described in her diary in a typical mixture of worldly wise respect and enthusiastic gossip. She says nothing about the work of these two giants of twentieth-century theater, but instead writes that Brook wore black turtleneck sweaters, had a fleshy face and pale blue eyes, and was very intense. What interests her about Grotowski is that there are no rumors about his sex life. The effects of this meeting, however, were lasting. The appearance of these two artists inspired Sontag to continue with her second novel *Death Kit,* which she had been working on since 1965, hoping that it would be her breakthrough as a writer. "I've got the Novel . . . I think! Thanks to Brook + Grotowski, the final pieces have fallen into place."[58]

Radical Chic

(1967–1969)

The Sixties were a terrific time.
It was the most important time in
my life. If perhaps in the end we were
too busy having a good time and
thought things were a little simpler
than they turned out to be, it doesn't
mean that most of what we learned
isn't very valuable.

Susan Sontag, in a 1978 interview

Over the next few years, Susan Sontag's unconventional private life and avant-garde aesthetic would find a parallel in her politics.[1] Here, too, she adopted increasingly radical positions. Like other American writers, artists, and students of the time, Sontag was forced out of her circumscribed urban enclave and into the political arena mainly by the Vietnam War, in which non-Communist South Vietnam, with the support of the United States, fought Communist North Vietnam. With her tendency to mythologize her life, Sontag would style herself thirty-five years later as one of the founders of the peace movement and claim that she was already taking part in political demonstrations in 1963, shortly after the beginning of the war and long before there was a real peace movement.[2] But if one compares the testimony of contemporaries[3] and the interviews she gave during those years, a different picture emerges. Although Sontag had already begun to participate in teach-ins by the end of 1964,[4] her political engagement did not really pick up steam until early 1966, after Harrison Salisbury revealed in the *New York Times* that the Johnson administration had lied about attacking only military targets in Vietnam. In her 1968 essay "Trip to Hanoi," Sontag still described herself as not a political activist even though she had signed petitions against the war. Thus, from the perspective of many political activists, Sontag came to political engagement in the peace movement relatively late.

Besides, Sontag surely was not one of the leaders of the antiwar movement, who tended to be members of the clergy and politicians such as Martin Luther King Jr. and John Kerry and performers such as Bob Dylan, John Lennon, and Jane Fonda. Among intellectuals, Noam Chomsky took an especially strong stand against the war. His February 1967 *New York Review of Books* essay on the responsibility of intellectuals for the Vietnam War made him one of the leading theoreticians of the peace movement and the New Left. Sontag's influence was more marginal. She was pursuing too many other interests, writing essays, working on her new novel, and traveling. But with her typical passion, she introduced the radical rhetoric of the movement to the bourgeois liberal intellectual scene and stirred up the somewhat stuffy universe of the *Partisan Review* with her polarizing opinions.

Sontag's political engagement included a wide variety of public activities. Together with Elizabeth Hardwick, James Baldwin, Norman Mailer, and others, she drafted and signed leftist protest letters, including one to the *New York Times* condemning police mistreatment of members of the Black Panthers.[5] She took part in many demonstrations and traveled to Hollywood in the spring of 1966 to give a speech at the dedication of the *Artists' Tower of Protest,* a six-story art installation designed by Mark di Suvero and others in protest against the Vietnam War. She accepted invitations to speak against the war at many college campuses. In February 1966, she was a co-organizer of one of those forms of sixties activism that now seems almost quaint, a "read-in" for peace in Southeast Asia at the New York Town Hall with twenty-nine other authors, including Arthur Miller and William Styron. And at a demonstration against the draft in December 1967 in New York, she got herself arrested amid much publicity along with 264 other protesters, including Allen Ginsberg and Jane Jacobs. The protesters had blocked the entrance to a recruitment center in Lower Manhattan.

When the news of Sontag's arrest reached Germany, the publisher Fritz J. Raddatz sent a worried telegram to his colleagues at Farrar, Straus and Giroux asking about Sontag's well-being. Lila Karpf wrote back that Sontag had only been held for two hours and later had to make a brief appearance in court, but that the whole thing had generated "a lot of publicity—which is exactly what it was meant to do."[6] Stephen Koch also has vivid memories of the orchestrated arrest that was captured in a famous photograph by Fred W. McDarrah.[7] Sontag was not the person to sign up for anonymous or obscure events. But in a sense, her notoriety was precisely the capital that she had to invest in the movement.

The first written evidence of Sontag's radical political positions was the famous essay "What's Happening in America," published as part of *Partisan Review*'s annual symposium and one of the principal reasons why Sontag became an "emblem of radical chic," as Elizabeth Hardwick called her.[8] In his 1970 book *Radical Chic & Mau-Mauing the Flak Catchers*, Tom Wolfe had reported on the absurd involvement of the New York haut monde with radical political groups like the Black Panthers, in which the members of high society lived out their fantasies of the raw, vital lifestyle of the lower classes.[9] Sontag was not part of that group, but "she was radical and she was chic," as Hardwick reported, and her thinking was "instinctively leftist."[10] There was a bull market for radical ideas, and Sontag exploited it with typical glamour.

The annual *Partisan Review* symposium was always an eagerly awaited event. The editors formulated questions on

important contemporary topics and sent them to a select group
of authors, then printed their replies over several issues of
the magazine. Sontag caused an uproar with her response to
the questionnaire of early 1967, which included questions on
Lyndon Johnson's foreign policy, the struggle for civil rights,
inflation, the role of intellectuals, and the "activities of young
people today."[11] Her essay was titled "What's Happening in
America."[12]

The essay became a foundational document of the New
Left and one of the most quoted of Sontag's works. Nothing
else summarized so well the mood of the young leftist generation in America. Sontag was the only respondent to mention
sex, drugs, and rock 'n' roll. She called Lyndon Johnson a "John
Wayne . . . in the White House."[13] Seldom had America been subjected to such a radical critique. She described the country as
"the arch-imperium of the planet, holding man's biological as
well as his historical future in its King Kong paws." Founded
on the genocide of its native inhabitants, America brutalized the
senses of its population and turned most of its inhabitants into
"gray neurotics" and the best of them into "perverse spiritual
athletes."[14] Its leading politicians were "genuine yahoos,"[15] its
culture a "tawdry fantasy of the good life."[16] Sontag went on
to say that she expected little from America's intelligentsia but
found hope in the student movement that was developing new
forms of protest through the revolution in popular music and
sexual mores. Sontag's sovereign and cold-blooded fury reached
its peak in a much-quoted indictment of Western culture as a
whole: "The truth is that Mozart, Pascal, Boolean algebra, Shakespeare, parliamentary government, baroque churches, Newton,
the emancipation of women, Kant, Marx, and Balanchine ballets
don't redeem what this particular civilization has wrought upon
the world. The white race *is* the cancer of human history."[17]

"What's Happening in America" also set the tone for the
political section of Susan Sontag's next volume of essays. At first
its title was going to be *Notes on a Definition of Cultural Revolution,* which was meant to emphasize Sontag's "radical chic"

position.[18] Originally the collection (whose working title *Made in U.S.A.* was later changed to *Styles of Radical Will*) was to have included pieces on Theodor W. Adorno, Antonin Artaud, and Gertrude Stein as well as three essays on literary criticism.[19] When it appeared in March 1969, it contained none of those essays. In their place, it had such brilliant works as "The Aesthetics of Silence" (1967), a lucid examination of the philosophical consciousness behind the artistic movement of the sixties centered on Jasper Johns and John Cage, for whom the only adequate expression of their seriousness ultimately became to fall completely silent. Other essays covered the films of Jean-Luc Godard and Ingmar Bergman and the pornographic imagination and its connection to the theme of death in literature from the Marquis de Sade to Georges Bataille.

The essays present a consciousness in the process of radical change, constantly seeking to better itself and find adequate responses to its environment. To that end, Sontag engages with difficult art and demanding films and seeks in such abstruse topics as pornography an alternative sensibility to capitalistic consumption. The essays, among the least popular of her works today, construct the image of an individual who subjects herself to a constant process of education and learning.

The reader of *Styles of Radical Will* seeks in vain for the panache that informed *Against Interpretation*. Sontag seems not to believe so firmly anymore that avant-garde aesthetics will promote artistic and political progress. She is concerned now with transforming her own consciousness, not revolutionizing the culture. Sontag no longer finds herself in the vanguard but now questions the permanent spiritual revolution of modernism and asks what its moral implications are for both art and life— an exploration that finds its clearest expression in her essay on the Romanian-French philosopher Emil Michel Cioran. She sees Cioran as an archaeologist of contemporary ruined landscapes and the downfall of societies. For her, his philosophy contains answers to the pressing question of how one manages to survive spiritually in an age of permanent apocalypse.[20]

The high point of the volume, however, is an essay on a trip to Communist North Vietnam that Sontag undertook in the summer of 1968 with the *New York Times* reporter Andrew Kopkind and the mathematics professor and antiwar activist Robert Greenblatt. It is indicative that "Trip to Hanoi" closes the volume, for the long piece specifies in a very personal way the bases of Sontag's role as an intellectual and her self-image in the national cultural and political arena. Although forty other prominent peace activists including Mary McCarthy and Jane Fonda had made the strenuous journey to Hanoi before Sontag, the trip into the war zone was by no means without danger at the time of her visit, when surprise bombing raids were still going on, as Andrew Kopkind would later report.[21] The complicated itinerary alone took ten days, with stops in Paris and Phnom Penh, and the group traveled under conditions that were precarious at best. The invitation came from a division of the North Vietnamese government that functioned as a sort of public relations team, and the guests were chosen on the recommendation of other Americans who either had already been to Vietnam or were considered prominent representatives of the peace movement.

At the very beginning of her essay, Sontag describes her role during the trip as exceptional since she is neither a journalist nor an Asia specialist. Of course, this statement is only half true. The FSG archives reveal that even before the trip, the plan was to publish the essay in the December 1968 issue of *Esquire,* so she was indeed traveling as a journalist.[22] Moreover, the essay was supposed to also appear as a softcover book under FSG's Noonday imprint in January 1969 and finally as part of the collection *Styles of Radical Will* the following March. According to Lila Karpf, the publisher had launched an extraordinary publicity campaign because both she and Straus were convinced that "Trip to Hanoi" would be one of Sontag's most important essays, a message to the large and growing number of people all over the world who were becoming politically engaged. At the same time, the essay was to be published as an affordable paperback in the most important foreign languages in January and February, to provide for the widest possible circulation.[23]

"Trip to Hanoi" was an essay of unusual importance for Sontag. In a letter to Roger Straus apologizing for how long it took to finish the piece, she writes that it was a new kind of writing for her, much more open and personal, which was what made it so hard to finish.[24]

"Trip to Hanoi" made Sontag a target for American neoconservatives for decades after its publication. In a sense, the text uses the methods of the New Journalism of Hunter Thompson, Norman Mailer, and Joan Didion, methods characterized by the reporter's personal involvement. But even if the text is written from a very personal and almost intimate perspective, it does not share the self-confident "I" that characterizes the texts of the New Journalism. Nevertheless, Sontag inserts herself for the first time in an essay and abandons her previous perspective of "we" or "one."[25]

First and foremost, the piece is concerned with "the dilemmas of being an American, an unaffiliated radical American, an American writer."[26] Years later, Sontag would still describe the trip as "the culture shock that one feels going to Asia for the first time."[27] In addition, Vietnam for Sontag was the first country where she witnessed real suffering, as she emphasized,[28] which radically called into question her assumptions about the aesthetic education of consciousness. The essay consists equally of an account of the experience, diary entries, and outlines of Vietnamese history.

Sontag is by no means uncritical of the trip's organizers. She is suspicious of the "political theatre" in which, she writes, while "they are playing their roles, we (I) must play ours (mine)" because of the circumstances of the war. She resents the travelers being cast in the role of "American friends of the Vietnamese struggle"[29] and analyzes the formulaic Communist officialese that all the Vietnamese she encounters seem to speak. Although in recent years she had again become accustomed to using Marxist and neo-Marxist vocabulary, as a writer she feels repelled by the flat, prescriptive language of the North Vietnamese.

On the other hand, Sontag sometimes succumbs to the North Vietnamese propaganda and commits some faux pas not untypical of the political thinking of those years. She describes the Vietnamese as "whole human beings" in contrast to Americans and West Europeans. She admires their sexual self-discipline and their generosity in giving American prisoners of war larger portions of food. She is impressed that they care for the grave of an American soldier, that they are little influenced by the Western culture of guilt, and that they are able to triumph over every material hardship. According to Sontag, the Vietnamese people, with their interest in justice and dignity, reinvigorate notions of heroism that can only be used ironically in the West. In short, North Vietnam seems to Sontag "a place which, in many respects, *deserves* to be idealized."[30] And so Sontag closes her essay with the perspicacious assertion that Vietnam and not America would win the war, a prophecy that almost no one at that point could credit, although seven years later it would prove to be true.

Sontag's idealization of North Vietnam continued upon her return to New York. She gave Stephen Koch one of two rings she had been given as a welcome gift in North Vietnam. They were made from the aluminum of American fighter jets that had been shot down and were stamped with their serial numbers. Koch says that he and Sontag wore these military totems for a long time as a sign of their commitment to the peace movement and their hope that North Vietnam would win the terrible war. Mary McCarthy, who had also traveled to Vietnam and written an essay about the trip, describes her shock when she was also offered such a ring. For her it symbolized not the inhumanity of the Americans' prosecution of the war but rather brought her into direct contact with the human life that had been sacrificed for this ring.[31] Sontag and Koch, in their absolute radical chic, did not consider such implications.

Sontag's activism against the Vietnam War also affected her literary work. In March 1967, Sontag finished her second novel, *Death Kit*.[32] She hoped it would convince the reading public that she was not just a critic but also a novelist to be taken seriously. Straus shared her optimism and was confident that the "important and original novel" would be a "success."[33]

The novel's suicidal antihero and antinarrator is Diddy, an ad writer from Pennsylvania who murders a railroad worker in a tunnel and is tortured to the end of the novel by the question of whether he really committed the murder or only imagined it. His name itself poses the symbolic question: Did he? The blind Hester, whom he meets on the train, shares his doubt about whether he did it. She claims she can see with her ears and she knows that Diddy never left the train car.

Although the novel is a linear narration, it gives the impression of a random series of imaginary events that follows a philosophic rather than a narrative logic. The motif played out in *Death Kit* is the idea that, without positive intervention, all social and natural systems tend toward chaos. A similar entropy can be found in many American novels of the sixties, such as Thomas Pynchon's *V.* (1963) and John Hawkes's *The Lime Twig* (1961). Sontag herself later described *Death Kit* as the product of "the lamenting mood—it's written in the shadow of the Vietnam war."[34] Even though the war is not explicitly mentioned, it is often present in the novel, especially on the television news Diddy is continually watching, which sometimes leads him to believe that his murder of a single individual is laughably insignificant on the larger scale of societal reality.

When *Death Kit* was published in the fall of 1967, it received catastrophic reviews. Only a few highbrow magazines even made an attempt to take it seriously as literature. The rest of the press referred to Sontag's intellectual accomplishments but judged the novel to be more or less unreadable. The *New York Times* critic Eliot Fremont-Smith wondered simply "how it happens that a critic of Susan Sontag's refined sensibilities can write fiction that is both tedious and demonstrably insensitive to the craft of fiction."[35] Others were harsher in their judgments and described the book as "less deadly than dull."[36] As in Sontag's first novel, the influence of French literature and philosophy are clearly visible. Sontag seemed to have repeated and even increased all the mistakes she had made in *The Benefactor*.

At the beginning and end of the novel, there are a few hints that the 312 pages are the hallucinatory dream of a coma patient shortly before his death. But as Sontag insisted in several interviews, that is only one possible reading of the book, which she had provided with "certain systematically obscure elements" to "leave several possible readings open."[37]

Alfred Kazin, one of the most important American critics of the time, aptly described Sontag's style as "entirely manifestations of Sontag's personal will" that bypass traditional literary principles such as inspiration and powerful narrative. "We do not experience a novel; we experience her readiness to see what she can think of next."[38] Indeed, in the sixties, literature seemed to be for Sontag a medium whose traditional demands she disparaged while failing to find functional means for their radical renewal. Sontag's literary texts from this period—the two novels and occasional stories like "Dummy" (1963)—give the impression that she is simply using them to seek another form in which to express her ideas, something she achieves so much more effectively in her essays. Even if she later extolled *Death Kit* in interviews and called it her "most intimate novel" in an afterword for the German translation,[39] Sontag had a clear sense of failure as a novelist. She seldom wanted to talk about her earlier works. As David Rieff said about his mother, she was not a woman who was nostalgic or liked to look back.[40] Stephen Koch says that the life of a novelist to which she aspired was a "painful topic" for her, a "special problem," and even "a rock on which she almost foundered."[41] Despite numerous attempts that she always had difficulty giving up, Susan Sontag would not write another novel for the next twenty-five years.

Behind the Camera

(1969–1972)

The typical formula of the new formalists of . . . film is a mixture of coldness and pathos: coldness enclosing and subduing an immense pathos.

Susan Sontag, *Against Interpretation* (1966)

Although in many respects "Trip to Hanoi" propagates the radical ideas with which Sontag's image remained connected into the late seventies, a certain ambivalence toward the New Left is also inscribed in the writing, an ambivalence that would increase over the next few years.[1] Sontag's provocative political writings cannot be subsumed under the largely anti-intellectual ideas of the antiwar movement, and they often give the impression of a mind seeking to regain its balance. On the one hand, they address current events, analyze contemporary discourses of the Left, and derive a position that Sontag considers generally valid. On the other hand, these texts often give the impression that she could not shake off a certain skepticism toward those discourses. By the end of the 1970s, Sontag was already distancing herself from "What's Happening in America" and "Trip to Hanoi" in interviews with *Rolling Stone*,

111

the French literary magazine *Tel Quel*, and French television.[2] From then until the end of her life, she no longer wished to be associated with the political positions she had espoused in those essays. For her, they were documents of a particular, radically inflected time whose fundamental attitudes were shared by an entire generation of authors, thinkers, and critics—a time she looked back on with a mixture of nostalgia and skepticism.[3]

In an interview with the *Los Angeles Times* from the early nineties, Sontag even said that the Vietnam War and its consequences had thrown her off course for about ten years.[4] And the following years were indeed marked by long-lasting bouts of depression and severe writer's block, serious financial worries, and a basic ambivalence toward her continuing popularity. Instead of continuing to pursue her career as an essayist and novelist, she decided to write and direct films and would spend the bulk of the next few years in Sweden and Paris.

American film scholars and critics are united in the opinion that Sontag's engagement with film cannot be overestimated in its significance for the medium. Her cineast's passion was manifest in her two influential essay collections, and not just because so many of the essays are about European avant-garde cinema and American underground films, but also in the way she applies the critical principles she had developed for film to literature and theater as well. For Sontag was convinced that film occupied an exemplary function vis-à-vis the other arts. At a time when movies were regarded in America as mere popular culture, she was one of a very small number of thinkers who took the medium seriously. Hardly anyone else had such a knowledge of European and Japanese films at his or her command and could thus lend the medium the status of an art form. Although a criticism that took films seriously as modern art had developed in the sixties, few of the well-known American film critics, such as Pauline Kael, Manny Farber, Dwight Macdonald, or James Agee, shared Sontag's comprehensive knowledge of the medium.[5]

Susan Sontag consistently applied rigorous philosophical methodology to cinematic phenomena as disparate as the work of Jean-Luc Godard and American science-fiction films of the fifties, thereby importing a quasi-academic element into film criticism. The testimonies to her passionate love of cinema, inflected by the film culture of Paris, form an essayistic compendium that is basically similar to her ideas about modernist literature. She admired the sensuous directness of films like Alain Resnais's *Last Year at Marienbad* (1961) and Michelangelo Antonioni's *L'Avventura* (*The Adventure*, 1960), a work that undermines traditional narrative structures and foregrounds the visual experience of the moviegoer. She esteemed the coolly experimental films of Robert Bresson, a coolness Sontag thought could reorganize the entire emotional world of the audience. She enjoyed the lyrical playfulness and serendipitous consistency of improvisation in the early films of Godard and admired the dark seriousness, self-referentiality, and atmospheric weight of Ingmar Bergman's films, especially when they abandoned traditional narrative modes, as in *Persona* (1966).[6] She believed strongly that, in their unique perception of reality, films could have an extraordinary educational function, not just an aesthetic education, but also—in their widening of sensibility—a sentimental education as well.[7] What Sontag brought together in her essays between 1961 and 1969 was a small catalog of modernist, mostly European, experimental films that for many film fans represent the golden age of the art film.

As Sontag told *New York Times* critic Mel Gussow, in her theoretical discussions of the medium she always wished she could make films herself.[8] It seemed to her a logical extension of her career. After all, European authors she particularly admired, such as Marguerite Duras, Pier Paolo Pasolini, and Alain Robbe-Grillet, had found their way from literature to film, making a name for themselves not just as writers but also as filmmakers.[9] With characteristic self-confidence, Sontag had early on begun to turn her wish into a reality. She watched Mike Nichols, her old friend from the University of Chicago, on the set and in the cutting room when he was gaining renown as the director of *Who's Afraid of Virginia Woolf?* (1966) and *The*

Graduate (1967). She developed several film scenarios of her own and began seeking advice about producers from European directors and actors she knew.

Sontag made these efforts especially in France and Italy, where she had been invited to be a member of the jury for the Venice Film Festival in 1967. She also had private reasons for spending more and more time in Italy. She was in a relationship with Carlotta del Pezzo, a duchess to whom Sontag dedicated her second film script *Brother Carl,* published by FSG in 1974 and illustrated with stills from the 1971 film.[10] Another reason that Sontag concentrated on the European film world was that she had almost no contact with American filmmaking. Aside from the flamboyant New York underground film scene, the movie industry was centered in Los Angeles, and at that time, before the great era of independent films, movies meant the big Hollywood studios. In addition, French, Italian, and Swedish filmmaking of the time was considered less industrialized, so it seemed easier for an outsider to gain a foothold. And compared to Hollywood, the considerably lower production costs in Europe, smaller film crews, and producers independent of the big studios meant that writers like Marguerite Duras were not automatically excluded as filmmakers. "Still a woman director is a freak in this country," said Sontag in 1972.[11]

Sontag did not have to wait long for an offer. The producer Göran Lindgren from the Swedish company Sandrew Film och Teater put a minuscule budget of $180,000 at her disposal and offered her complete artistic freedom. Susan Sontag enjoyed an impressive reputation in Sweden since the Swedish edition of *Against Interpretation* and the publication of subsequent essays in the culture journal *Bonniers Litterära Magasin,* and Lindgren obviously had great hopes for his investment. Sontag did not care where the film was shot. "I would have taken any offer just to show I could do it . . . I would have gone to Afghanistan," she later commented.[12]

Only a few weeks after returning from Vietnam in August 1968, she was in Sweden to begin work on her first film, *Duet for Cannibals,* and planning the shooting schedule with Lindgren. She wrote the script in just three weeks and moved to Stockholm, where she lived in October and November 1968 and again in February and March 1969, to begin shooting. Sontag did not find it easy to work on the film. The Swedish actors and film crew, whose language she did not understand, worked seven days a week, and a typical workday began at 6 A.M. and ended at midnight.[13]

Set to the music of Antonín Dvořák, Gustav Mahler, and Richard Wagner, *Duet for Cannibals* is a grotesque chamber piece about the psychic and sexual games in which Arthur Bauer (Lars Ekborg)—a mysterious, egomaniacal German revolutionary with a presumably fascist past—and his mute wife, Francesca (Adriana Asti), entangle their young assistant (Gösta Ekman) and his wife (Agneta Ekmanner). From the voice-over perspective of the younger couple, Sontag develops a surreal black-and-white scenario that abandons traditional psychological development in favor of the characters' mysterious emotional vacuum and replaces action with a catalog of disjointed psychic disturbances, elaborate abuses of power, and sexual fantasies.

As the product of a cinematic novice who was scriptwriter, director, and film editor rolled into one, *Duet for Cannibals* displays remarkable professionalism and stylistic strength. Despite its fashionably contemporary motifs, it has neither the unsteady camera work nor the amateur acting and careless cutting typical of the New York underground films of Mike Kuchar and Jonas Mekas, who treated similar themes. The atmosphere of the film is more reminiscent of Ingmar Bergman. But perhaps that is precisely the problem with *Duet for Cannibals.* From today's perspective, the film seems like a leaden collection of clichés from European art films of the sixties. So much so, indeed, that it is sometimes unintentionally funny, for example, when the protagonists stare intently and silently into the camera or indulge in inscrutable dialogues loaded with what sounds like philosophy.

When *Duet for Cannibals* was screened as a noncompetitor at the Cannes Film Festival in May 1969, at the New York

Film Festival in September, and finally for a week in Carnegie Hall, the reaction of both audiences and critics was mainly negative. A reviewer for the *Harvard Crimson* surmised that Sontag had seen so many films and thought about them for so long that she had unconsciously produced a hodgepodge of all the cinematographic, atmospheric, and narrative elements she admired in the films of Bresson, Godard, and Bergman. *Duet for Cannibals* seemed like an imitation, the product of someone "more interested in Making Movies than in making a particular movie."[14] Nevertheless, at the end of shooting Göran Lindgren offered to finance another Sontag film the following year.

During this time, Sontag spent only brief periods in the United States. During her absence, Roger Straus took care of her daily affairs with the help of the FSG bookkeeping department and scheduled her lectures from his office in New York. She spoke about her film at Harvard and other American universities and made stops at her European publishers in Amsterdam, Rome, and Paris when a translation of one of her books was about to appear. Straus arranged the publication of shorter articles in American and European magazines; kept an eye on David, who was now seventeen; and even established an FSG account that paid Sontag's taxes as well as the utility and telephone bills for her apartment on Riverside Drive.[15]

Even when the exhausting work on her first film was finally over, Sontag did not cut back her schedule of trips to Europe, publishers' events, university lectures, and political meetings. David, who always maintained an intense relationship with his mother and whom she often called her "best friend," began to imitate her lifestyle as well. He traveled by himself through Europe, South America, Afghanistan, and Africa, crossing paths with his mother as often as possible. Their meetings were frequently organized by Roger Straus, who would keep them informed of each other's whereabouts.[16]

Most of Sontag's journeys took her to the countries where her political sympathies lay. In particular, her fascination with Cuba (where she had spent three months in 1960) and enthusiasm for its revolutionary heroes Che Guevara and Fidel Castro (the latter in the meantime declared an official enemy by the American government) culminated in a second trip there in January 1969. The two articles Sontag wrote about this trip are testimony to her admiration for the social and economic justice she presumed to exist in the Cuban socialist model. Moreover, Sontag believed that Cuba possessed a heretofore unimagined store of potential personal and erotic energy. In an article about the agitprop posters of the Cuban revolution, which first appeared in *Artforum* and was later reprinted as the introduction to a collection of Cuban posters, Sontag describes the "liveliness and openness" of a country that was fundamentally different from the Soviet Union. The artistically sophisticated Cuban posters, so different in character from the banal and conformist propaganda posters in the U.S.S.R., expressed this difference.[17]

A certain skepticism, however, begins to creep into "Some Thoughts on the Right Way (for Us) to Love the Cuban Revolution," an essay she wrote for *Ramparts*. A glossy-format organ of the radical Left published in San Francisco, *Ramparts* in its heyday at the height of the Vietnam War had 300,000 subscribers and was the ideal place for Sontag's political articles. She had met its editor in chief Bob Scheer in Cuba and promised to write about her experiences on the Caribbean island for the magazine.[18] Although she ended her essay on Cuban posters with a rabble-rousing "Viva Fidel!" the *Ramparts* article foreshadows her gradual disenchantment with the American Left and its radical movements. Sontag's tone is critical, especially when she writes about Americans' obsession with personal freedom. According to Sontag, the New Left neglects to put the emphasis on justice and lays claim for itself to "one of the fundamental promises of American society—the promise to protect each person's right to non-participation, disaffiliation, selfishness."[19]

During the next few years, Sontag's enthusiasm for the Cuban model, on which she had set such hope as an alternative to Soviet and Eastern European socialism as well as to American capitalism, waned. In May 1971, along with sixty other intellectuals from Europe and the Americas, including Jean-Paul Sartre, Julio Cortázar, Simone de Beauvoir, and Mario Vargas Llosa, she signed a protest letter against the imprisonment of the Cuban writer Heberto Padilla, which appeared on the title page of *Le Monde* and the *New York Times*. Padilla had been tortured by the Cuban police and forced to sign a confession in which he identified himself as an enemy of Cuba and admitted having contacts with American intellectuals who worked for the Central Intelligence Agency.[20]

In later years, Sontag would repeatedly cite this letter as proof of her opposition to Communist regimes, yet despite signing it, her attitude remained ambivalent. According to the *Village Voice,* at a meeting of the Socialist Workers Party in November 1971, Sontag encouraged those present to reaffirm their support for the Cuban revolution. She declared that she had only signed the Padilla letter because she thought it was addressed to Fidel Castro personally and would not be published. In retrospect, she added, she regretted her decision because the letter now served as propaganda material for the enemies of Cuba.[21]

What made Sontag increasingly uncomfortable about radical political movements, however, was their striking anti-intellectualism.[22] Richard Nixon and his "silent majority" ruled America in the early seventies, plunging it deeper and deeper into the Vietnam War, which continued to cost hundreds of lives each year with no prospect of success. Meanwhile, the New Left developed more and more obscure and self-congratulatory forms of expression that resulted in shifting coalitions between hippies, yuppies, antiwar groups, and the Black Power movement. On the cultural level, representatives of the New Left began to attack film, art, and literature in general as bourgeois and repressive if those art forms fulfilled no ideological educational function and had no express intention to change consciousness or the world. In a certain sense, the ideology of the New Left echoed Sontag's own political ideas at their most radical, when she saw the cultural achievements of the West as inseparably connected to colonialism and imperialism. But despite her fascination with popular culture, political radicalism, and underground art, Sontag could no longer maintain this position. Especially for the New York Intellectuals, who for decades had defined themselves as "leftist," this anti-intellectualism led to a change in their image of themselves. It marked a separation between the Old Left and a neoconservative camp that saw itself as the victim of the radically liberal faction to which Sontag belonged.

Sontag's development can only partially be understood as an intellectual about-face. The change in her political thinking seems like a reaction, years in the making, to the gradual radicalization of aesthetic discourse. Her change of heart manifested itself in a clearly oppositional stance but did not result in a new political position for the next three years. In an interview with *Salmagundi,* Sontag said that concepts such as "reactionary" and "progressive," in her opinion, "always support ideological conformity, encourage intolerance." To reproach artists for "having an insufficiently radical relation to the world" was for her a "complaint about art as such."[23] "Rebellion," she would elsewhere state with certainty, "does not seem to me a value in itself, as—say—truth is."[24]

What is difficult about Sontag's intellectual development is her tendency to not explicitly acknowledge that she has changed her mind. Instead, she claimed in the same interview that she had always held such a position, even when that was clearly not the case. Again and again at such turning points, she tried not to identify errors or changes of opinion as such but rather to rewrite her own intellectual history. Only later did she claim the right to change her mind, defending it as a fundamental condition of intellectual existence—a right seldom granted Sontag by American public opinion because of her importance as a symbol of the aesthetic and political movements of the sixties.

At the same time, Sontag's private life was also becoming more and more unsettled. She dedicated her first film script, *Duet for Cannibals,* to Susan Taubes. Taubes—one of her closest friends since their days together at Harvard—had belonged to Sontag

and Fornés's first writers' group and she became Susan's colleague at Columbia University. Taubes had suffered from severe
depression for some time. Whenever Sontag was in New York,
she tried to support her friend and also help Taubes's two teenage
children, who had remained with their mother after her divorce
from Jacob Taubes and his return to Germany. Susan Taubes had
already threatened several times to commit suicide. Shortly after
publishing *Divorcing* (1969), her first and only novel, in which
she described in great detail her marriage and difficult divorce,
she unexpectedly made good on her threats.

Six days before Taubes took her life, the novel had been sav-
aged in the *New York Times*. The reviewer seemed eager to take
revenge on Sontag through Taubes, since in his very first sentence he began to take bitter sideswipes at Sontag's literary style,
which he claimed to identify in Taubes's novel as well. She was
for him, like Sontag, a "lady novelist" writing a "pop mobile."[25]

On November 8, 1969, Susan Taubes drowned herself off
Long Island.[26] Sontag had to drive to East Hampton to identify
the body. Stephen Koch went with her and recalls that Sontag
was so stricken that her entire body was trembling. The police
had found a half-empty bottle of pills where Taubes committed
suicide. As they were leaving the police station, the shocked Sontag kept repeating over and over, "Now she's finally done it, that
stupid woman."[27]

How close Sontag had felt to Taubes can be seen not just in
the fact that she kept in contact with her friend's two children
until her own death and tried to help them as best she could.
Her struggle with her friend's suicide also left traces in her artistic work. In Sontag's second film, *Brother Carl,* again shot in
Stockholm, there are clear reminiscences of the incident. Göran
Lindgren had put a larger sum of money at her disposal this
time, and it allowed a longer shooting schedule and more time in
postproduction.

Sontag had begun work on *Brother Carl* in September 1969
and finished the script in Sweden in January 1970. Shooting
and cutting took place between July and December 1970. If the

work on her first film was grueling, the production of *Brother Carl* turned out to be even more so. The letters Sontag wrote to her mentor Roger Straus paint a picture of genuine depression. In the foreword to the published script, Sontag relates that in Stockholm in January it was still dark in the middle of the day and during work on the film she was always searching for some light. In her letters, she writes of being gradually overcome by a difficult period, so difficult that she can hardly function.[28] She feels more and more impatience and sometimes even a real antipathy toward Stockholm and thinks of New York with enormous longing, something that has not happened to her before anywhere else in Europe.[29]

In her second film, Sontag came much closer to finding her own cinematic voice, perhaps because the movie deals with the problem of finding a language that will effectively reach an interlocutor. All the figures in the film suffer from a failure to communicate, an aspect that is heightened by the Swedish accents and the real difficulties the actors had with English, the language Sontag intentionally chose for the film.

Most of the movie takes place in an almost oppressively picturesque black-and-white Scandinavian landscape and depicts the repeated failure of two groups of people to relate to each other: the attorney Peter (Torsten Wahlund); his wife, Karen (Geneviève Page), who suffers under their bourgeois lifestyle; and their mute daughter; as well as the director Lena (Gunnel Lindblom); her former husband, the choreographer Martin (Keve Hjelm); and his mute friend Carl (Laurent Terzieff). The center of *Brother Carl* is a spiral of self-destruction upon which Lena embarks when she tries, with Karen's help, to take up her relationship with Martin again. Martin, for his part, reacts to this attempt in a typically sadistic way. The film ends with Lena's suicide after she tries to make Martin jealous by having an affair with Carl.

The consequences of this suicide are enormous. Carl, who finds her body floating in the water, loses his faith in a scene filled with pathos and sets out to heal Karen's mute daughter.

As for Karen, her eyes are opened by the self-destruction of her friend. As in Sontag's own case, her response to Lena's suicide is furious shock at the hopeless stupidity of the act. Karen finally returns to her husband. The events in Martin's summer house prove the catalyst for the opening up of her restricted emotional world.

Brother Carl follows a rigid logic of cruelty within a careful, almost classic structure that has the power to draw viewers into its spell. Nevertheless, the film was not a success when it was shown at festivals in Cannes, San Francisco, Chicago, and London in 1971 and 1972. Critics and audiences agreed that its characters spoke too much in philosophically inflected aphorisms that lack context in the film. The mysterious atmosphere that pervades the film often seems meaningless, unnecessary, and sometimes even willfully out of place. Sontag herself admitted that *Brother Carl,* while functioning in an imaginary psychological universe, was "partly realistic in the sense of everyday psychology and partly kind of fantastic psychology which I also believe is true—yet not true on the level of plausibilities of daily life."[30] The title of the review in the *Village Voice*, "Child Admitted Only with College Graduate,"[31] suggested how difficult the film was to understand. Although Sontag's friend Daniel Talbot bought the American rights to *Brother Carl,* it closed after only a week at his New Yorker Theatre for lack of an audience.

In Semi-Exile

(1972–1975)

*We know more than we can use.
Look at all this stuff I've got in my
head: rockets and Venetian churches,
David Bowie and Diderot, nuoc mam
and Big Macs, sunglasses and
orgasms . . . And we don't know
nearly enough.*

Susan Sontag, "Debriefing" (1973)

Susan Sontag's two Swedish films were strongly indebted to the "new sensibility" of the sixties.[1] However, that sensibility was fast becoming obsolete. At the beginning of the seventies, it became clear that the hoped-for aesthetic revolution had not occurred and the former avant-garde had lost its momentum. What remained was self-referential recourse to an aesthetic that no longer seemed appropriate to the times. The formerly predominant high modernism that achieved a late flowering in abstract expressionist painting, the *nouvelle vague* in film, and the *nouveau roman* in literature now also seemed a relic of the past. Caught between a more and more radical aesthetic discourse on the one hand and a conservative majority opinion on the other, modernism was being replaced by a turn toward realistic narrative and conventional artistic practices. Sontag reacted to this more conservative view of art by labeling it a "mean-spiritedness" that was "so discouraging" it derailed her own creative work.[2]

Despite the disappointing reception of her films, Sontag now defined herself as a filmmaker and defended her new profession with the same passion she had brought to the pursuit of her ambitions as an intellectual and writer. With her typical tendency to make ex cathedra pronouncements, she told the *New York Times*, "If I want to be in total control of something, I write." This turn away from her intellectual work went hand in hand with a turn away from her earlier aesthetic ideas, a move that was easier for her than the shift in her political positions. Now she said that her essays "don't interest me at all. You see, I don't *love* my work, I like it. But I'm not attached to it in the sense that I feel a responsibility *now* to be consistent with my past work."[3]

In this respect, *Duet for Cannibals* and *Brother Carl* can be seen as the products of the aesthetic and intellectual crisis Sontag found herself in at the beginning of the seventies. Another sign of that crisis was that when shooting was completed in Sweden, she moved her primary residence to Paris, the city to which she owed her most important aesthetic inspiration and intellectual experiences. From 1972 to 1975, she returned to New York only for a few months at a time.

Sontag's friend Richard Howard interpreted her decision as an escape from celebrity and the public scrutiny that went with it.[4] Indeed, Sontag's abandonment of essay writing and her semi-emigration were the signs of a deep-seated conflict with her own fame. On the one hand, she played the role of public figure with a great deal of conviction. She loved the recognition that went along with fame and used her popularity to support cultural and political projects of all kinds. She told the journalist Helen Benedict that she firmly believed she was "performing a public service."[5] Although Sontag was aware that she needed to excite the attention of the media so that her writings would be read, her films watched, and her opinions seen as coming from an important person in the public sphere, she was increasingly uncomfortable with people's image of her as a radical intellectual. She could modify that image only to a certain extent, so firmly had it become entrenched during the sixties. For a long time now, she no longer recognized herself in it. That discomfort with her image emerges most clearly in an interview with Edwin Newman for NBC: "I think publicity in general is a very destructive thing, for any artist . . . It always is a problem. Because even if it's good, the extent to which you get all this attention is an extra thing for you to take account of. You start thinking about your work as an outsider—you start being aware of . . . what other people think of you. And you become self-conscious . . . it's taking your attention away from your own business."[6]

Her whole life long, Sontag was unable to resolve this conflict. It led Robert Brustein to dub her a "fairy princess of the kingdom of cultural schizophrenia" in 1971. He criticized her for distancing herself from her celebrity status on the one hand but at the same time seeking media attention for her projects and opinions on the other.[7] Sontag wanted to be taken seriously by the public for her intellectual and artistic work, and at the same time be accepted as the person she considered herself to be at any given point in her development. She desired an extent of control over her image that was impossible in a continuously expanding media environment. What seemed to suffer most during these years of conflict was her work as a writer.

Another reason for Sontag's return to Paris was a new personal relationship. In the small world of European film, Nicole Stéphane had been a constant since the fifties. She projected an androgynous glamour seldom seen on the French screen. Her best-known film, *Les enfants terribles* (translated as *The Terrible Children* or *The Holy Terrors*, 1950) was an adaptation of the novel by Jean Cocteau directed by Jean-Pierre Melville. It depicted the incestuous love of a brother and sister and earned her cult status among cineasts for her hypnotic acting. Following a serious automobile accident in which she was almost killed, Stéphane gave up acting and began to work as a producer. She was born a Rothschild, and the fortune of that famous banking family provided her financial support her whole life. The first film she produced, Frédéric Rossif's Spanish Civil War documentary *To Die in Madrid,* earned her an Oscar nomination in 1966.[8] Even before the production of *Brother Carl,* Sontag had planned to produce her next films in France with Stéphane.[9]

Partly through Stéphane, Susan Sontag was able to establish contacts in Parisian intellectual circles famous for their rigorous exclusion of outsiders. She even lived for a time in Sartre's former apartment in the rue Bonaparte in Saint-Germain-des-Prés. In a letter to Roger Straus, she writes as though it were only a coincidence, but she betrays her excitement when she remarks ironically that the dentist from whom she was renting has thoroughly exorcized the ghosts of Sartre, de Beauvoir, Camus, Merleau-Ponty, and all the literary film stars who had been there.[10] Even at a time when she was internationally famous in her own right, she still approached her models with an exaggerated respect. In a certain sense, she never lost the starstruck enthusiasm of the girl from California worshipping her cultural heroes. When she met the new wave director Robert Bresson at a film screening, for instance, she greeted him with an effusive "*Cher maître!*"[11]

Richard Howard introduced Sontag to Roland Barthes, whose works he would later translate into English. Sontag was a great admirer of the legendary literary critic and semiotician, and courted him with all the charm she could muster, while Barthes's nonchalance toward her sometimes bordered on ironic indifference.[12] Sontag would often relate how Barthes always greeted her with a sardonic, "Ah Susan. Toujours fidèle," a remark she took as a sign of his egotism.[13] But that never stopped her from seeking contact with the admired author and later seeing to it—through her connection to FSG and her two influential essays "Remembering Barthes" (1980) and "Writing Itself: On Roland Barthes" (1982)—that Barthes became known throughout American universities and not just on the Upper West Side.

Despite these stimulating encounters with Barthes and others, Sontag's crisis seemed only to be exacerbated by her move to Paris. Her letters to Roger Straus contain bitter laments about her dark phases, her lack of productivity, and her writer's block. In interviews, she described this time as "a great crisis"[14] in her life, a time of "great grief" and "intense depression."[15] One reason lay in the hard facts of Sontag's financial situation. Her work on the two films had earned her essentially no income. She depended primarily on royalties from her four books, which all continued to sell but never earned her very much money. Not only did the films not recoup their production costs but also the scripts that Roger Straus published under the Noonday imprint of FSG sold next to no copies. Sontag's British publisher reacted with outright anger when Straus suggested the scripts be published in England as well. Despite the popularity of their author, such an idea made no economic sense.[16] Yet Sontag's extravagant way of life had to be paid for. Her travels were only partially underwritten by publishers, universities, and film festivals, and it was costly to maintain apartments in both New York and Paris. Sontag tried to improve her finances by signing a contract to write a film script for her acquaintance Henri Carter Carnegie. After she had missed several deadlines and finally announced she would not write the script after all, Carnegie threatened legal action, so that Roger Straus had to intervene and pay Sontag's debts in installments from her FSG account.[17]

Nevertheless, Sontag continued to turn down invitations to deliver well-paid lectures because she obviously did not want to. They would require her not only to travel into the American hinterland but also to have contact with academics, who represented a world she had rejected. Many journalists, professors, and friends report that she seemed to be in a bad mood and was easily annoyed. Especially when she had to answer questions from the audience after a talk, she gave the impression that she was surrounded by complete fools.[18] Sontag was a passionate devotee of big cities. Giving lectures at universities represented the same compromise for her as granting interviews to the tabloid press or on television, a medium she described as the "death of western civilization."[19] At such times, she would often remark, "Beckett wouldn't do it."[20] In a letter to Straus, she was even more explicit. After he had urged her to accept an especially lucrative offer from the University of Michigan in Ann Arbor, she wrote back promising to be in the United States on September 10 so that she could "fly to Ann Arbor and prostitute myself for 1,500 dollars."[21] Sontag's financial troubles finally became so serious that she had to move into Nichole Stéphane's townhouse in the rue de la Faisanderie, where at first she inhabited a garden house and later a separate living and working space on the third floor.[22]

It appears that between her life in France and her activities in the world of film, Sontag had lost her way. It had actually been her dream to succeed as a writer. Later she described her situation thus: "Where am I, what am I doing, what have I done? I seem to be an expatriate, but I didn't mean to become an expatriate. I don't seem to be a writer anymore, but I wanted most of all to be a writer."[23] Naturally, Sontag's abstinence from writing was also a thorn in the side of her publisher. Straus wrote countless letters reminding her of long-promised writing projects.[24] Robert Silvers and Barbara Epstein from the *New York Review of Books* (which had dropped Sontag as one of its authors during her time as the intellectual representative of "radical chic") also tried their hardest to win her back. Sontag agreed, among other things, to write pieces on feminism and the American moon landing, but never did.[25] In the end, Robert Silvers flew to Europe in the summer of 1972 and met with Sontag in Paris. He made her an urgent offer of peace along with a contract to write something on a topic of her choice.[26]

And in fact, after her long stretch of silence, Susan Sontag finally responded to the pleas of her publisher and editors—although she did so by going to the other extreme, a reaction that in retrospect seems like nothing but a blind and excessive emphasis on action instead of sameness. On July 5, 1972, she wrote to Straus from Paris that she was calm and working more productively. The bad time was past, and she was back in the running for the most important writer of her generation "and all that shit."[27] The next year, although she finished only a few texts, she churned out so many ideas for books—and even signed contracts for some of them—that it seemed impossible to realize even half of them. She planned to finally edit and write a foreword for a selection of Artaud texts she had been promising Straus since 1967. After a trip to India, where she produced a program on Indira Gandhi for the French ORTF network, she decided to edit the memoirs of the Indian prime minister, who had become world famous through her overwhelming reelection in 1972 and her success in concluding peace with Pakistan. Sontag also received an advance of $15,000 for a novel with the working title *The Temptation of Ricardo Torres*. She planned to write a book about Adorno and one on China. She outlined a new collection of essays and a volume of short stories. On May 21, 1973, she wrote to "Roger Darling," asking if he realized that four books of hers would be appearing in the next two years. "It's not a comeback, it's a blitzkrieg!"[28]

None of these books was destined to appear in the two following years, much to the annoyance of Roger Straus. But sometimes such periods of disorientation and writer's block can serve as catalysts for new ideas, voices, and registers. That was the case with Susan Sontag. During her bout of depression, she laid the bases for three books that would be published at the end of the seventies and prove to be some of her best work. In them, she continued her tentative turn to more personal and autobiographical subject matter, which she had already initiated with the essay "Trip to Hanoi." Instead of putting her authorship at the service of something that lay outside of her—as she described her working method during the sixties—Sontag now set off in search of her own voice. The first result was an article that appeared in the *New York Review of Books* in 1972 and would become the first essay in her next collection, *Under the*

Sign of Saturn (1980): "On Paul Goodman" was her obituary for the author, thinker, and cofounder of Gestalt therapy known for his open homosexuality and refusal to assimilate into the New York intelligentsia. With the great success of *Growing Up Absurd* (1960), he had become an exemplary figure for the radical youth movement of the sixties.

Sontag begins her essay with a description of her small study in Paris, in which, aside from some manuscripts and notebooks, there is no written matter except two paperbacks, one of which is by Goodman, because she is trying "better to hear my own voice and discover what I really think and really feel."[29] Every morning, she writes, someone delivers the *New York Herald Tribune,* where she follows the continuing bombing of North Vietnam as well as the irresistible rise of Woody Allen and also discovers that Paul Goodman has died. Goodman, says Sontag, "was our Sartre, our Cocteau."[30]

The subtext of the obituary is a covertly new and intimate stance in which Sontag sees herself and her own writing reflected on several levels in Goodman and his life. Sontag writes that Goodman, like her, had been a fixture of Vietnam demonstrations and teach-ins. He also wrote openly about his homosexuality even "before the advent of Gay Liberation made coming out of the closet chic," as Sontag wished to, but in the end was unable to do for considerations of both career and her private life. Sontag considered this essay a breakthrough for herself and her writing,[31] and indeed, her strategy of covert self-reflection in writing about Goodman would become a model for a series of essays she wrote on Walter Benjamin, Elias Canetti, and Antonin Artaud.

Shortly thereafter, Sontag began experimenting with another literary form, the short story. The first work she wrote in this genre was "Project for a Trip to China" (1972), one of her best works of short fiction. It was published in her 1978 collection *I, etcetera.* This story grew out of her plans to visit China, a journey Sontag undertook in January 1973 after having been to Vietnam a second time in 1972. The trip completed her tour of the "Axis of Evil" of those days—Cuba, Vietnam, and China.

But "Project for a Trip to China" is the document of an imaginary inner journey that takes place before the actual excursion to the Far East, and is based on the model of the Halliburton travel books Sontag so loved as a child. In the story, she explores her memories of her father, who had died in China. What is so impressive about the story is not its memoirlike aspects but the assured and moving voice in which Sontag describes her fantasies about the land in the Far East. They yield a pastiche of quotations, headlines, geographic references, and intentionally stereotypical thoughts about Chinese life. Sontag attains a formal freedom in this story that is completely new to her writing. In many respects, this voice reflects Sontag's narrative temperament so well because the methods of fiction are mixed with the tools of the essayist. What results is a testimony to autobiographical experience as well as a little cultural history of the fantasies and imaginings that connect the West to China.[32]

Sontag abandoned the "real" reportage she had agreed to with FSG and promised to write for *Ms.* magazine, although the publisher and the magazine had together underwritten her trip. Despite the revolutionary impulse that Sontag still maintained at this time, she could hardly get over her shock at how totalitarian the Chinese system was and how much it resembled the Soviet Union's state apparatus and ideology. Her trip to China made it very clear to her, she reported, "that the moralism of *serious* communist societies not only wipes out the autonomy of the aesthetic, but makes it impossible to produce art (in the modern sense) at all" and that "the autonomy of the aesthetic is something to be protected, and cherished, as indispensable nourishment to intelligence."[33]

Sontag wrote three more autobiographically inflected short stories in a similar associative style, replacing linear narrative with the evocation of intense emotional and intellectual atmosphere: "Baby" (1973) and "Old Complaints Revisited" and "Debriefing" (both 1974). She wrote to Roger Straus that she was so enthusiastic about the stories that she was planning to continue writing short fiction for a while, postponing the novel until the following year. She said they came to her almost faster than she could type and she was chained to her typewriter day and night.[34]

In "Baby," Sontag reworks events from both her own childhood and that of her son and depicts the disorientation of the young parents in a fictitious therapy session. "Old Complaints Revisited" presents a similarly retrospective self-examination inspired by Sontag's visit to Israel in October 1973 and coming to terms with her Jewish identity. "Debriefing" revisits the suicide of Sontag's friend Susan Taubes. The narrator of the story reflects on her own reaction of stoicism, mourning, and incomprehension at the suicide of her friend Julia and rehearses a series of reasons to stay alive—among them the necessity of learning more, experiencing more, and knowing more. "Debriefing" testifies to the helpless fury Sontag felt at the suicide of her friend. "That late Wednesday afternoon I told Julia how stupid it would be if she committed suicide. She agreed. I thought I was convincing. Two days later she left her apartment again and killed herself, showing me that she didn't mind doing something stupid."[35]

Susan Sontag's film career now developed a similar creative dynamic. For two years, she had explored various ideas for films, among them a political documentary on Vietnam. With Nicole Stéphane as producer, she had acquired the film rights for Simone de Beauvoir's first novel, *She Came to Stay* (1943), in which the author fictionalizes a love triangle between Sartre, herself, and another woman. De Beauvoir granted Sontag the film rights gratis.[36] Sontag also had plans for a science-fiction film and even a Western.[37]

When the Yom Kippur War between Israel and the allies Syria and Egypt broke out in 1973, Sontag decided to make a film in which she would explore her role as a Jewish intellectual and the product of a nonreligious Jewish upbringing. Nicole Stéphane offered to underwrite the production costs and encouraged Sontag to pursue the idea. Within a few days, Sontag assembled a film crew—recruiting her son, David, as assistant director—and flew to Israel, where the hostilities were still going on. The result was the documentary *Promised Lands*, which at least among critics proved to be a great success at the Chicago Film Festival. *Promised Lands* is regarded by many as Sontag's best film. It plumbs the relationship between the history of the Jews in Israel and their situation during the Yom Kippur War. In purely associative sequence, Sontag presents images of dying on the Israeli side of the war. Instead of examining the Arab-Israeli conflict from an objective perspective, for the most part she allows despairing Israelis to speak about the war. The result is an extremely personal film showing the frustrations, contradictions, and helplessness of the Israeli Jews, an essay that was utterly partisan without conceding that the Israelis were right. The New York magazine *Time Out* bore the headline "Must Be Seen." The *Financial Times* was impressed by Sontag's refusal to get involved with which side was right or wrong and by the film's images, which remained burned into the viewer's memory. And the leftist *Jewish Chronicle* called *Promised Lands* "the rare phenomenon of an objective film about an inflammatory topic."[38]

In a sense, Sontag was working her way out of her own deep crisis. Between 1973 and 1975, she wrote a brilliant essay on the French poet and theoretician of theater Antonin Artaud and several articles on feminism for such magazines as *Partisan Review, Vogue,* and *Cosmopolitan.* And last but not least, she began to write a series of essays for the *New York Review of Books* on the topic of photography.

One result of this phase of enormous productivity was the temporary achievement of financial stability. The seventies were, in a certain sense, the golden age of American magazines. Glossy publications such as *Vogue* and *Cosmopolitan* published long articles by serious authors like Sontag and paid them extremely generous fees. Even the *New York Review of Books* and such literary magazines as *American Review* and the *Atlantic Monthly,* where Sontag published her short stories, provided lucrative outlets for her work. According to a bill in the FSG files, the *New Yorker* paid the record amount of $7,500 for the Artaud essay.[39]

Sontag urgently needed the money, and Straus found nothing dubious about asking for large sums for her pieces nor about publishing them where they would fetch the highest fee. He sold *Playboy* the rights to Sontag's short story "Baby" for $2,500. It made Sontag a bit uncomfortable when she received her specimen copy in Paris, but she never regretted the decision. She was, after all, in financial straits.[40] Straus also managed to secure a Rockefeller Fellowship as well as a Guggenheim Fellowship for his author through American PEN. Together they provided Sontag with a secure income for 1974 and 1975.

Public debate in the early seventies was dominated by feminism. The founding generation of American feminists—such authors as Betty Friedan, Kate Millett, Gloria Steinem, and Germaine Greer—wrote the basic texts defining the emancipation of women as a radical liberation movement. It seems curious that Sontag was not part of this group, for in a certain sense she was one of the models for their generation, a woman who had already realized the promise of emancipation on her own, making her way as a single mother and a woman of letters in a world dominated by men. There was never any doubt that she strongly espoused feminist positions and was familiar with the barriers faced by young women who wanted their own careers. Susan Sontag would react with extreme verbal abuse whenever she felt herself being patronized as a woman. "God help anyone who tried!" says Stephen Koch.[41] In interviews as well as her 1974 *Partisan Review* essay "The Third World of Women," she clearly articulated the inequality of women and compared the feminist movement to the abolition of slavery. She called herself a "nigger in a room full of whites" because she belonged to the small minority of women who were part of a professional world dominated by men.[42]

And yet Sontag's biography cannot be subsumed under the discourses of social change that dominated the women's liberation movement, even though she supported it heart and soul. The main reason was that after her political engagement in the sixties, Sontag was moving away from her former ambition to change society toward a decidedly more individual approach. This new focus was incompatible with the social impetus of feminism. It is clear from Sontag's comments on the topic that she hoped to achieve an initial rethinking of women's roles among women themselves, not in society as a whole: "It's built into our bodies, into our way of moving. Fear, low self-esteem, insecurity, inability to localize our full energies for achievement . . . Every woman, no matter how enlightened she is, faces these problems," she said in an interview with the *SoHo Weekly News*.[43] In another interview, she carried this critical thought further when she said that women were too afraid of articulating their anger while anger in men was considered a normal, active behavior.[44]

In private conversations, Sontag could sometimes express herself more openly and even a bit smugly about the feminist movement. These commentaries often seemed motivated by her own status as an exceptional woman. According to Sontag, feminism was without a doubt one of the most important developments of our era, but at heart it was concerned with mediocrity. While men of second- or even third-class intelligence held positions at the center of power, such status was not possible for modestly talented women. Stephen Koch says his friend regarded feminism as a movement for the rights of women of average intelligence who also had a claim to positions of power. But one must not forget that Western European and American women with excellent educations had been occupying important positions in science, the arts, journalism, and the economy for more than 150 years—women like George Eliot, Simone de Beauvoir, Hannah Arendt, Madame Curie, and of course Susan Sontag herself.[45]

It must be added that Sontag measured such women by the same standards as she did men. This assessment became a central although largely unspoken argument in one of her most brilliant essays. In the mid-seventies, the German filmmaker and photographer Leni Riefenstahl was enjoying a pronounced renaissance in America. Her propaganda films *Triumph of the Will,* on the National Socialist convention in 1934, and *Olympia,* on the

Berlin Olympic Games of 1936, were screened at several film festivals. Feminist artist Niki de Saint Phalle's poster for the New York Film Festival in 1973 ecstatically announced the presence of "Leni." In Telluride, Colorado, in 1974, Riefenstahl was the guest of honor, and she attended the Chicago Films by Women Festival the same year. There was an increasing consensus that the Nazi ideology Riefenstahl had so effectively presented in her propaganda films was merely the product of the zeitgeist of the Third Reich and of secondary importance compared to the beauty, classical composition, and technical perfection of the films themselves. Sontag herself had made this claim in the 1965 essay "On Style." To be sure, even at that time she made it clear that Riefenstahl's films must be considered Nazi propaganda. But she saw in them something else that forced the propaganda into the background and let the fascist contents shrink to a purely formal role. Riefenstahl's films, according to Sontag, were masterpieces "because they project the complex movements of intelligence and grace and sensuousness" and "transcend the categories of propaganda or even reportage."[46]

"Fascinating Fascism," Sontag's Riefenstahl essay of 1974, can be read as an elaborate footnote to this thesis that both refines and revises it. This time, Sontag's focus was not on Riefenstahl's impressive stylistic achievements but on why her films exert such a hold on us. Sontag's answer: Riefenstahl's style itself is shot through with fascist ideology, reflecting it at every moment and enveloping the viewer unconsciously in the sadomasochistic ideology of power and superiority through its seductively beautiful images. When the essay first appeared in the *New York Review of Books* in 1975, that issue achieved the highest circulation numbers the *Review* ever had—before or since. Up to the last minute before press time, Robert Silvers and Barbara Epstein had been on the telephone with Sontag discussing revisions and exchanging galley proofs. It was clear to them that the piece was one of the best things she had ever written.[47]

In 1973,[48] Riefenstahl had published a large-format book of glossy photographs of the Sudanese people called the Nuba to much fanfare. Using *The Last of the Nuba* as her starting point, Sontag describes the troubling rehabilitation of the German filmmaker as a cinematic genius. She identifies the social impulse that underwrote this development as a new and growing cult of beauty. Sontag's critique of Riefenstahl's photographs and her foreword to the Nuba book is directed at their unabashed celebration of physical strength, ethnic loyalty, and collective and ecstatic subjugation. Sontag argues that these are the very stylistic elements Riefenstahl had used in her monumental propaganda documentaries. A critical assessment of the book must not gloss over such elements of fascist ideology, Sontag argues. She says that all Riefenstahl is doing is translating them into the romantic ideals of yearning, attractiveness, and physical perfection that every observer understands intuitively. Such ideals now, under a different guise, reappear in popular culture, for example, in the form of pornographic magazines that reinvigorate the cult of Nazi uniforms as a variety of sadomasochism.[49]

Peripherally, "Fascinating Fascism" also addressed the acclaim Riefenstahl was supposedly enjoying among feminist circles. This provoked a response from the poet Adrienne Rich. In a letter to the *New York Review,* Rich set the record straight, saying that the entire feminist movement did not share this view. Rather, radical feminists criticized Riefenstahl as an example of "male-identified 'successful' women." Moreover, Rich directly challenged Sontag to state clearly her own position vis-à-vis the feminist movement.[50] Adrienne Rich had thrown down the gauntlet, and Sontag responded with a fierce letter in which virtually every sentence exudes cold-blooded fury, especially when she comes to the topic of women who identified with men. Sontag accused Rich of "the infantile leftism of the 1960s" and using demagogic rhetoric. More than that, the streamlined ideology of the feminist movement and its intellectual banalities seemed to Sontag to be themselves like "the roots of fascism."[51]

Sontag's response caused as much uproar as the Riefenstahl essay itself. Richard Howard summarizes the dispute between the two women by saying, "Susan wiped the floor of the ring with Adrienne."[52] But Nadine Gordimer recalls how important her friend and colleague's critical attitude toward feminism was for the ongoing discussion among writers.[53]

In a 1975 interview, Sontag declares that she wishes there were armies of women ready to do battle against the patriarchal stereotypes, but she says, "Feminists have tended to perpetuate these philistine characterizations of hierarchy, theory, and intellect. What was denounced in the 1960s as bourgeois, repressive, and elitist was discovered to be phallocratic, too. That kind of second-hand militancy . . . means a surrender to callow notions of art and of thought and the encouragement of a genuinely repressive moralism."[54]

Steve Wasserman says there is a sense in which Sontag remained a radical at heart all her life, one who "never lost her ability to open the newspaper in the morning and be outraged."[55] Still, the Riefenstahl affair marks her final break from the radical movements of the sixties and early seventies. She was never the follower of a party line or a subscriber to a particular ideology. For Sontag, the sixties finally ended in 1975, and, with their end, it became possible for her to reinvent herself as an intellectual.

The Kingdom of the Sick

(1975–1979)

> *Everyone who is born holds dual*
> *citizenship, in the kingdom of the*
> *well and in the kingdom of the sick.*
>
> Susan Sontag, *Illness as Metaphor*
> (1978)

Sontag's return to the intellectual scene continued in a series of essays on photography she had been working on since 1972 that appeared in the *New York Review of Books*.[1] The initial impetus for Sontag's engagement with this medium was an exhibition of Diane Arbus photographs at the Museum of Modern Art. The show was immensely popular, attracting more visitors than any previous exhibition in the museum's history, and its catalog became a surprise best seller. Arbus, born in 1923, was famous for oppressive head-on portraits of freaks and outsiders from the margins of society and had become a mythic figure since her suicide in 1971. But for Sontag, Arbus was little more than a voyeur from the Upper West Side with a practiced eye for the marginal. Moreover, the photographs seemed to her ethically problematic. Sontag interpreted their popularity as a voyeuristic reflex that suggested a new status for the medium of photography in Western societies, a status of which she did not approve.

With a few exceptions—among them Walter Benjamin's "Short History of Photography" (1931) and Roland Barthes's semiotic essay "The Photographic Message" (1961)—almost nothing had been written about the history of the medium. Sontag collected photos and sorted them into piles on the floor of her study, looking through them again and again during her work on the essay series. Robert Silvers and Barbara Epstein were so enthusiastic about the pieces they suggested Sontag publish them as a book under the *Review*'s imprint. She declined, citing her relationship with Roger Straus.[2] Straus meanwhile had been growing impatient waiting for at least one of the many books she had been promising him for years, and he urged Sontag to finish the manuscript. But she struggled with the project. For each essay, she wrote ten to fifteen drafts, interrupted by long periods of writer's block.[3] There was no doubt of the difficulties she was having, although Sontag also tended to exaggerate them. In interviews, she claimed to have written twenty or forty drafts and expended thousands of pages for a thirty-page essay.[4] It took her five years to complete the six essays that comprise *On Photography* (1977).

While Sontag was working intensively on the photography book, a routine doctor's examination revealed she had an advanced case of breast cancer. It was a shock for the forty-two-year-old, and her reaction was "Panic . . . animal terror."[5] As she told the *New York Times,* she had thought she was in the best of health—she had never been seriously ill—and the check-up had been a completely routine one. After the diagnosis, she had at first felt the need to do "very primitive sorts of things, like sleeping with the light on the first couple of months." Her fear of the dark reflected her personal experience in a situation in which "You really do feel as though you're looking into that black hole."[6] With this black hole Susan Sontag's struggle with the disease began, a battle she would ultimately lose almost three decades later. David Rieff, Stephen Koch, and a few other friends accompanied her to Memorial Sloan-Kettering Cancer Center in New

York, where she was to undergo a diagnostic operation. During an hour alone with Koch in her room, she talked openly about the possibility that she might die. "She always talked about what was buzzing around inside her head. And that evening it was about dying," he said. They were discussing the manuals for dying that had been traditional in Buddhist cultures for centuries when she suddenly sat up and said there was still something she had to do. She had promised Peter Hujar she would write an introduction for his collection of photographs *Portraits in Life and Death* (1976). It contained photos of his New York friends, including Sontag herself, Robert Wilson, Paul Thek, William S. Burroughs, and John Waters. Sontag had let the deadline for the manuscript slip by, and now, in less than an hour, she wrote by hand a text about the intimate connection between photography and death. In the face of her own possible demise, she described Hujar's photos as a memento mori.[7]

The exploratory operation revealed that Sontag had an advanced and aggressive tumor with several metastases. The prognosis was that she had perhaps a half year to live. The chances of a two-year survival were ten percent. Sontag reacted on the one hand with an optimism bordering on sarcasm. After all, she said, "somebody's got to be in that ten percent."[8] At the same time, she tried to maintain objective clarity about her situation. Her son, David Rieff, recalls that his mother was furious with the way the doctors talked to her. She felt patronized and kept in the dark, deprived of her independence. She rebelled and began to read everything she could find about breast cancer in reference works and articles from American and European medical journals. She also discussed her situation with as many oncologists as possible.[9] In the end, Sontag underwent a radical mastectomy and five subsequent operations. Nicole Stéphane recommended she see the French specialist Lucien Israël, one of the best oncologists of the time. He had achieved good results with high-dose chemotherapy.[10] Her American doctors advised against it because the treatment was grueling and painful and for that reason not yet approved in the United States. Sontag ignored their advice, and finally her doctors at Sloan-Kettering reluctantly agreed to complete the chemotherapy she had begun in Paris. The painful procedure lasted two and a half years.

Sontag, like most freelance American authors, had no health insurance—for one thing, because she had lived abroad for so long; for another, because she had never thought she would need it and considered it, along with savings accounts and life insurance, as bourgeois folderol.[11] She now had to pay the cost of her treatment out of her own pocket, to the tune of $150,000. Naturally these medical bills caused immense difficulties since she had always had just barely enough money to pay her living expenses and David's college tuition. Especially during her first year of chemotherapy, she was unable to work. So Robert Silvers and Barbara Epstein, along with Arthur Miller, Roger Straus, Diana Trilling, William Phillips, Joe Chaikin, and others set up a fund for Sontag's medical expenses and solicited contributions. Many friends, acquaintances, and fans donated to the fund, which paid the greater part of her doctors' bills.[12]

Sontag later described the experience of feeling near death: "One moment you are in a boat, and the next moment you are in the water. But if you can take in the idea that you're going to die, there is a euphoria in it as well as great terror. Nothing else is real except the most intense experiences, so you reach out for the intimacy. It can be exalting, even as you are reduced to this damaged body that is being cut up and made ugly and made to hurt and feel vulnerable. But it's passionate and turbulent and intense."[13] Elsewhere, she said the time of her first cancer treatment had been "a great adventure. It was the adventure of being ill and probably dying."[14]

Sontag's need to experience everything as intensely as possible grew even more pronounced during these years, according to Sigrid Nunez. At the time, Nunez was David Rieff's girlfriend and lived with him and his mother in their penthouse on Riverside Drive. In the period following her therapy, Sontag went out every night she was physically able to do so—to the opera, to dinner with friends, to the movies or the theater.[15] Steve Wasserman remembers some wild evenings with Sontag and David Rieff in the Lower East Side punk club CBGB.[16] When Hans-Jürgen Syberberg's seven-hour film *Our Hitler* arrived in New York movie theaters in 1977, Sontag saw it so often and forced so many of her friends to come with her that Richard Howard started calling it "Her Hitler."[17] "Sontag always wanted to be in the middle of the action in the most profound sense," Howard said.[18] At a time when the gay subculture, with its dark rooms, bars, and sex clubs, was causing a furor, Sontag's ravenous curiosity even led her to disguise herself as a man to visit a gay bar called the Toilet that she could not have gotten into as a woman.[19]

This period of intense living was also one of increased productivity. Sontag planned to write about her experiences with the illness. Three times a week, she was going to the hospital for chemotherapy injections and watching other patients dying. Then, as now, cancer, "the big C," was fraught with many myths and taboos. This situation often led patients to accept their ignorance and resign themselves to what their doctors ordered instead of actively seeking better treatments. It also provided Sontag with the idea for *Illness as Metaphor* (1978). But before she wrote that book, she finished work on the last two essays in *On Photography*, work her illness had interrupted.

When it finally appeared in the fall of 1977, *On Photography* ushered in another wave of fame for Sontag after her "radical chic" period, more fame than she had ever expected. It is nearly impossible to summarize the intellectual journey Sontag undertakes in these six multifaceted and detail-rich essays. She elaborates connections between the history of photography from Stieglitz to Arbus and painting from Eugène Delacroix to Jackson Pollock, film from Jean Cocteau to Michelangelo Antonioni, philosophy from Ludwig Feuerbach to Walter Benjamin, and literature from Marcel Proust to Vladimir Nabokov. Sontag succeeds in analyzing the photographic medium from every conceivable angle, examining pictures taken by security cameras as closely as vacation snapshots, war photography, and the extravagant aesthetics of commercial photography.

As Sontag states in the famous opening chapter, humankind is still living in "Plato's cave," preferring pictures to real things. Plato had polemicized against artistic images and likened them to the shadows on the wall of a cave instead of the real objects that cast the shadows. Plato, she remarks laconically, has lost out to the power of images, and photography is at fault. Photography has trained society with "a new visual code" and, as an indispensable component of daily life, has developed a "grammar . . . of seeing" and given us the feeling that we can hold the world in our hands as an "anthology of images."[20]

If there is a common thread running through *On Photography,* it is Sontag's view that photographs are, above all, the means by which a culture of consumption makes reality and the past consumable; it replaces them with images. The power of photography has "in effect de-Platonized our understanding of reality." It becomes more and more difficult even to distinguish between image and reality. Images are "more real than anyone could have supposed." They turn "the tables on reality," turn "*it* into a shadow." Logically, Sontag ends the volume with a plea for an "ecology not only of real things but of images as well."[21]

The irony of the situation was certainly not lost on Sontag. As a young author, she had marketed herself partly through glamorous photographic portraits, and now she was subjecting the medium to critical analysis. One may guess that it was precisely Sontag's personal experience of having an image—partly evoked by photographs—that bore no relation to her own conception of herself that made her such a close observer of our interaction with images in general. The book, dedicated to Nicole Stéphane, was well and even enthusiastically reviewed by almost all American magazines and newspapers. Even the *New York Times Book Review,* which had often been extremely critical of Sontag in the sixties, called the new volume "brilliant" and praised Sontag's "clarity, skepticism and passionate concern." "Every page . . . raises important and exciting questions about its subject and raises them in the best way," said the *Book Review,* "with an admirable pungency of thought and directness of expression that sacrifices nothing of subtlety or refinement."[22] *On Photography* was included in the *Book Review*'s list of the twenty best books of the year and also received the National Book Critics Circle Award and the prestigious Arts and Letters Award of the American Academy of Arts and Letters.

Not surprisingly, the only dissenting voices were those of professional photographers and those who regarded photography as an art form, a status Sontag refused to grant the medium. Inspired by a critique in the *New York Times,* a quip made the rounds in artistic circles that the book should actually have been called *Against Photography.* Many art photographers, such as Irving Penn, vigorously objected.[23] Others, including Peter Hujar, took more drastic measures and ended their friendships with Sontag.[24] Despite these protests, *On Photography* is still considered a groundbreaking contribution to the history and theory of photography and has become a standard text in academic critical studies of art, culture, and photography. Twenty-five years later, Sontag would take up the topic again in *Regarding the Pain of Others* (2003), her essay on war photography.

By the time *On Photography* appeared, Susan Sontag had completed the most difficult phase of her treatment for breast cancer. She not only belonged to the ten percent who survived for two years but also the illness itself had been successfully arrested and the chances of a cure increased. Nevertheless Sontag also knew that a complete cure was impossible, since the danger of recurrence remains for every cancer patient. For the rest of her life, she would be very sensitive to the signals her body was sending and pay regular visits to her doctors as well as undergo exploratory surgery.

Sontag had been able to observe firsthand the shame cancer patients felt at having the disease. Hardly any of them read the medical journals in which Sontag immersed herself, looking for alternative therapies. Instead, many patients accepted the diagnosis as a death sentence, although it was often not necessarily so. It was customary not to divulge details of the diagnosis or the probable survival rate to the patients, but only to certain members of their families. The Memorial Sloan-Kettering Cancer Center, the leading cancer hospital in New York and one of the best in America, sent its bills out without a return address on the envelope so that neighbors or relatives would not discover the diagnosis by accident. Susan Sontag rebelled against this deep-seated stigmatization of the disease that was perpetuated by all concerned. She became a "crusader for the sick," as she once described herself.[25] In her view, it was not only the disease that killed but also, above all, the taboos associated with it, especially when patients refused treatment in the belief that they were going to die anyway.

The first campaign of Sontag's crusade against the stigma of cancer consisted of three informational essays—"Illness as Metaphor," "Images of Illness," and "Disease as Political Metaphor"—that she wrote in the space of three months and published in January and February 1978 in the *New York Review of Books*. In revised form, they appeared as a book in the fall of that year under the title *Illness as Metaphor*. These essays were nothing like the then-fashionable memoirs of cancer patients. Such a memoir would have been a basic contradiction to Sontag's stance. She was not interested in writing a subjective report on her experience as a patient. Rather, she wanted to communicate her thoughts on the topic in a way that could be helpful and stimulating for other people with the disease as well as their friends, partners, and relatives.[26]

Illness as Metaphor is an impassioned plea for dealing straightforwardly with cancer as well as an intellectual roller-coaster ride through the cultural history of the disease. Adducing ancient Greek theories of disease, medieval medical lexicons, psychoanalytic texts, modern medical studies, and literary, philosophical, scientific, and musical examples from every conceivable language and epoch—from Leo Tolstoy to Boris Pasternak, Novalis to Nietzsche, Kafka to Mann, John Keats to Lord Byron, Robert Koch to Rudolf Virchow, Giovanni Boccaccio to Filippo Tommaso Marinetti, Frédéric Chopin to Giacomo

Puccini, and Victor Hugo to Charles Baudelaire—Sontag analyzes the metaphorical levels associated with the disease. She
compares cancer to tuberculosis, another disease with painful
connections to her personal history. Tuberculosis was the disease
that had killed her father, a disease whose stigmatization was
still virulent in the thirties—so much so that Mildred Sontag did
not tell her five-year-old daughter, Susan, what her father had
died of—and a disease about whose all-embracing mythology
Thomas Mann had written in *The Magic Mountain.*

But for Sontag, the mythologizing of cancer is different in
kind. She argues with particular sharpness against the widespread belief that cancer had something to do with a depressive
personality or that tumors could develop from unprocessed
psychic energies. She told several interviewers that, after her initial diagnosis, she asked herself whether she had lived her life
wrongly and the breast cancer was somehow the result of the
depression she had experienced in Paris.[27] Beyond that, *Illness
as Metaphor* pillories the equation of the illness with "radical or
absolute evil." In discussing cancer, people would invoke images
of economic catastrophe: uncontrolled, abnormal, and incoher-
ent growth and its deadly consequences for the body of society.
They would avail themselves of the jargon of military colonialism and speak about "invasion," "colonization," "attacks," and
"counterattacks." Even the language of science fiction was used
to talk about cellular "mutations." Conversely, the cancer patient
was daily confronted by the use of the illness as a simplistic metaphor for complex political situations, and here Sontag cites her
own famous sentence from "What's Happening in America,"
"The white race *is* the cancer of human history." Depicting cancer as an unconquerable evil, Sontag argues, was hardly helpful
for an active struggle against the disease.[28]

When *Illness as Metaphor* appeared, dedicated to Robert Silvers in gratitude for his financial and organizational support, its
success was equal to that of *On Photography.* Sontag received
hundreds of letters from cancer patients, many telling her that
they had switched doctors or decided to get treatment after

reading it.[29] *Illness as Metaphor* became required reading for patients and doctors the world over. Beyond entering the public discussion with her book, she also became engaged in helping patients privately. Lucinda Childs says Sontag spoke daily with friends who had been diagnosed with cancer and also with patients who were strangers to her. Anyone who wanted to share his or her experiences or needed advice found a ready listener in Sontag. Richard Howard says that Sontag sometimes even carried her engagement too far, actually forcing herself on patients to make sure they were exhausting all possibilities for treatment. When Leonard Bernstein's wife, Felicia Montealegre, got cancer, Sontag spoke with her almost every day until her death.[30]

Sontag described her convalescence as an intense and upsetting experience. Finding out she would continue to live after having come to terms with the prospect of dying, she felt a need for more intimacy and contact with others.[31] She made many new friends, especially among young authors. "One of the most exciting things in New York was to go out with her until late at night," reports the essayist and author Darryl Pinckney. Sontag possessed an enormous amount of energy. For several days, the two of them sat in a theater for hours watching Rainer Werner Fassbinder's thirteen-hour film version of Alfred Döblin's novel *Berlin Alexanderplatz*.[32] Sontag was a wonderful mentor for young authors. Sigrid Nunez recalls that "when you spent time with her, you could learn more than from a university."[33]

Nunez also said, however, that Sontag had difficulty combining this increased need for social contacts with her work: "She was very dissatisfied and restless and constantly in need of diversion, unable to be alone."[34] Sontag had always been undisciplined in her work and now procrastinated until the last minute with every piece she wrote. To meet the deadlines for her articles in the *New York Review of Books* and the *New Yorker,* she turned to amphetamines (in their medical but nevertheless still illegal form, Benzedrine), like thousands of writers before her, including Jean-Paul Sartre. Sontag told her friend Victor Bockris,

"It eliminates the need to eat, sleep or pee or talk to other people. And one can really sit 20 hours in a room and not feel lonely or tired or bored. It gives you terrific powers of concentration."[35] However, she added that she always tried to be careful with it because, in Sartre's case, the lifelong use of amphetamines had produced the dubious result of thousands of pages of inconsequential prose.[36]

Susan Sontag's cancer also left visible traces in her appearance. Her hair had fallen out during the chemotherapy, and it grew back white. Sontag decided to have it dyed black. A hairdresser suggested leaving one strand white because it looked more natural. She agreed, and for the next twenty years, her jet-black hair with the eccentric white strand over her forehead would become what Americans call her signature look, a trademark that was immediately recognizable and much caricatured. After numerous new photos, interviews, and profiles of her in the press and a few appearances on television—including Dick Cavett's legendary talk show—a Susan Sontag wig became a regular feature on the late-night comedy show *Saturday Night Live*. Films in which Sontag made cameo appearances, such as Gina Blumenfeld's *In Dark Places* (1978), Woody Allen's *Zelig* (1983), Néstor Almendros's *Mauvaise Conduite* (*Improper Conduct*, 1984), and Edgardo Cozarinsky's *Sarah* (1988), continued the march toward her iconization as a glamorous intellectual.

Despite Sontag's lack of disciplined work habits, this was a phase of enormous productivity. In 1978 and 1979, she laid the groundwork for her next essay collection, *Under the Sign of Saturn* (1980), and completed *I, etcetera*, the volume of short stories she had been working on for almost seven years. Except for "American Spirits" and "The Dummy," formal experiments from the early sixties decidedly in the style of her novels that could be characterized as existential comics, the stories in the collection represent a new literary voice in which Sontag combines autobiographical details with essayistic passages. The last story she wrote for the volume was "Unguided Tour." An eccentric, touching, and witty story that nonchalantly makes use of

established American clichés about trips to Europe, it appeared
in the *New Yorker* in October 1978. It concerns the destruction of beautiful things, the unstoppable change and decay of
old European cities, and the feeling that they may not be there
much longer. "Unguided Tour" is a requiem for the history of the
Old World, but also for a love affair. The subtext of the short
story is the ending of a relationship in which romantic desire has
withered.

There is strong evidence that Susan Sontag was here coming
to terms with the end of her relationship with Nicole Stéphane.
The fact that Sontag had shifted her center of activity back
to New York put a strain on the relationship. Sontag's and
Stéphane's interests had also diverged more and more. Sontag,
again working exclusively as a writer, reacted in annoyance to
Stéphane's suggestions for new film projects.[37] Mutual friends
describe a tense and sometimes bitter mood between the two
partners, with Sontag often striking out at Stéphane with relent-
less verbal attacks. According to Stephen Koch, it was mainly
Sontag who was unfair to Stéphane, once accusing her in front
of other people of saying something stupid. The process of separation was difficult, Koch said, because "they really loved each
other."[38]

When *I, etcetera* appeared in the fall of 1978, critics and
readers generally received it with surprise. Although most critics
noted the uneven quality of the stories in the collection, "Debriefing," "Project for a Trip to China," and "Unguided Tour" were
praised as important stories, the first successful fiction Sontag
had written. Anatole Broyard wrote that "Unguided Tour" was
Sontag's "apotheosis as a fiction writer" and "one of the most
modern stories I have ever read—perhaps one of the best. For
the first time, Susan Sontag . . . is entirely at home in fiction."[39]
Sontag had discovered her fictional form, one that combined her
debt to literary modernity with the power of her intellect and an
urgent, sometimes poetic, but above all approachable voice, in
contrast to her first two novels. Some of her stories can still be
regarded as leading examples of the genre. She had dreamed all

her life of being a successful author, and now she had reached her goal.

Sontag followed the fate of her works in Europe and especially in Germany with great interest. Her German publisher Michael Krüger, head of the Hanser Verlag, recalls "more and more urgent letters from Sontag . . . asking us to do more for her." After several visits to Germany, especially to Munich and Berlin, and once her essays had appeared in German magazines and the influential Hamburg weekly *Die Zeit*, Hanser was able to "gradually . . . promote her with more success."[40] In November 1979, the Mainz Academy of Sciences and Literature awarded Susan Sontag the Wilhelm Heinse Medal for essay writing, the first of numerous prestigious German awards that would culminate in the Peace Prize of the German Book Trade in 2003.

The Last Intellectual

(1980–1983)

*I do not want to be a professor
and I do not want to be a journalist.
I want to be a writer who is also
an intellectual.*

Susan Sontag, in a 1980 interview

The world of American arts and letters was undergoing profound changes in the late seventies.[1] While popular culture was
becoming an all-encompassing phenomenon, serious discussion
of literature, art, and film was increasingly relegated to academic
publications. In the rapidly shifting media landscape, the formerly important coterie of New York Intellectuals was slipping
into insignificance. The uniform and stable intellectual scene that
had reigned—with shifting personnel, of course—from the thirties to the sixties no longer existed. To earn their bread, most
intellectuals now sought positions at universities or received
support from neoconservative think tanks such as the American
Enterprise Institute, the Project for the New American Century,
and the Jewish Institute for National Security Affairs. Writers,
too, found themselves increasingly forced to accept university
teaching positions. Only a few were in a position to continue
working as freelance authors. Not only were publications like

Partisan Review steadily losing subscribers, but also the intellectual style they represented was out of fashion. Under the editorship of Norman Podhoretz, one of the most vociferous of the neoconservatives, *Commentary* became a partisan organ of the incipient Reagan revolution.[2]

During the Vietnam War, the *New York Review of Books* alone had become an important forum for political and critical debates that resonated beyond the confines of New York. The publication was able to maintain its dominant position in the journalistic landscape by paying increased attention to political topics and representing the interests of the academics scattered across the country. In its early years still confined to the New York scene, the *Review* became and remains to this day obligatory reading for university faculty and ambitious graduate students.

Moreover, the solidarity of the New Left had vanished. There were no more grand issues holding the movement together. The ethos of dissent and rebellion that had been a foundation for leftist thinkers for the past two decades had lost much of its attraction. Most leftists had abandoned their radical heritage or become nostalgic. Many of them, especially bourgeois-liberal thinkers from the Old Left who had always had certain reservations about the radicalism of the New Left, began to adopt increasingly conservative attitudes. The influential neoconservative movement, bolstered by the rise of the previously mentioned think tanks and lobbying groups, made its political influence felt. The movement celebrated its first overwhelming victory with the election of the former actor and California governor Ronald Reagan as president in November 1980.

Although this so-called neocon movement cannot be considered unified by any means, its multiplicity of splinter groups was held together by their deep dislike of the political radicalism of the sixties and their utopian vision of the future. Neoconservative authors such as Hilton Kramer, Norman Podhoretz, and Irving Kristol styled themselves the genuine heirs of the New York Intellectuals, leading the way forward for the middle class.[3]

A similar development was taking place in Europe. The aging Roland Barthes would complain repeatedly that the spe cies of traditional intellectuals and writers was dying out and being replaced by a new breed, most of whom held university positions. Sontag agreed with this prognosis. In a 1980 interview, she declared it her aim to defend the universal role of the writer against the opposition of her times.[4] It was by no means an easy assignment. Sontag's audience had changed. They were now reading the next generation of Europeans, writers who came along after Sontag's heroes but whose ideas did not particularly interest her. These Europeans included the Frankfurt School, a group of German-American neo-Marxists; Lacanian psychoanalysis, practiced by followers of the French psychiatrist Jacques Lacan; Michel Foucault's discourse analysis, which studied power relationships in society as expressed through language. They also included the up-and-coming deconstructivism of Jacques Derrida, Julia Kristeva, Gilles Deleuze, and Michel de Certeau, who questioned traditional assumptions about truth, instead stressing ambiguities and contradictions in literature, and arguing that the meaning of a piece of writing depends on the reader.[5] Specialized academic journals, such as *October, Artforum, Camera Obscura,* and *New German Critique,* were the forums for these writers. The often-cited "theoretical revolution" was under way in the humanities departments and research institutions of America, celebrating the collapse of the "Great Narratives" of identity, family, nation, and authorship as a positive aspect of postmodernism. Under its auspices, political agendas like feminism turned into academic disciplines with names like gender studies. The goal of effecting real change in the world, so important to the previous generation, no longer took precedence.

Sontag was one of the few figures able to maintain her public status as an intellectual in the new era of theory. One reason was that, as her essays had always shown, she believed implicitly in her mission, namely, to bring together art, literature, film, and politics and communicate their interrelatedness to her readers.

And she accomplished that mission. Her conception of herself as an intellectual and writer on the French model whose passing Barthes mourned and her irresistible combination of braininess and hipness proved compatible with the changing public taste. Characteristically, the art critic Hal Foster describes Sontag as a "figure of the interregnum."[6] Both the old and the new generation found a common denominator in her thought and writings. She was capable of building a bridge between the moribund New York Intellectuals of the "old school" and the academic disseminators of cultural studies, semiotics, and deconstructivism. As a transitional figure, she was both the object of a kind of nostalgia and the creator of new impulses, both the relict of a bygone era and the media star of a new one.

One of the academic institutions that illustrate this development is the New York Institute for the Humanities at New York University (NYU). The sociologist Richard Sennett had founded the institute in 1976 precisely to counter the trend toward academic specialization by bringing together writers and academics. Sennett describes the early years of the institute as consisting essentially of informal get-togethers of a small group of thinkers and writers who debated with one another and gave free seminars. Sennett's friend Susan Sontag was one of the first people he invited to participate, and she contributed in essential ways to the success of the institute. She not only facilitated ties to European authors and filmmakers, including Roland Barthes and Hans-Jürgen Syberberg, she also helped assemble New York intellectuals at the institute. Among others, she brought along such fellow FSG authors as the later Nobel laureates Joseph Brodsky and Derek Walcott. Other members of the institute were Robert Silvers and a handful of his authors from the *New York Review of Books,* professors from New York University and Columbia, and Roger Straus, who lent the institute his talent for practical organization and finding sources of financial support. Straus had hired Sontag's son as an editor at FSG when David graduated from college in 1978. David edited books by his mother,

Joseph Brodsky, Philip Roth, Mario Vargas Llosa, and Elias Canetti, among others. He also became interim director of the institute.

The New York Institute for the Humanities quickly became one of the city's most important intellectual venues. Intimately connected to it were the legendary informal soirees at Sennett's house near the NYU campus, where participants would go after a seminar to continue their discussion over a gourmet meal cooked by their host.

Sennett's main goal for the institute was to rescue New York from its literary and intellectual provincialism. According to him, the city's theater, dance, and art were already very cosmopolitan, but "writers from Europe and South America were widely ignored."[7] Thanks largely to the engagement of the Soviet émigré poet Joseph Brodsky, one of the most important aspects of the institute's work was to support East European and Soviet dissidents who had fled their native countries for the West. Sennett says that, after martial law was declared in Poland in 1981, it became a priority for the group to help writers from "the communist empire" become U.S. citizens. Members of the institute signed petitions, established contacts, and helped the dissidents obtain teaching positions at American universities. Among the many authors who received such help was Adam Zagajewski. In 1983, the group worked with Senator Edward Kennedy to bring the Cuban Heberto Padilla to America. Sontag had protested against his imprisonment as early as 1972.[8]

For Sontag, the institute's engagement in support of writers persecuted in their Communist homelands marked a final break in her sympathy for such countries as Cuba and Vietnam. This break had already begun in the mid-seventies and was exacerbated by a trip to Poland in 1980 and the reports of the exiles, including Alexander Solzhenitsyn, whose *Gulag Archipelago* (1973) was published by FSG. This change of direction cost Sontag a difficult struggle, a battle manifest in the many contradictory statements of her and her friends. Sennett and Edmund White recall an institute seminar she gave on the topic of "The

Visit," in which she subjected herself to the same passionate and sometimes scathing criticism she usually reserved for others.[9]

The seminar dealt with the trips organized by Communist countries for visitors from the West, during which only selected locations were presented, careful doses of propaganda were administered, and the travelers sent home laden with gifts and books. What especially fascinated Sontag was the literary genre that resulted from these visits, for instance, a whole series of books about China that appeared in France during the fifties and sixties. These travelogues were remarkably similar for the simple reason that the French intellectuals who wrote them had all been given the same tour. In retrospect, Sontag's own informational trips to China, Cuba, Poland, and Vietnam seemed to her like visits to the "Disneyland of revolution."[10]

Following this seminar, Sontag was supposed to write a book on her investigation of this phenomenon on the model of André Gide's memoir of his disillusion after a 1936 trip to the Soviet Union. The book had been long in the planning, but she kept postponing its completion because of her ambivalence about the topic. In the end, she wrote only a short article titled "Model Destinations" that appeared in the *Times Literary Supplement* in 1984. Sontag also planned to write a novel about Eastern European writers who had left for the West. She had begun to work on it in the seventies and had high hopes that *Toward the Western Half* would mark her return to writing fiction. Sontag worked on the project for more than ten years but was never able to finish it.

Edmund White, at the time a close friend of Sontag's, says that her change of heart about Communism was influenced both by Joseph Brodsky and by her relationship to French intellectuals.[11] While French thinkers had been openly criticizing the totalitarian regimes in Eastern Europe since the mid-seventies, most American leftists still hoped for an alternative, socialist society, especially in light of a growing conservative movement and the increasing consolidation of a culture of consumption in the United States.

Brodsky's political conservatism was the result of his clashes with the Soviet authorities, his banishment into "inner exile," and his eventual expulsion from the Soviet Union in 1972. Richard Sennett says he "would have made a good monarchist."[12] Sontag described Brodsky as having a temperament very like her own. Their encounters were examples of irresistible "mental acceleration."[13] After an initial romantic relationship (Richard Howard says Brodsky was so besotted with Sontag that he even asked her to marry him), they remained close friends and saw each other often from the mid-seventies on.[14] An iconic anecdote for Sontag's change of heart, often repeated by Sontag and her friends, was when Brodsky dispelled her doubts about the credibility of Solzhenitsyn's *Gulag Archipelago* with the words, "Think whatever you want to about him on a political level, but what he witnessed, what he describes, are *facts*."[15]

Another manifestation of Brodsky's influence was Sontag's newly awakened passion for the classics of Russian literature and Eastern European literature in general. Here she found confirmed an ideal of literary quality she considered more and more rare in American literature. In her opinion, American authors concentrated too much on the demands of the marketplace, and as a result "few contemporary writers" tried "to write books that are first-rate" or belonged to the "international class" of writers.[16] She shared Brodsky's view of the writer's prophetic authority. In Sontag's opinion, one had to look to the past for the source of literary and ethical standards, where one discovered "higher standards than the present affords" that empowered the writer to write "to please not one's contemporaries but one's predecessors."[17]

Echoes of this rather exalted authorial ideal can be found in Sontag's essay collection *Under the Sign of Saturn,* published in 1980 and dedicated to her Russian friend. The volume collects essays she wrote in the wake of her obituary for Paul Goodman and ends with another obituary for a friend and colleague, "Remembering Barthes." Except for her essays on Riefenstahl and "Syberberg's Hitler," all the pieces are portraits of writers and intellectuals whom Sontag admired and with whom she strongly identified—in addition to Goodman and Barthes, Antonin Artaud, Walter Benjamin, and Elias Canetti. The essays are romantic and quite anachronistic exercises in old-fashioned admiration for great representatives of (except for the American Paul Goodman) European intelligentsia. Sometimes one has the impression that Sontag is using her discussions of these authors to come to terms with her own life, so evident is the tone of self-interrogation. David Rieff says that he often kidded his mother that she revealed more about herself than she thought in these essays. Although she laughed, he was never quite sure if she saw it that way too.[18] Other statements by Susan Sontag, however, show that she did, but with certain reservations. The *New York Times,* for instance, quoted her concerning the essay on Benjamin: "I felt I was describing myself . . . I know I am drawn to the part of people that reminds me of myself."[19] In Europe, *Under the Sign of Saturn* was one of Sontag's most successful books because of its European themes. But it received mostly lukewarm reviews in America when it first appeared in 1980 because its challenging subject matter was too exotic for most American readers. Typical was John Leonard's review for the *New York Times.* Although he notes a pleasing irony and lightness of tone, he criticizes its obvious eclecticism and Sontag's tendency to exaggerate and absolutize. He adds sarcastically, "She is also, suddenly, a moralist. And a fine one, and she is much more fun than the surgeon or the dentist."[20]

The important thing about the book, however, is not its lack of popularity but its long-lasting influence on intellectual and academic discourse. Sontag's portraits made most of their subjects known in America for the first time. For years after the appearance of *Under the Sign of Saturn,* Barthes, Benjamin, and Artaud continued to be fashionable in American departments of literature.

Many regard the essay "Mind as Passion" on Elias Canetti (until then virtually unknown in America) as an important impulse for the Nobel Prize for Literature he was awarded that same year. The essay's title can be read as a condensed description of Sontag's own intellectual and authorial project. Moreover, her discussion of Canetti's works is punctuated by observations that apply equally to herself, for example, the ardor of his admiration for other authors. In an even more personal observation connected to her own experience of illness, she describes how consistently Elias Canetti pursues his idea of absolute longevity, literally compelling his body to continue living, not because he secretly expects, like Faust, "the return of youth," but because he wants to keep his intellect alive as long as possible.[21]

In "Remembering Barthes," this selective method that occasionally slips into pure self-reflection is even more obvious. Here, for example, she is writing about Barthes's autobiography *Roland Barthes by Roland Barthes* and his essay collection *A Lover's Discourse* (both 1977), calling them "triumphs of modernist fiction . . . which crossbreeds fiction, essayistic speculation, and autobiography,"[22] just as her own recent stories had done. Or she recalls how Barthes genuinely enjoyed being famous but at the same time defended his private sphere and found it uncanny to open a newspaper and read his own name in it.

Very often Sontag uses the phrase "the life of the mind" and means by that both the intellectual life and a certain style of living. The title essay on Walter Benjamin, "Under the Sign of Saturn," is especially revealing in this regard. Not only does she portray Benjamin's passion for collecting in a positively erotic way, interpreting it as an immersion in a "geography of pleasure"[23] very similar to her own bibliophilia, she also quotes Theodor Adorno on how Benjamin was plagued all his life by the "perfidious reproach of being 'too intelligent.' "[24] What especially fascinates Sontag about Benjamin is his "Saturnine temperament"[25]—the melancholy with which she so strongly identifies. According to Sontag, the melancholic is predestined by his self-conscious and unforgiving relationship to himself to decode himself like a text and simultaneously to adopt contradictory positions to keep them open as possibilities for consideration. Sontag ends the piece with a portrayal of how much Benjamin feared that

the freelance intellectual as a species was becoming extinct. Ironically, she imagines him standing before the Last Judgment as
the "Last Intellectual" and declaring that he had defended the
life of the mind to the end.[26] How fascinated she was by the idea
of "the last intellectual" on the basis of her own experience is
manifest in the fact that she gave the essay that title when it first
appeared in the *New York Review of Books*.

Despite the romantic glorification of the life of the mind running through Sontag's *Sign of Saturn* essays, they also contain a
certain indecisiveness. The celebration of artistic outsiders and
the duty of the intellectual seem to be wedded to a feeling of insecurity. Perhaps Sontag was, for one last time, so stoutly defending
the ideal of what intellectuals and authors do because she fore-
saw that she would not be able to maintain it herself under the
changed circumstances of her own writing. In the following
years, she often said she wanted to stop writing essays to have
more time for her fiction. One can see what problems the *Sign
of Saturn* essays caused her from the way she sought help with
them: her son edited the pieces and the author Sharon DeLano,
a longtime close associate, helped revise them.

Sontag seemed to have exhausted the essay form that had
made her famous. While she was working on the portraits in
Under the Sign of Saturn, she was thinking, "Why am I doing
this so indirectly? I have all this feeling—I'm in a storm of feeling all the time—and instead of expressing it I'm writing about
people with feeling."[27] Although she had been trying to concentrate on writing fiction for a long time, she had failed in the
attempt. "Essay writing is part of an addiction that I'm trying to
kick. My last essay is like my last cigarette."[28] In the case of both
essay writing and cigarette smoking (which she had repeatedly
tried to give up since being diagnosed with cancer), she would
backslide repeatedly during the next twenty years. Never again,
however, would she achieve the stylistic polish and complexity
of content of her early essays. "In other words," she said after
publication of *Under the Sign of Saturn,* "I'd come to the end of
what the essay form could do for me."[29]

The consequence of this insight was that Sontag reoriented herself as an intellectual and public person and redefined her image. She had always had a tendency to provoke controversy by changing her opinion on impulse, using strong language, and engaging in polemics. But her experience as a provocateur on the Vietnam War and feminism did not prepare her for the scandal she kicked loose on February 6, 1982, with a controversial speech at Town Hall in New York, where writers, intellectuals, and activists had convened in support of the Polish Solidarity movement. After its founding in September 1980, Solidarność, the first independent trade union in the entire Eastern Bloc, had quickly developed into a protest movement of the entire Polish society. In December 1981 in Warsaw, General Wojciech Jaruzelski, after being chosen prime minister, had declared martial law. The leaders of Solidarność were arrested overnight. The media, universities, and schools were subjected to a purge. Employees' attitudes toward the Polish government were investigated, and more than two thousand workers lost their jobs. Military courts sentenced Solidarność sympathizers to long prison terms. Coal mines were put under military oversight, and a six-day workweek and comprehensive censorship were reintroduced.

Through her connections to Polish dissidents at the New York Institute for the Humanities, Sontag was fully informed of these developments. On the other hand, Ronald Reagan had been inaugurated only a month earlier and the Town Hall meeting was in the difficult position of reconciling its support for Solidarność with its opposition to the Reagan administration's military intervention in El Salvador. Besides Sontag, other invited speakers included Allen Ginsberg, Kurt Vonnegut, E. L. Doctorow, and Gore Vidal, all of whom simply declared their support for Solidarność while also poking fun at Reagan.[30] Sontag, however, gave a speech in which she sharply attacked that easygoing New Left position. She began with the thesis that since the fifties, both she herself and most of her colleagues had misjudged the Communist regimes, especially because of the bad memories she and her colleagues had of McCarthy-era propaganda. Leftist intellectuals had not been sufficiently critical of the repression under Eastern European regimes, Sontag said, comparing them to the military dictatorships in Argentina and Chile: "We had identified the enemy as Fascism . . . We believed in, or at least applied, a double standard to the angelic language of Communism . . . What the recent Polish events illustrate is something more than that Fascist rule is possible within the framework of a Communist society . . . What they illustrate is a truth that we should have understood a very long time ago: that Communism is Fascism—successful Fascism, if you will . . . 'Fascism with a Human Face.' "[31]

With this speech, Sontag disrupted the unspoken agreements that held together the Town Hall meeting and the majority of New York political discussions. Moreover, she committed the sacrilege of declaring to her comrades-in-arms that their hopes for Communism and socialism as alternatives to capitalism were futile, hopes they had nourished for decades and often used to explain away the unsettling reports coming from Eastern Europe. Sontag's provocative speech was greeted with loud boos, and she was barely able to read it to the end.

The storm of indignation continued unabated into the following week, when Sontag's statements were criticized in various media. The bitterest protests appeared in the *SoHo Weekly News* and *The Nation,* both of which reprinted the speech and published responses to it from prominent writers, academics, and journalists. Despite their differing political positions, they unanimously criticized Sontag for her polemical jargon and inaccuracies. The friendliest writers, such as Christopher Hitchens, allowed that Sontag's conscious exaggerations were only meant to shake up the audience.[32] Although neoconservative commentators were pleased that Sontag had finally seen the light and bid her welcome, as Diana Trilling put it, "into her new difficult life as an anticommunist,"[33] even they took issue with her conviction that leftist antifascism had once provided a justification for the existence of Communism. For most of those present and for the commentators who followed, it looked as if Sontag—the poster girl for chic radicalism since the days of her support for Cuba and Vietnam—was trying to turn a possibly justified *mea culpa* into a presumptuous *nostra culpa*. Moreover, she seemed to have gone over to the side of the neoconservatives like many of her former colleagues at *Partisan Review*. An editor at *The Nation* remarked acidly that Sontag risked becoming "Norman Podhoretz with a human face."[34]

As so often before, Sontag made contradictory statements about the contentious speech. She told Helen Benedict that she had actually only gone to the Town Hall meeting for Brodsky's sake because together they hoped to "make a ruckus," and that afterward she had "sat backstage for an hour, giggling," and enjoyed herself immensely.[35] On the other hand, she told Charles Ruas of the *New York Times* that the only explanation she could find for the "grotesque attacks" was that they were a reaction to her notoriety.[36] Nevertheless, Sontag had never before been the object of such unanimous condemnation, and her deliberately defiant commentary on the attacks reads like a denial of the fact that she was deeply hurt by their animosity. Edmund White says that she came to his place after the speech and told him that she had just done something very dangerous.[37] Sontag knew who her audience was and also that she had lost a large part of her leftist supporters with the Town Hall speech.

In the long run, however, her image suffered little from the controversy. The laws of the media landscape in America were so well established by that time that even negative publicity could turn out to have a positive effect. The brouhaha simply reminded the American public that Susan Sontag was still good for savage and quotable aphorisms. Sontag's nose for publicity was getting even better. In October 1983, for example, Sontag—still an extraordinarily beautiful woman at 50—had her picture taken by Irving Penn for the cover of *Vanity Fair*. Alexander Cockburn sneered that he was expecting an aerobics book from Sontag next.[38]

Sontag's flirting with public opinion, however, was always in controlled doses. Although she enjoyed notoriety and obviously sought it, she would never have playacted to achieve it. Jonathan Galassi, who became her editor at FSG in 1988, says, "She was absolutely aware of the effect of what she said and in that sense, was also certainly calculating, but I would say that she was not at all one of the great culprits in this regard . . . Privately she was quite open about finding fame erotic, but she wanted to be famous for what she did. She never lowered her standards. She wanted to be famous for her seriousness."[39]

By the time *A Susan Sontag Reader*—a collection of her best essays and stories of the previous twenty years—was published in the fall of 1982, her reputation as the "last intellectual" was already well established. One critic remarked that this name was made possible by "the absence of an American intelligentsia."[40] At the same time, however, Sontag was increasingly trying to separate herself from that image.

When Sontag was introduced as an intellectual at lectures, conferences, or readings, she often brusquely objected that she was a writer. Sometimes she did so because she hated such labels in general. Occasionally she objected, she added, because the word "intellectual" had acquired such a bad taste in America and was sometimes even used pejoratively.

Small-Scale Politics

(1984–1988)

*Fame, prestige and sheer seniority
make the writer a public figure . . .
And this is when writers not only
tend to get more service-minded but
are expected to be more collegial.*

Susan Sontag, "When Writers Talk
Among Themselves" (1988)

Sontag's professional and private crises had obvious effects on her friendships.[1] Even in her personal relationships, she had always evinced a certain narcissism and a great deal of self-assertion. When she felt herself discriminated against or unjustly attacked, she was always prepared to participate in verbal sparring to defend her interests. But even her best friends, such as Stephen Koch and Richard Howard, say that in these years, Sontag's egotism was "difficult" or even "unbearable."[2] At the time, Edmund White was working on his angry roman-à-clef *Caracole* (1985), in which he portrays Sontag, Rieff, and their New York world. It began a now-famous feud between him and his former friend. He recalls that Sontag "wanted more and more to be treated like royalty" and sometimes would upset the harmony of an entire party or dinner when she felt she was not

being treated with the proper respect.[3] Many friendships foundered at that time, but others survived. Most of Sontag's friends
knew what she was like and learned to live with her outbursts.
Darryl Pinckney recalls, with a mixture of criticism and love,
"Sometimes her demands could be monstrous, but at the *New
York Review of Books* we felt that she was our monster."[4] Karen
Kennerley, who as the director of American PEN often worked
with Sontag in those years, describes things this way: "Susan
was like the weather in England. A storm cloud could always
blow up. And then you just kept out of her way until the rain
was over. It was just Susan."[5]

In the eighties, Sontag's interest turned increasingly to specialized topics sometimes bordering on the esoteric. She published a
series of shorter articles, directed theater productions, and wrote
television commentaries that lacked much of the intellectual
intensity for which she had become famous.[6] She often let it be
known that she thought of these small works mainly as putting
bread on the table. Her income was modest for the style in which
she lived in New York, so she was under constant and serious
economic pressure.[7] Extremely esoteric articles such as "A Place
for Fantasy," however—an exploration of her fascination with
grottoes as an element of garden architecture, which appeared in
House and Garden in 1983—remained the exception. Richard
Howard says that his friend was above all strongly concerned
with retaining a comprehensive overview of the cultural landscape. "Film, literature, opera, dance, theater—her bibliography
contains something for everyone."[8]

Sontag herself explained her extraordinary attention to every
art form not as the fear of missing something (which Howard
recalls with amusement) but mainly as due to her obsessive personality and her need for intensity and distraction. She did not
own a television. Books, movies, plays, and operas were her TV.[9]
Whenever she discovered something new that ignited her interest, according to Howard, she would literally immerse herself
in the topic. She watched new films and plays as many times as

possible. She always read books several times before she wrote about them. Once her work had appeared, however, her excitement dissipated. She no longer felt she was in the avant-garde because now the rest of the world was talking about the same thing.[10]

The fruits of this "cultural addiction" usually appeared as articles in *Vanity Fair.* Tina Brown, the magazine's editor in chief and a friend of Sontag's, had breathed new life into the magazine in the eighties, making it into a flagship of cultural chic in which portraits of Hollywood stars appeared cheek-by-jowl with articles such as Sontag's long piece on Rainer Werner Fassbinder's 1980 film *Berlin Alexanderplatz.*

In the fall of 1982, the Italian TV network RAI asked Sontag to make a film about Venice that would be shown in conjunction with a film Marguerite Duras was making about Rome. Sontag loved Venice and had fond memories of the time she had spent there with Carlotta del Pezzo.[11] Sontag decided to make a film version of her short story "Unguided Tour" and asked Robert Wilson whom she should choose to play the lead. He suggested Lucinda Childs, one of America's best-known dancers and choreographers. Wilson had worked with Childs on the production of the 1976 opera *Einstein on the Beach,* and the choreographer recalls with a smile Sontag's exaggerations about how often she had seen that production—sometimes she claimed it had been forty times, sometimes a hundred.

In the film *Unguided Tour* (1983), a somber-looking Childs wanders aimlessly through Venice. It was a great disappointment for Sontag, Childs says. Even Sontag's close friend Tom Luddy, director of the Telluride Film Festival, did not like it and chose not to invite it to the festival. But the shoot in Venice did result in Sontag and Childs falling in love. They would spend the next few years together and remain close friends even after their separation.[12]

Sontag's relationship with Childs marked the renewal of her interest in dance and the beginning of a close artistic collaboration. Childs choreographed Sontag's 1983 short story

"Description (of a Description)," and Sontag wrote the short, atmospheric article "A Lexicon for *Available Light*" about Childs's dance piece of the same name. The article appeared in *Art in America* in December 1983 and in its associative use of rubrics followed by brief chunks of text is strongly reminiscent of Roland Barthes's *A Lover's Discourse*. Dance as a genre was at the center of Sontag's interest in those years. That interest resulted in charming articles displaying a good deal of technical knowledge, written in Sontag's preferred tone of admiration, but they cannot compare with her earlier essays. She published the cursory "Dancer and the Dance" on Lincoln Kirstein, founder of the New York City Ballet, in the December 1986 edition of the French *Vogue*. Another piece on Kirstein followed in the May 1987 *Vanity Fair*. For an exhibition about John Cage, Merce Cunningham, and Jasper Johns—to whose circle she had belonged in the sixties—she wrote "In Memory of Their Feelings," a somewhat puzzling text in which she tries to approach her friends, especially the choreographer Merce Cunningham, intellectually. Sontag even planned to write a novel with a dancer as its central character. Like her novel about émigrés from Eastern Europe, however, it never got off the ground. In August 1986, she wrote and produced a video essay for the English Channel 4 about the German dancer and choreographer Pina Bausch and the Wuppertal Dance Theater, a company she particularly revered.

As if sensing she would not complete the novel *Toward the Western Half*, she was simultaneously planning a new collection of shorter pieces including short stories and reminiscences of her youth.[13] As before, this manic activity would come to nothing and only lead to further delays. Another project Sontag often spoke about at the time was a book about Japan. Inspired by her immense fascination for Japanese culture, she made a total of six trips to that country in the course of the 1980s. Robert Wilson, who was often working in Japan at that time, says that on a trip to Japan together, he introduced Sontag to Madame Kalikito from the Japanese Film Society. Kalikito was amazed by Sontag's knowledge of Japanese silent films and said there was hardly anyone in Japan who knew as much about them. Wilson recalls fondly the brilliant ease with which Sontag was able to absorb foreign cultures. "She was a marvelous cultural critic of boundless interests and knowledge," he says. She could analyze the dress or body language of a foreign culture with great acuity and recall years later the look of a certain marketplace or the course of a particular conversation.[14]

Sontag's friendship with Wilson reflected her continuing interest in theater. Later, she would try her own hand at directing. In January 1985, she directed Milan Kundera's *Jacques and His Master* (1971) at the American Repertory Theater in Cambridge, Massachusetts, but without great success. Although her famous name automatically made Kundera's playful homage to Denis Diderot's novel *Jacques le fataliste et son maître* (1796) an important cultural event, it was criticized in the press and by the audience as too "pompous."[15] Sontag's theatrical ambitions were also clear in her desire to write the American section for Robert Wilson's mammoth operatic production *the CIVIL warS,* although, like so many of her plans, it came to nothing. Nevertheless, her enthusiasms for Wilson, for theater, and for Japan all found expression in her 1983 program essay "A Note on Bunraku" for a theater festival at the New York Japan Society.

Another lifelong interest was opera. Even during her most radical avant-garde years, she had regularly attended the Metropolitan Opera and, whenever she could, international opera houses as well. She was a frequent visitor to the Festspielhaus in Bayreuth. The somewhat puzzling "Wagner's Fluids," written for the program of a 1987 production of *Tristan und Isolde* at the Los Angeles Opera directed by Sontag's friend Jonathan Miller, bears witness to her fascination with the composer. During these years, she often spoke about wanting to direct an opera herself.

Sontag's turn to smaller forms was also evident in the short stories she published in the *New Yorker.* In these writings, she continued to follow the autobiographical impulse that had always informed her short fiction. "The Letter Scene" (August 1986), for instance, revolves around the romantic fusion of

letter writing and ending a relationship. The end of her marriage to Philip Rieff thirty years earlier comes into focus, and
the short story becomes an intimate account of dealing with
painful memories. Sontag stretches the autobiographical impulse
into something like a fragmentary memoir. With a view to in
fact writing a memoir of her childhood and youth, she wrote
"Pilgrimage" (1987), a highly regarded reminiscence of her formative teenage years in California and her meeting with Thomas
Mann.

Sontag's most successful mixture of zeitgeist and classic
short-story form, however, is "The Way We Live Now." The
story was so successful that Roger Straus decided to publish it
three years later in book form, illustrated with etchings by the
British artist Howard Hodgkin. Although Sontag borrowed her
title from Anthony Trollope's 1875 novel, what she described
could not have been more contemporary. The story is a literary
treatment of the merciless 1980s AIDS epidemic. The widespread disease, demonized at first in the tirades of right-wing
ideologues declaring it to be divine punishment for deviant lifestyles, extinguished an entire generation of gay artists, authors,
photographers, actors, and directors.

"The Way We Live Now" is Susan Sontag's testimony to very
personal experiences. While at this point there seemed a high
probability that her own cancer was cured, those around her
were increasingly falling victim to catastrophic illness and death.
In 1984 her friend Joseph Chaikin suffered a stroke during car-
diac surgery and was seriously disabled for the rest of his life.
Sontag's mother, Mildred, died of lung cancer in 1986 without
a reconciliation with her oldest daughter, according to Sontag's
sister Judith.[16] And more and more friends and acquaintances
were dying of AIDS. At that time, no one knew what was causing
the illness, which in the beginning was often called "gay cancer"
because of the increased incidence of Kaposi's sarcoma among
those affected. Susan Sontag reacted to the AIDS crisis with the
same active concern she had earlier shown for friends suffering from cancer.[17] She advised HIV patients to seek aggressive

treatment and became a member of the Board of Directors of the AIDS Community Research Initiative of America, founded by her friend Dr. Joseph Sonnabend to search for new treatments for HIV and AIDS.[18] She sat at the bedside of Paul Thek and other close friends dying of AIDS.

The catalyst for "The Way We Live Now" was the news that Robert Mapplethorpe had contracted AIDS. The story captures the atmosphere of those years through the example of an unnamed protagonist dying of an unnamed illness. Sontag concentrates on the friends and lovers of the dying man—their fears, hopes, and conflicts. She draws up an alphabet of lovers, friends, and acquaintances from Aileen to Zack whose lives are changed by the life-threatening illness. Their comments constitute the body of the text, testifying not only to their social interrelationships and the all-pervasive consternation that AIDS provoked in those years, but also to an eerie feeling that death presented a latent threat seemingly synonymous with sexuality. At the same time, however, the friends constitute a characteristic phalanx of mutual support. The story is an alphabet of simultaneous death and hope.

Sontag's story evoked an avid response because she had struck the tenor of a time out of joint as no one else had. Not only was it chosen as the introductory story for *The Best American Short Stories, 1987*, but it was also included in *The Best American Short Stories of the Eighties* and *The Best American Short Stories of the Century*.

But the greater part of Sontag's authorial and intellectual energy in these years was spent enthusiastically promoting other writers and artists, an activity in which she took pleasure. It was possibly due to such active cultural advocacy that, despite her best efforts, she was unable to achieve consistency and write longer works of her own. She wrote a series of forewords for authors she wanted to support with her popularity, for example, for an edition of the Russian poet Marina Tsvetaeva, for a Roland Barthes reader, and for a volume of stories by the Swiss author

Robert Walser. According to Richard Howard, it was Sontag's explicit goal to make European authors she found interesting better known in America and to find publishers for them. Sontag and Howard often strategized how they could convince Roger Straus that FSG should publish certain authors. Straus was willing to listen to them and accept their advice, not always to his own financial advantage. Sontag and Howard persuaded him, for example, to acquire the rights to *The Day of Judgment* by the Sardinian novelist Salvatore Satta, and FSG published it in 1987. Straus had only a restricted budget for Italian books and had to decide between Satta and Umberto Eco's *The Name of the Rose*. Howard and Sontag assured him that Eco was not in the same class with Satta. Straus noted with sarcastic humor that *The Name of the Rose* went on to become a best seller in America, and he never missed an opportunity to rag his two friends about it.[19]

But it was Susan Sontag's work as president of the American PEN Center between 1987 and 1989 that represented an "especially interesting moment in her life as a public intellectual," according to the poet Robert Hass, her colleague in PEN.[20] The special emphasis of her presidency was a campaign for freedom of speech, promoted at various writers' conferences and PEN meetings and reaching its high point in the middle and late eighties through the incipient thaw in the Eastern Bloc countries. Sontag succinctly and self-ironically characterized such conferences in a January 1986 *New York Times* article, "When Writers Talk Among Themselves," written to draw attention to the upcoming PEN Congress in New York. "With age, and with a certain volume of accomplishment . . . comes a stack of invitations to board planes, cross borders and sometimes oceans, check into large hotels, in order to palaver . . . with each other."[21] Nevertheless, she continues, such meetings seem to have a greater political significance, since currently they are "dominated by the issue of dissidence and human rights" and attempt to draw the attention of the public at large to these issues. She herself considered PEN as above all a "human-rights organization."[22]

Sontag was certainly also motivated by a desire to give her political existence a new direction after her decisive split with the New Left. Instead of supporting large political movements, she now became engaged in more practical projects. Together with other authors, she organized public readings of the texts of imprisoned writers from all over the world[23] and drafted and signed stirring letters to the editor calling for the release of Miklos Duray, the Hungarian minority leader imprisoned in Czechoslovakia; Ali Taygun, a member of the peace movement imprisoned in Turkey; Zbigniew Lewicki, a literature professor in jail in Poland; and the South Koreans Kim Hyon-Jan and Kim Nam-Ju.[24] She protested against the persecution of the Hungarian poet and politician Sándor Lezsák. She campaigned against the threatened deportation of the Bengali poet Daud Haider to Bangladesh, where certain death awaited him at the hands of Islamic militiamen. Nadine Gordimer says that such engagement was a deeply felt moral imperative for Sontag. "She used her intellectual power to fight for many causes. She decided against a merely private life. It was an existential dilemma for Susan, unlike most authors . . . She was not able to be just an author. She felt a personal responsibility to become publicly engaged against prejudice and suppression."[25]

When Sontag declared herself willing to be the PEN president in 1987, her instinct for publicity and dramatic statements, her good relations with the American press, her cosmopolitan knowledge, and her talent for behind-the-scenes pulling of strings all stood her in good stead. Some PEN members, including Francis King, were irritated by Sontag's cantankerous arrogance, explosive temperament, and the self-righteousness with which she pushed through her own political agenda and demanded to be flown first-class to conferences. Using the classic tactic of authorial revenge, King published the thinly veiled roman-à-clef *Visiting Cards* (1990).[26] But Karen Kennerley, longtime director of the American PEN Center, recalls how skillfully and seriously Sontag went about her work. She "was the only president in the history of PEN who knew how to speak to the rest of the world,"

Kennerley said. "When she flew to a conference in Europe, she didn't participate as an American but as an international author. Above all, she knew the European psyche inside and out."[27]

The main focuses of PEN during those years were the naturalization of dissidents from the Eastern Bloc and the rarely successful protests against the political persecution and imprisonment of authors in those countries. During Sontag's presidency, Mikhail Gorbachev was the most frequent addressee for the letters of protest sent by the American PEN Center, letters he never answered.[28]

Sontag's most memorable moment as PEN president came in February 1989. The Iranian head of state Ayatollah Ruhollah Khomeini declared a fatwa against Salman Rushdie, then the most famous novelist in Great Britain and a friend of Sontag's, sentencing Rushdie to death. His controversial 1988 novel *The Satanic Verses* tells the story of certain Koran verses that, according to legend, Satan whispered to the prophet Muhammad while he was writing. Rushdie implies that the entire Koran was not written by God himself, but by Muhammad. The title alone was blasphemous in the eyes of Islamic fundamentalists. Khomeini put a price of a million dollars on Rushdie's head and threatened death to everyone involved in the novel's publication. What followed was an international crisis. In India and Pakistan, there were huge demonstrations against the imminent American publication of the novel. Demonstrators stormed the American embassy. Muslim groups in Great Britain, where the work was first published in September 1989, organized mass book burnings. European publishers, including the prestigious Kiepenheuer und Witsch, Heinrich Böll's publisher, abandoned plans for translations.[29] The Canadian government ordered a halt to the import of the novel. The American publisher Viking received bomb threats, as did the bookselling chains Barnes & Noble, Waldenbooks, and Dalton, who thereupon withdrew the book from their shelves. But while some European writers and even the Egyptian Nobel laureate Naguib Mahfouz publicly condemned the restrictions to free speech that followed the fatwa, most American writers remained silent. Sontag organized an emergency meeting of the PEN steering committee and called for a public statement. Kennerley recalls that this statement would never have come to pass without Sontag. "Almost everyone else hesitated . . . But Susan was never afraid of anything."[30]

Sontag was subsequently invited to testify at a congressional hearing on the matter. Seven years later, when Bill Clinton was being inaugurated president and the initial wave of consternation had passed, Sontag tried once more. The American administration had done nothing, although the novel's Italian translator had been murdered, its Japanese translator had been attacked, and the price on Rushdie's head had been raised to $5 million. Sontag wrote an open letter advocating a political solution such as the British government had chosen by ending diplomatic ties to Iran. But the kind of engagement that Sontag had made her trademark seemed to have gone out of fashion.

Sontag's cultural and political advocacy, her PEN presidency, and frequent trips to various writers' meetings around the world cemented her image in Europe as a militant intellectual, where she gradually became more popular than in America. If America's longing for Europe, on which Sontag had invested large parts of her career, was becoming more and more a thing of the past, Europe's longing for America was unbroken. The Europeans greeted Sontag as a needed voice from America, a voice capable of speaking the intellectual language of Europe.

Sontag's own writing stagnated during this period. She finished only one book between 1982 and 1989, and it was not one of the projects she had planned. In interviews she gave when *AIDS and Its Metaphors* was published in 1989, she called it an "accidental text." Roger Straus had decided to reissue Sontag's books as a paperback series with elegant covers designed by the graphic artist William Drenttel. For the paperback edition of *Illness as Metaphor*, Sontag intended to write a three-page epilogue about AIDS in September 1986. But the three pages eventually swelled to ninety-five. Without meaning to, she had returned to her old essay form, interrogating a contemporary development with the help of classics of literature and philosophy. *AIDS and Its Metaphors* also appeared in the *New York Review of Books,* for which Susan had not written anything for eight years except letters to the editor on political topics. In the essay, she continues to develop the ideas that informed *Illness as Metaphor,* countering the prevailing metaphors of plague and apocalypse with the voice of rationality. Sontag once again deplored the military metaphors of attack and invasion she had already criticized in her book on cancer. She compares the discussion of AIDS with the way syphilis and the plague were attributed to imaginary causes and describes the use of the virus as a metaphor in other areas of life, most notably in computers. The essay ends with the speculation that AIDS would lose its metaphoric power once medical research had produced an effective treatment and the illness was no longer invariably fatal.

AIDS and Its Metaphors is a strangely anachronistic book. On the one hand, its ideas were already out of date by the time it appeared. The AIDS discussion had advanced significantly beyond them through the work of the journalist Randy Shilts and others. Members of the AIDS community felt themselves attacked because Sontag consistently used the word "homosexual" rather than "gay" and worse, wrote about "sex regarded as deviant."[31] On the other hand, however, her essay was in a certain sense almost farsighted. It was above all its calm tone, which had replaced the cold fury of her cancer book, that many readers found disturbing or otherworldly. Although Sontag would be proved right about AIDS losing its metaphoric attraction, when the volume appeared in 1989, dedicated to the memory of her deceased friend Paul Thek, the diagnosis of AIDS was still essentially a death sentence. The apocalyptic metaphors were less metaphorical than simply the best way to describe the mood that united those affected. The essay evinced little feeling for that mood and failed to provide the moral support that Sontag had captured so well in "The Way We Live Now."

Accordingly, reactions were primarily negative or at best respectfully skeptical. It was once again the *New York Times* review that dealt Sontag the hardest blow. Its longtime reviewer Christopher Lehmann-Haupt, already the author of several unfavorable reviews of Sontag works, wrote that "she never quite defines whatever it is that ultimately concerns her. Which leaves this reader with the sense that either he has missed some essential point she is making, or else that something in her otherwise closely reasoned argument is lacking."[32] It was a typical reaction. Sontag was extremely disappointed by the reviews of her first book in seven years. She attacked Lehmann-Haupt as "a hack,"[33] but also protested that she was not a journalist like Randy Shilts but a literary essayist whose work deserved to be judged as such.[34]

The world in which Sontag had built her career had basically disappeared. Some of her friends had died, she had financial problems, and it looked as though her career as freelance intellectual and writer would not last much longer despite Roger Straus's generous support. And although her glamorous image had given way to a beautifully aging face, she said in a 2002 interview that she was now at a time of life when "men stop fancying you."[35] There are traces of a new crisis in the remarks of Sontag's friends and acquaintances from those years and in her own interviews as well, in which she is sometimes rude and often slides into smugness. She was capable of lashing out at interviewers who were not sufficiently deferential. When annoyed, she also indulged in silly comments such as that she had written her famous AIDS story in just two days or that she did not need to do research for her essays because she had "all the books" in her library (about 10,000) "in her head" and could quote them "from memory" when she wrote.[36] It was a time when Susan Sontag's passionate defense of her life as an independent intellectual often shaded into exaggerated caricature and even self-glorification.

Return to the Magic Mountain

(1989–1992)

> *I don't want to write a lot of books. I want to write a few wonderful books that people will read 100 years from now.*

Susan Sontag, in a 1992 interview

Susan Sontag, the vehement champion of popular culture in the sixties, was not prepared for the speed with which times were changing.[1] The pop culture industry, not elite high culture, was becoming dominant and pushing intellectual discourse into the background. It became more and more difficult for Sontag to maintain her position as a critic with the traditional authority to recommend, rank, categorize, and define. Many of her friends report how depressed she was at the unstoppable rise of an entertainment culture that had abandoned its earlier avant-garde position and moved into the mainstream. Sontag herself sometimes seemed to be caught in the dilemma of the sorcerer's apprentice, unable to stop what she had helped to start. Steve Wasserman tells how annoyed she was that American pop culture had made "the most unseemly aspects of human behavior . . . into a worthwhile goal for the general public." In the sixties, Wasserman said, she had not been able to foresee "how traditional forms and traditional aesthetic hierarchies that constituted the Western canon would be besieged by the entertainment culture and that one would suddenly have to fight for the right to make aesthetic judgments." She "didn't think that everything was of equal value. She believed that history would have the last word."[2]

Not that Sontag's love of popular culture disappeared completely. She continued to go to Patti Smith's concerts in the punk club CBGB and to an occasional Hollywood film. What disturbed her was that pop culture had gained such a huge influence that it was shouldering high culture onto the sidelines. Despite that, however, Sontag's healthy pragmatism would at least partially come to terms with the cultural facts of life in the years that followed. She not only wrote a best seller but also fell in love with the most famous photographer in the world.

Susan Sontag met the thirty-nine-year-old Annie Leibovitz at the end of 1988 when Leibovitz was to take her photo for the dust jacket of *AIDS and Its Metaphors*. Leibovitz's work for *Rolling Stone* and *Vanity Fair* had already made her internationally famous. She had, of course, read *On Photography* and prepared for the shoot by reading *The Benefactor* as well. Leibovitz had a good instinct for the dynamics of fame. Her cover photos for *Vanity Fair,* with their characteristic mix of classical composition, powerful conceptuality, subtle theatricality, and tongue-in-cheek irony, had helped to define the concept of celebrity in the eighties. At twenty-four, she had already become the leading photographer for *Rolling Stone,* and she took some of the most famous photos of the pop culture era, including pictures of an extravagant Rolling Stones concert tour and the last double portrait of Yoko Ono and John Lennon.

When Leibovitz left *Rolling Stone* for *Vanity Fair* in 1983, she quickly became one of the best-paid photographers anywhere. No one else was able to stage such glamorous portraits of Hollywood stars and prominent politicians. At the same time, she often included teases that provoked controversy and gave her pictures a trademark style. She shot Whoopi Goldberg in a bathtub filled with milk and Bette Midler engulfed in a pile of roses.

Of course, the fifty-five-year-old Sontag also knew Leibovitz's work and thought highly of it. Leibovitz would later describe their early time together as a phase of uncertainty. Only after she met Sontag did she begin to feel comfortable in New York. She was looking for direction, and Sontag spurred her on with critical encouragement. Sontag is supposed to have told Leibovitz the first time they met that "she was good but could be better."[3] Coming from Susan Sontag, that criticism sounded to Leibovitz like high praise. She felt encouraged to work harder, become more personal in her photos, and dig deeper. She had encountered someone who supported her in her aesthetic impulses.

Many contemporaries describe Leibovitz as very much like Sontag: a self-confident and sometimes arrogant woman who had fought hard to get to the top of her profession and expected to receive the corresponding recognition.[4] Leibovitz says they admired each other's ambitions and artistic goals despite obvious differences in lifestyle that sometimes led to dramatic scenes. During arguments, Sontag could sometimes accuse her friend of ignorance, for instance, when she had to explain to her the difference between the French Revolution and the October Revolution.[5] On the other hand, the private photos of Sontag that Leibovitz published in her 2006 photographic memoir *A Photographer's Life* document a relationship of open and natural intimacy, tender devotion, and great love. The two women became an instantly recognizable couple. They attended numerous public events together—openings, theatrical premieres, fund-raisers, lecture tours, or simply visits to restaurants. An entourage of close friends, including Patti Smith and the editor and author Sharon DeLano, often accompanied them. But despite their appearances together, the couple never publicly acknowledged their relationship although often urged to do so by gay and lesbian activists who were regularly "outing" public figures at the time. Richard Howard reports that he and other

PEN members asked Sontag to take this important step for the movement, in the hope that it would increase public acceptance of gays and lesbians.[6] But Sontag refused. After all, she had had serious relationships with men as well as with women throughout her life. Most journalists Sontag granted interviews to knew about her relationship with Leibovitz or were even friends of theirs. It was considered bad form, however, to report about it although it was common knowledge in New York that the two women were partners.

Sontag's resistance to talking about the relationship publicly even when asked about it directly went so far that, in interviews, she would begin talking about her marriage to Philip Rieff thirty years ago as if wanting to divert attention from her current life. According to Sigrid Nunez, Sontag wanted to live out her sexuality in private and not have to talk about it in public; amazingly, despite her notoriety, she succeeded.[7] Terry Castle says that Sontag would have found it in a certain sense vulgar to come out publicly.[8] Only toward the end of her life, after the 2001 advance announcement of a scandal-mongering, gossipy, and unauthorized biography by Carl Rollyson and Lisa Paddock, did Sontag tell Joan Acocella of the *New Yorker* and Suzie Mackenzie of *The Guardian* that she had been with both men and women in the course of her life, adding that she never considered it worth discussing.[9]

Moreover, it seems that Sontag was resisting the identity politics widespread among homosexual artists. In the early eighties, she had already told Edmund White that she did not understand why it was so important to him to be known as a "gay writer."[10] Just as she had avoided the label "feminist author," she now resisted the label "lesbian writer" being urged upon her by the gay and lesbian movement. Her works were addressed to a wider public. She did not want them to be read through the lens of identity politics as they undoubtedly would have been had she come out.[11]

For her part, Annie Leibovitz did not publicly acknowledge their long relationship until after Sontag's death and after Leibovitz herself had been made fun of on the satirical TV program

The Daily Show for acting as if Sontag had been "only a friend." At the end of 2006, Leibovitz told the *San Francisco Chronicle*, "We never liked words like 'companion' or 'partner.' Susan never used them. I never used them . . . It was a relationship in all its dimensions. It had its ups and downs . . . I mean, we helped each other through our lives. Call us 'lovers' . . . I like 'lovers.' You know, 'lovers' sounds romantic. I mean, I want to be perfectly clear. I love Susan. I don't have a problem with that."[12]

Sontag's new life went hand in hand with a change in the city where she had lived for so many years. She loved New York to the end of her life and often said in solemn tones that there was nowhere else in America she could live. She said you only needed to go out into the street in New York to be reminded by the presence of so many immigrants that the rest of the world really existed.[13] For her the metropolis was "this boat anchored off the coast of the United States."[14] But if she could still write in her diary at the end of the sixties that "NYC with its intelligentsia, its liberal consensus, is in relationship to the rest of U.S.A. like Vatican in the midst of Italy, a tiny private state with immense power + wealth, but separate,"[15] by the end of the eighties it was clear that it was now wealth above all else that had won the upper hand, radically marginalizing the influence of the intelligentsia.

Sontag suddenly found among her acquaintances former students of literature at Yale or Princeton universities who had become real estate bankers.[16] After having to give up her beloved penthouse on Riverside Drive in the late seventies, Sontag began an odyssey through several apartments in Greenwich Village, the West End, and Gramercy Park. She found herself increasingly unable to afford the rising rents. Although she still lived a relatively well-to-do life, most of her travels were paid for by publishers, PEN, or the organizations that invited her to events. Even with her iconic status in America and the rest of the world, she never managed to establish lasting financial security. She had arguments with Roger Straus about royalties and advances that, while they might be appropriate for the number of copies her books sold, made her feel like "a charitable organization" and forced her to continue writing newspaper articles and art show catalogs instead of devoting all her time to her new novel, *The Volcano Lover,* which she had begun to plan after the appearance of *AIDS and Its Metaphors.*[17] Her financial situation became really serious following a fire in her apartment early in 1989. The firefighters had to cut a hole in her roof to extinguish the flames, and she did not have enough money in the bank to afford a hotel room while the roof and the half-destroyed apartment were being repaired.[18]

At about that time, Sontag met Andrew Wylie, who would become her agent. She confided to him with a sigh, "I'm sick of being Susan Sontag. I can't get any work done. I'm trying to write a novel but I get thirty phone calls a day. They want me to read some book and write a blurb for it. They want me to give speeches. They want me to support this political campaign or that one . . . And a lot of it is important to me. But I end up doing nothing but being Susan Sontag."[19]

Sontag seemed to be stuck in a situation that no longer corresponded to her original dreams and motivations. From earliest childhood, she had wanted to be a writer, and although she had become a literary eminence she had not written a novel in more than twenty-two years. The eighties, when she had devoted herself largely to political causes, had passed by without a new book of any great significance.

Andrew Wylie and Susan Sontag met through David Rieff. Wylie was already a legend of American publishing. In just a few years, he had made his midsize literary agency into an empire through a combination of chutzpah and unparalleled ambition. By the time he met Sontag, he was representing 150 of the best authors in America, including Philip Roth, Norman Mailer, and Saul Bellow. Frank Bruni even suggested in the *New York Times* that Wylie, with his "nondescript gray suit," efficient manner, unconventional way of doing business, and breathtaking advances negotiated for his authors, "was to literary agency what Michael Milken was to investment banking."[20]

In the rapidly changing landscape of American publishing, with its bookstore chains and the huge market share enjoyed by works of escapist entertainment by the likes of Danielle Steel and Dean R. Koontz, authors of challenging books were usually offered relatively low advances. But Wylie, like a Hollywood agent, represented his clients as literary stars, breaking the taboo against putting a price tag on serious literature. He doggedly negotiated fees of several hundred thousand dollars for Salman Rushdie and Philip Roth, fees the publishers recouped when their novels became best sellers. For another thing, Wylie kept a close eye on his clients' backlists with foreign publishers. Wylie introduced a practice that has since become widespread among American literary agents: he saw to negotiating the foreign contracts himself rather than working with sub-agents. He often got promises from foreign publishers to reissue his authors' backlisted titles in new editions. Such an agent seemed ideal for Susan Sontag.

Wylie says that Sontag was especially interested in the international market. He also offered to organize the scheduling of interviews and lecture tours for her so she would finally have the time to devote to her novel. Wylie describes the difference between his and Roger Straus's association with Sontag in this way: "There is always a slightly paternalistic relationship between the writer and the publisher. My relations with Susan were different. I'm the gardener and you own the land . . . I work for you. If I say to you, 'Tulips would be nice,' but you say, 'No, I want roses,' then there's no question I'm going to plant roses."[21]

Of course the relationship between Sontag and her agent was not always a smooth one, but in Wylie she had found an ally and friend who represented her interests with the same conviction that had inspired Straus through the years, with the difference that Wylie obtained for her a degree of economic stability she had never had before. One of his first official acts as her agent was to negotiate a new contract with FSG. He advised Sontag to stay with the publisher not just because of her longtime friendship with Roger Straus but also because of the value of her backlist, which she would no longer control if she switched to another publishing house. Wylie negotiated a six-figure advance for her next four books, an amount that was less a reflection of her sales figures than her enormous prestige.

Although, after the contract was signed, Sontag often claimed that Straus had given his blessing to the new arrangement,[22] the publisher was of course not particularly pleased with the development. "It was a difficult process," according to Wylie. But after a while, the resentments had healed. Wylie recalls that Straus finally realized the inevitability of the situation and agreed that if Sontag had to have an agent, Wylie was the right choice. Jonathan Galassi, by then the chief editor at FSG, agrees. "Andrew and Roger got along well. In a certain sense they were the same type of person."[23]

With her generous advance, Sontag was finally able to buy an apartment that met her requirements. In 1990 she moved into a penthouse in the London Terrace complex on 23rd Street in Chelsea, near a neighborhood becoming known for its art galleries. The five-room apartment was roomy, bright, and surrounded by terraces, and it had a breathtaking view of the Hudson River. Sontag now had room for her gigantic library and could even retrieve the books she had been forced to store in a warehouse. And she had a good arrangement with Annie Leibovitz, who had her own penthouse in the same complex. The couple could live together without living in the same apartment. In the same year, Susan Sontag was awarded a MacArthur Fellowship, also known as the "genius award," America's most desirable and highest paid fellowship for artists, writers, and academics. Sontag received $340,000, to be paid out over the next five years, as well as health insurance. With this financial and personal security and with the help of Wylie and two assistants who took over organizational tasks, Sontag was finally in a position to concentrate on her novel.

Steve Wasserman traces Susan Sontag's return to literature partly to the spirit of the late eighties and early nineties, an intellectual climate no longer conducive to her kind of essay writing. The whole media landscape had changed dramatically. Although she could have continued writing essays, the magazines that would publish them—the newly founded *Threepenny Review* in California, the reinvigorated *Times Literary Supplement,* the familiar *Harper's* and *Paris Review,* and of course the *New York Review of Books*—had slipped completely from the consciousness of the mainstream and were reduced to a relatively small group of highly educated but marginalized readers. A novel, on the other hand, promised wider public recognition and the mixture of seriousness and glamour that Sontag strove for while also giving her a sense of a personal liberation. Wasserman said, "I think she was more and more convinced that the novel form would give her more freedom to try out various ideas. She could invent many voices for various and contradictory ideas. She was no longer arguing theoretically, but in the dialogue of her figures instead. Like life, novels do not demand a single, focused conclusion."[24] Sontag also had more respect for the novel as a form. Only the king of literary genres promised entry into Olympus. "She sought the highest form of literature in the empire of the novel rather than the republic of the essay," Wasserman explained. "Susan had the feeling of being in a dialogue with the greatest representatives of the genre. It was that dialogue she wanted to be part of."[25] Jonathan Galassi agrees that Sontag regarded the novel "in a certain sense as her higher calling."[26] David Rieff remarks that his mother always wrote with an eye to her posthumous reputation. "I don't want to write a lot of books," she said, "I want to write a few wonderful books that people will read 100 years from now."[27]

Sontag had already begun to work seriously on *The Volcano Lover* at the end of 1989, and this time she was determined to stick with it. Since 1979 she had had an open-ended offer from the German Academic Exchange Service of a stipend to go to Berlin. Already the site of sweeping changes that would culminate in the fall of the Berlin Wall, the German metropolis had increasingly attracted her interest. In the summer of 1989, Sontag accepted the stipend and began to use her time in Berlin intensively despite the political distractions all around her.

A year later she returned, again with the help of the German Academic Exchange Service, and wrote further sections of the novel. With Annie Leibovitz, she also undertook a trip to Italy to do extensive research for the novel.

"When I started the novel, it seemed like climbing Mount Everest," Sontag told Leslie Garis of the *New York Times*. "And I said to my psychiatrist, 'I'm afraid I'm not adequate.' Of course, that was a normal anxiety. What worried me was that I would not be writing essays, because they have a powerful ethical impulse behind them, and I think they make a contribution. But my psychiatrist said, 'What makes you think it isn't a contribution to give people pleasure?' "[28] Garis describes how Sontag fought back tears with this confession. Jonathan Galassi confirms that he often heard his author exclaim passionately, "I want to give joy!" when she talked about the novel.[29] This new element in her motivation for writing also is echoed in the novel's subtitle, "A Romance," an ironic reference to the genre of historical romance and to Sontag's image as an intellectual amazon.

Sontag drew the inspiration for *The Volcano Lover* from copper engravings of Mount Vesuvius she had purchased in a London antiquarian bookstore near the British Museum in 1980 and hung in her penthouse. The bookstore owner told her the engravings were by Pietro Fabris and originally came from William Hamilton's book *Campi Phlegraei* (*Flaming Fields,* 1776), in which he describes the volcanic landscape surrounding the mountain. Later Sontag read a biography of Hamilton, a British diplomat, and discovered that she already knew his story from the 1941 Hollywood classic *That Hamilton Woman* with Vivien Leigh and Laurence Olivier, which she had seen as a child. "Until *The Volcano Lover,* I wasn't able to give myself permission to tell a story, a real story, as opposed to the adventures of somebody's consciousness."[30]

The Volcano Lover tells the story of the famous and well-documented love triangle between the British consul, collector, and amateur natural scientist Sir William Hamilton; his wife, Emma Hamilton, one of the most beautiful women of the eighteenth century; and the British naval hero Admiral Horatio Nelson. Sontag keeps her text close to the historical figures and the dramatic developments of the time, but she gives each of the main characters aspects of her own personality. William Hamilton is a depressive, withdrawn collector of antique objets d'art who attempts to treat his melancholia with an obsessive preoccupation with philosophy, literature, and natural science. What fascinated Sontag about Emma was her career: she began as the daughter of a village blacksmith, by the age of seventeen had worked her way up to being one of the most sought-after models for the painters of her time, and in the end became a genuine star. Her beauty and social aplomb made her a muse for the most famous writers of the day, until at last she married Hamilton, the British consul to the Neapolitan Kingdom of the Two Sicilies.[31] Nelson interested Sontag because of the extreme passion and perseverance with which he pursued his goals. With a wealth of detail, the novelist describes the small Italian kingdom against the background of the French Revolution, the era in which the foundations of modern European culture were being laid. Sontag achieves a light, nimble narrative style unlike anything she had previously written. For the first time, she was writing a genuinely entertaining book, backed up by thorough research in biographies, historical works, and the correspondence of her characters. She describes bloody battles, elaborate rituals at the Neapolitan court, and voluptuous scenes of lovemaking.

But she would not have been Susan Sontag if she had not also been pursuing a theoretical goal with the book. She said she had borrowed the structure of the novel from Paul Hindemith's 1940 ballet *The Four Temperaments*. Interpolated in her historical narrative are miniature essays on the nature of collecting, on melancholy, and on beauty and humor. In the early sixties, Sontag had ridiculed the omniscient and omnipresent narrator, but now she applied that very technique with great panache and skill. Her narrator is a late twentieth-century and sometimes ironic adaptation of the classic omniscient narrator, commenting upon her story with contemporary glosses.

This perspective and the essayistic voice that sometimes steers the text away from the purely literary led many commentators to place Sontag in the company of essayistic novelists from Milan Kundera to V. S. Naipaul. In an interview with the *Paris Review,* however, she saw herself as part of a larger tradition that includes Honoré de Balzac, Leo Tolstoy, Marcel Proust, and Thomas Mann. She mentions Mann's *Magic Mountain* in particular, a novel that had spellbound her as a teenager.[32] It seems no accident that the motif that runs through the novel is Hamilton's passionate interest in investigating Vesuvius. In a certain sense, the volcano can be thought of as a variation on the Magic Mountain, not only in the imagination of the eighteenth-century contemporaries who actually believed in the mountain's magic powers, but also in its central significance for the culture of Old Europe. As on Mann's Swiss mountaintop, travelers from all over the continent meet in Naples and live out an idyll of high culture before Europe is again plunged into war. Sontag's novel is a very European book, written from the perspective of an America determined to get to the roots of European culture. It thus completes the arc that began with Sontag's reading of Thomas Mann's *Magic Mountain*—a book she called "the thinkiest great novel of all"[33]—and ends as she rediscovers the Europe of her youthful imagination.

The Volcano Lover was published in the fall of 1992 to much media fanfare and received effusive reviews. The major dailies published interviews with Sontag about her new role as the author of a historical novel. Almost all the critics praised the quality of her prose, and the consensus was that she had found a convincing narrative voice.[34] The *Los Angeles Times* described the novel as "the repository of much of Sontag's 59 years' worth of stored-up wisdom on the business of living" and added, "Never before has Sontag been so readable."[35] And Michiko Kakutani of the *New York Times,* arguably the most influential reviewer in America, called *The Volcano Lover* "a delight to read . . . it throws off ideas and intellectual sparks, like a Roman candle or Catherine wheel blazing in the night."[36] The novel remained on the *Times* best-seller list for eight weeks and was translated into twenty languages. Twenty-five years after the failure of *Death Kit,* Sontag was at last enjoying success as a novelist in her native land.

Reviewers in Germany were considerably harder on the novel. Most found it lacking in literary empathy, a lack that often left readers dissatisfied despite the extravagant descriptive passages. They wrote that all too frequently, the essayist would get the better of the novelist and that Sontag's prose seldom penetrated beneath the surfaces she described with such skill.

And in fact, few readers in America today find either of Sontag's late novels an unqualified success. Even good friends such as Nadine Gordimer admit that her "wonderful intellect got in the way of writing her novels."[37] The enthusiastic American reception of *The Volcano Lover* seems indebted to the good story that the almost sixty-year-old Sontag offered the cultural critics. In response to the changing times, she had once again reinvented herself. The formerly hypermodern writer tinged with existentialism, the protagonist of radical chic, the pensive theoretician and rigorous intellectual had now become a classic writer of big, romantic page-turners. That impression was reinforced by Sontag's own remarks about the novel, remarks that often sound less as if they come from a writer than from a publicity agent. She repeatedly supplied the press with stories about how certain themes or figures "came to her" or how she had written the book "in a fever" after its final sentence—"Damn them all"—occurred to her and she needed a novel to go with it. Such commentaries about her work seem an inadequate and unreliable description of her creative process. All too clearly, they represent a self-stylization based on transcendently romantic aesthetic ideals.

Theater at the Spiritual Front

(1993–1997)

*Maybe it's the single most surprising
thing I've witnessed in my life. The
death of high-mindedness. It's my
impression that most people now find
quite alien, almost incomprehensible,
the idea that you might do something
out of principle, something altruistic,
whatever the financial incentives
to do otherwise, or the degree of
inconvenience or discomfort or
personal danger.*

Susan Sontag, in a 1995 conversation
with Tony Kushner

One of Susan Sontag's most striking characteristics was her restlessness and the positively obsessive way she pursued her wishes, dreams, and goals.[1] David Rieff says his mother was always strongly oriented toward the future and seldom looked back. She never rested on her laurels or waxed nostalgic.[2] This attitude contributed largely to Sontag's success as well as to her ability to stay always abreast of contemporary discourse and reach new generations of readers. Sontag's friend Terry Castle

calls her "an intellectual marathon runner always trying to better her time."[3] And so, after *The Volcano Lover*'s sensational
success in America, Susan Sontag turned deliberately to areas of
endeavor where she thought she had not yet achieved what she
was capable of. One of those areas was the theater. Sontag had
written essays about the theater and was an enthusiastic play-
goer, knowledgeable about the theater scene in both Europe and
America. She had also directed two productions: Luigi Piran-
dello's *As You Desire Me* in Italy in 1979 and Milan Kundera's
Jacques and His Master in Cambridge, Massachusetts, in 1985.
But despite some attempts, she had yet to write a play of her
own. Ariel Dorfman, the Chilean writer best known in America
for his 1991 play *Death and the Maiden*, which was made into
a film starring Sigourney Weaver, relates the determination with
which Sontag carried out her plan to write a play.

The two of them often discussed the technical aspects of
writing for the stage. While Sontag had written *The Volcano
Lover* in a realistic style unusual for her, in her work for the theater she returned to her modernist roots. According to Dorfman,
plays were primarily intellectual projects for her. "She would not
sacrifice a single comma to make her dramas more attractive
for the stage," he said.[4] Instead of adopting the naturalism traditional in the American theater, Sontag wanted to experiment
with language in a way that would allow her to raise philosophical questions and foreground the materiality of speech sounds.
Her focus was formalistic. The play's theme was less important
than reducing the dialogic or monologic material and allowing
a multiplicity of possible meanings and readings to emerge. This
emphasis resulted in an intentional, programmatic incomprehen-
sibility of the kind that had already proved problematic in *The
Benefactor* and *Death Kit* as well as her films *Duet for Cannibals, Brother Carl,* and *Unguided Tour.*

In many respects, Samuel Beckett can be regarded as the primary model for Sontag's dramatic conception. The productions
she liked best were those of her friend Robert Wilson. Since the
sixties, he had become one of the most successful directors in

American theater and a sensation in Europe as well. His style was ultramodern, combining abstract sets, impressive lighting effects, distant microphone voices, and machinelike choreography to produce effects of spare beauty, cool atmosphere, and dense intellectuality. Wilson became Sontag's closest collaborator in her theatrical projects.

The realization of those projects had actually begun as far back as 1979, when she had the idea of a play about Alice James, the sister of Henry and William James. Alice died of breast cancer in 1892 at the age of forty-three, only eight years after moving to England with her longtime friend Katherine Loring. Her reputation as a writer rested primarily on her posthumously published diary, in which, with a sharp pen, she described the rituals and traditions of her time, the traumatic events in her family, and her experience as the victim of a misogynistic society. Along with her letters and a biography, the diary made her a much-discussed figure in feminist circles in the 1980s. The biographical parallels between Sontag and Alice James promised to be fertile soil for a theater project. Sontag herself remarked, "I think I have been preparing to write *Alice in Bed* all my life."[5] *Alice in Bed* (1991) was intended as a play about "the grief and anger of women" and "the reality of the mental prison" in which women found themselves.[6]

In her typical self-stylization as a romantically inspired artist, Sontag often said she had written *Alice in Bed* in just two weeks while in Berlin,[7] although the play went through several drafts after Sontag had read from it in Berlin and New York.[8] She described her fascination for the theater at that time, "Yes. I hear voices. That's why I like to write plays."[9]

Alice in Bed premiered in Bonn in September 1991. Two years later, Robert Wilson directed it at the Berlin Schaubühne. It had to wait nine years for its U.S. premiere at the New York Theatre Workshop under the Belgian-Dutch director Ivo van Hove. All these productions garnered an impressively long list of negative reviews that ran the gamut from polite to malicious. The play leaves one with the impression that Sontag has completely neglected the Alice James material and her personal connection to it, replacing them with a series of disconnected pseudo-experimental images, dialogues, and clichés with which she tries to conjure up the desperation of the bedridden James. The play begins with the confusing image of a woman lying under a pile of mattresses. Another scene is a tea party attended by the nineteenth-century protofeminists Margaret Fuller and Emily Dickinson. There is no unifying concept tying together the play's eight scenes. Instead, one is confronted with pretentious language and a great deal of pathos. Sontag's claim that she wrote the play in only two weeks suggests not a romantically inspired creative rapture but aesthetic dilettantism.

Also problematic are extensive borrowings, not just from the biographical material about Alice James but from other sources as well. The tea party scene, for instance—according to Sontag a reference to that other famous Alice of the nineteenth century, Lewis Carroll's creation—displays strong similarities to an imagined group scene in the play *Top Girls* (1982) by Caryl Churchill, the British playwright who successfully combined feminist themes with experimental stage techniques. Reviews that criticized Sontag for her "brittle stage prose"[10] or joked that she "actually doesn't let Alice say anything, but has her say it again and again"[11] still seem relatively restrained. John Simon's piece for *New York* magazine threw off all restraint: "Miss Sontag . . . must have set herself the task of writing a difficult work worthy of Dadaist, Surrealist, absurdist, and postmodern arcana. If they could be opaque, preposterous, illogical, and shocking, why, so could she make them—in spades."[12]

Sontag's collaboration with Robert Wilson began with *A Parsifal,* a short, six-page play she wrote for the catalog of the 1991 Wilson retrospective at the Boston Museum of Fine Arts. In a sense, *A Parsifal* is a deconstruction of Richard Wagner that was inspired by Wilson's production of *Parsifal* at the Los Angeles Opera. Sontag interprets Parsifal as an ignorant and violent soldier. Her little drama was first performed after her death by the experimental group the Hotel Savant Theatre Company at the off-off-Broadway P.S. 122. The miscalculation Sontag made with the piece is evident both on paper and on the stage, proof that to be a good experimental playwright you have to be a good realist first. Sontag gave Wilson the play with the words "No one will ever produce it; if anyone does, then it will be you."[13]

The high point of their collaboration was an adaptation of Henrik Ibsen's *The Lady from the Sea* (1888) that Sontag and Wilson developed with a few actors at a workshop at Wilson's Watermill Center on Long Island. They took on a successful tour to Italy, Spain, Poland, Norway, France, Turkey, and Korea after its premiere in Ferrara, Italy. Wilson says he very much liked working with Sontag because her plays always left great mental and virtual space, which he could fill in with his staging.[14]

It is difficult to guess whether the keen-eyed critic Sontag had any idea of the questionable quality of her plays. It is not unusual, after all, that sharply honed critical judgment with respect to others' work fails with respect to one's own. Sontag admitted in some interviews that she had not read reviews of her own work for years, leaving that job to her son, David, who would tell her if they were good or bad.[15] She also seems to have received little critical feedback from her friends. Dorfman and Wilson, with all their theater experience, could not bring themselves to criticize her work even when Sontag complained bitterly that her plays were not performed or her stories not turned into plays often enough (her short story "Baby" was staged in Hamburg in 1994). Ariel Dorfman reassured her that her theater was too avant-garde for the majority of theatergoers and required an especially intellectual audience.[16] Robert Wilson told her that her time would yet come, for her pieces were "philosophically oriented" and would "therefore never age, just like Shakespeare's plays."[17]

The play with which Sontag achieved a breakthrough was not one of her own compositions, but a production she directed that achieved unparalleled media attention. When Susan Sontag staged Samuel Beckett's *Waiting for Godot* in occupied Sarajevo in August 1993, theatrical artistry was not of central importance. Instead, she channeled her predilection for grand symbolic gestures—sometimes uncomfortably obvious in her own plays—into a political statement that could not have been more effective.

Sontag first traveled to war-torn Bosnia in April 1993 to visit her son. David Rieff was reporting from Sarajevo for several American newspapers and writing a book on the civil war in the heart of Europe, in which hundreds of people were brutally killed every week before the eyes of the Western media.[18] Sarajevo was encircled by Serbian militias and subjected to daily bombings and round-the-clock sniper fire. Both out of concern for her son and because of her deep ties to Europe, Sontag felt compelled to do something tangible to help. "What was happening in Rwanda was far worse than Bosnia, but I found it unbelievable that in modern Europe there could be genocide and death camps 50 years after the end of the Second World War."[19] It was self-evident that Sontag would want to gather her impressions firsthand. The German war reporter Carolin Emcke describes this obligation to bear witness as something basic to Sontag's nature: "She couldn't stand to be a sheltered foreigner while others were suffering. She was not satisfied with a role as 'First World intellectual.' She wanted to know what was happening in these war zones, to really understand it."[20] To do so, Sontag was willing to run potentially fatal risks such as entering Sarajevo by an unpaved road through the Dinaric Alps, under fire from the Serbs, because the airport had been destroyed.

Sontag was a friend of the United Nations director of humanitarian programs and asked if she could accompany a mission on their flight to the besieged city. At sixty, with the experience of her two visits to Vietnam and her documentary film work during the Yom Kippur War, Sontag was wondering how she could spend her time in the war zone in a meaningful and "morally decent" way. "What can you do in Sarajevo," she asked in *The Guardian*, "if you are not a journalist or a worker with a humanitarian organization?"[21] Her two weeks in Sarajevo proved to be a decisive experience for her, and she sought ways to return to the city and make a tangible contribution. She said, "I met up with some theatre people and I asked them if they would like me to come back and work with them for a while. They said 'Yes.' The play itself occurred to me without thinking about it too much; *Waiting for Godot.*"[22]

Sontag's sojourns in the besieged and ruined Bosnian capital would become some of the most important events in her life, as she told interviewers years later. She described the overwhelming power of the experience, "It wasn't simply an experience of war—it was an experience of the continuity of human life . . . At every level you would see people continuing with their lives."[23]

According to the journalist Mark Danner, who spent time with her in Sarajevo, "Sontag was marvelous. She didn't just feel she was fighting on the right side, she was intensely engaged. It may sound strange, but it was *the* time of her life."[24] Danner was impressed by Sontag's expertise in introducing him to life in the war zone. She showed him how to duck behind the cargo containers scattered around the city as protection against the ubiquitous sharpshooters and how to reconnoiter the terrain before dashing to the next safe location.

The journalists lived in the half-bombed-out Holiday Inn, the only hotel still operating, although, like the whole city, it had to make do without water, heat, or electric power. They used flashlights, got their water at public pumps, and brought it back to their rooms in bottles and wastebaskets so they could wash and flush the toilets. "It was a big adventure for Sontag. She believed in the effectiveness of her efforts."[25]

Sontag's engagement was indeed admirable even if it sometimes met with practical obstacles. For a long time, she intended to start an elementary school, but parents were afraid their children would be shot by snipers on the way to school and the project never got off the ground. She was more successful at organizing a fund-raising campaign among New York writers to benefit the PEN group in Sarajevo. She personally carried the desperately needed funds back to the city—in cash, so purchases could be made on the black market.[26]

Sontag harshly criticized the French intellectuals André Glucksmann and Bernard-Henri Lévy for flying into Sarajevo for a twenty-four-hour tour and then holding a press conference. She saw herself in the tradition of George Orwell and Ernest Hemingway, actively fighting against Francisco Franco's forces in the Spanish Civil War, as she told the *Washington Post*.[27] She could not understand the inaction of intellectuals all over the world and she persuaded Annie Leibovitz to come to Sarajevo for two weeks to document the city's physical destruction and human misery. "People told me they thought I was crazy to come here," Sontag said, "but they didn't understand that I couldn't not come here. Once I understood what was happening, it was the obvious moral choice. It was the only choice."[28]

But Mark Danner says that some inhabitants of Sarajevo also viewed Sontag skeptically. They had the feeling she was only using the situation to enhance her own public image. And she sometimes made herself unpopular with journalists in the city. Although she was not reporting on the war herself and for long stretches of her nine separate visits to the besieged city had nothing specific to do, she gave some colleagues the impression she thought she was having the most authentic experiences and was the only one "on the front line."[29]

Sontag's idea to stage *Waiting for Godot,* however, was greeted enthusiastically by both inhabitants and journalists. When she visited Sarajevo for the second time in July 1993, she began rehearsals for Beckett's play in the Pozorište Mladih (Youth Theater), one of two Sarajevo theaters still able to function. Plays continued to be performed even during the siege. Her production was supposed to be a part of a small festival organized by the director Haris Pašović. Sontag described the rehearsals as extremely difficult. Not only did the theater lack the most basic equipment, such as spotlights and costumes, but also the actors were in a permanent state of exhaustion caused by personal losses, lack of food, and fear. Sontag and her set designer Ognjenka Finci filled the stage with the everyday insignia of the new life of Sarajevo: munitions boxes, sandbags, and a hospital bed. To emphasize the collective nature of the waiting, Sontag cast three actors each in the roles of Vladimir and Estragon, and had them repeat the text one after the other. The six actors were arranged in three pairs: two men, a man and a woman, and two women. All of them wore the uniforms of concentration camp inmates. Instead of Beckett's original two acts, each of which ends with Godot failing to appear, Sontag made do with the first act in view of the audience's long and dangerous way home after the performance. The stage was illuminated with candles and flashlights.[30]

Even if the Bosnian director Davor Koric thought the production tended slightly to "stiffness and unnecessary seriousness,"[31] Sontag's *Godot* was a forceful symbol both of the cultural normality of theater in Sarajevo and of the city's painful helplessness. *Godot* showed the world what was at stake in the multicultural, cosmopolitan city in the former Yugoslavia, namely, the urban way of life and artistic multiplicity. It was a model of resistance against encirclement and destruction. The choice of play served as a mordant commentary on NATO, Bosnia's European neighbors, and the United States, all watching the slaughter in Sarajevo more or less without lifting a finger. When they finally deployed troops to Bosnia two years later, it took only a few days to put an end to the siege. Meanwhile, Sarajevo waited for Allied air raids against the Serbian army and for liberation. It was also waiting for water, gas, electric power, food supplies, cigarettes, and gasoline, for an end to the bombardment and the snipers, and for an end to its constant terror.

Sontag's popularity and the symbolic value of her *Godot* attracted much attention in the media. Journalists from the press, radio, and television flocked to the tumbledown Youth Theater. Hardly a newspaper or news broadcast in the West failed to report on Sontag's theater work. She readily granted numerous interviews in which she talked almost euphorically about Sarajevo and her activities there. This publicity boom struck many of the city's inhabitants and some journalists as frivolous. Sontag seemed to them less interested in the fate of Sarajevo and more interested in promoting herself as the heroine of a city in ruins. It was not just the conservative press in America—for whom she had long been a thorn in the side—who jumped on this bandwagon, but also leftist cultural reporters in Europe. A prime example was the *Süddeutsche Zeitung* in Munich, which dubbed Sontag, with biting sarcasm, "the courageous moralist with the media-mane, putting the world to shame as a director in the besieged city."[32] For her part, Sontag reacted angrily to such attacks. She wrote a long essay in her own defense for the *New York Review of Books*. Although in earlier interviews she said she had asked Sarajevo's theater people for permission to stage a play,[33] now and in all subsequent interviews she declared somewhat pompously that they had come to her with the request. Moreover, she insisted that the press attention was not her fault. She had not wanted any reports or interviews whatsoever, but the actors and staff of the theater had asked her to allow journalists into the theater.

Of course it is cynical to accuse Sontag of undertaking her protracted, dangerous, exhausting work in Sarajevo solely out of her own need for attention. On the contrary, her popularity was the greatest currency Sontag had at her disposal to help bring the war-ravaged city to the attention of the West. In retrospect, her interviews and the testimony of her colleagues in Sarajevo paint the picture of an enthusiastic and sometimes naive woman. Sontag seemed to believe so earnestly that her mission was in the tradition of intellectuals' engagement in the Spanish Civil War that she did not realize how pretentious that anachronism could sound. She was extremely hurt by the accusations.

At least once a year after the end of the Bosnian war, Sontag and David Rieff would fly to Sarajevo to maintain the contacts they had made during the siege and provide practical help in rebuilding the life of the city. For her engagement in Sarajevo, Sontag was granted honorary citizenship and also received the Swiss Montblanc de la Culture Arts Patronage Award. She donated the prize money to Sarajevo humanitarian organizations. After her death, a public square in the center of the capital of Bosnia and Herzegovina was renamed in her honor.

Sontag's works over the following years show the dramatic impact of her experiences in Sarajevo. She often said in interviews that she considered the war in the former Yugoslavia as more or less the end of the European culture she had admired all her life. The indifference of the West European cultural and political elite toward the war marked for her a growing disillusion with European ideals that is palpable in her later writings. The disappearance of serious high culture that Sontag had observed in America, a culture whose original model she had found in Europe, now seemed to be in evidence there as well. As early as in the speech "The Idea of Europe (One More Elegy)," which she delivered at a Berlin conference in May 1988, she declared that the serious aesthetic, ethical, and personal values of old Europe were now being pushed aside by "Euroland," a theme park that turned the champions of European high culture into emigrants and exiles in their own geography.[34] Sontag's text is less an exact description of a process than a document of leave-taking from a dream that had motivated her work from the beginning.

In the wake of the Yugoslav wars, this change can be seen most clearly in Sontag's intense work on a new novel significantly titled *In America*. It traces the career of the Polish actor Maryna Zalezowska, modeled on the historic figure Helena Modjeska (born Helena Modrzejewska, 1840–1909), who emigrated from Russian Poland to America in 1876 and there enjoyed a meteoric rise to become one of the most famous actors of the nineteenth century. Sontag had discovered her heroine in a small bookstore in Boston as she leafed through a monograph on the Polish author Henryk Sienkiewicz. As a young man, he had accompanied Modjeska as part of her entourage and cofounded with her a short-lived utopian agrarian community in Anaheim, California.

Especially in the introductory chapter of *In America*, Sontag inserts herself into the novel and points to parallels between herself and her protagonist. Superficially, *In America* seems like a meditation on fame and the life of a diva. But in a sense, the novel stages Sontag's own spiritual return to America as well. Its most moving passages are the descriptions of Maryna's forced departure from old Europe and its cultural ideals and the difficulties of a public life in America.

The turn in Sontag's career represented by her time in Sarajevo is evident, above all, in her surprising insight that the Western culture in which she had grown up had changed so much that intellectual engagement such as hers in Bosnia seemed to have lost its credibility and value. This note of disappointment seems very authentic, for instance, when she complains in an interview with the dramatist Tony Kushner that most people now found it positively unimaginable to do something from altruism or on principle. Sontag blames this moral decline for the ebbing of a rhetoric that writers and intellectuals had used with confidence since the days of Émile Zola. She said, "'My principles forbid . . .' or 'I believe this is the right thing; therefore I'm going to do it,' or 'I have to do it even though it's dangerous . . .'—that kind of language, of thinking, is dying. It actually makes no sense to most people."[35]

Sontag expressed this opinion in speeches, lectures, interviews, and roundtable discussions, often adducing her experiences in Sarajevo and attacking the statements of other participants with aggressive indignation, even when they were on her side and agreed with her political arguments. Many contemporaries, such as the journalist Paul Berman, who had organized the fund-raiser for Sarajevo PEN with Sontag, describe this behavior as intolerable despite their admiration for her.[36]

Sontag's friends, however, were amused by her bizarre behavior. According to Wendy Lesser, Sontag simply did not acknowledge the opinions of people who had not been in the war zone.[37] For Lesser this attitude was not self-righteousness but rather the expression of a moral conviction that sometimes shaded over into egocentrism. Sontag believed too firmly in her ethical principles to want to see them diluted in conversation.

Lesser recalls a lunch Sontag invited her to in San Francisco because she wanted to meet Lesser's friend, the poet Thom Gunn. After the meeting, Gunn was visibly exhausted. He found Sontag to be a really good person with firm moral principles, "but being a good person doesn't make it any easier to have lunch with her."[38]

Even Sontag's close friend and defender Andrew Wylie had to admit that, despite her great human warmth, personal lack of pretension, and curiosity, she could definitely also play the imperious grande dame. "She showed her aggressiveness in the same way that Callas would have," Wylie said. "You always knew you were with someone who knew exactly what she wanted. If something didn't please her, she launched an attack."[39] Terry Castle agrees that Sontag was always prepared to be critical, aggressive, impolite, and harsh if she did not like something. Castle said, "She never stopped being the self-appointed 'critic of the world.' She reserved the right to treat her fellow human beings badly if they said something that didn't meet with her approval or something she thought was stupid or banal . . . That was part of her aura."[40] In the end, Sontag's affectations became a recognized literary genre in academic and intellectual circles and, according to Castle, the subject of gossip and a clandestine source of amusement. Thus, when a distinguished Stanford professor asked Sontag at an official dinner whether she had had any news of her friend Jonathan Miller (who enjoyed a similar status in Great Britain to Sontag's in the United States), she asked him testily if he did not read the newspapers. Another time, in front of a group of students at the University of Norfolk, she accused the English professor Dana Heller of stupidity when the latter asked her if she had known that Cathleen Schine had already used her play *Alice in Bed* as the title of a novel.[41] Sontag even walked out of an official banquet at the PEN Center because the person sitting next to her, a Doubleday editor, did not know who she was.[42]

Both Stephen Koch and Sigrid Nunez say that Sontag was an extremely talented and well-connected power politician.[43] A call from her, for example, could persuade editor Tina Brown to put a controversial Annie Leibovitz photo of the nude and very pregnant Demi Moore on the cover of *Vanity Fair*. Sontag's advocacy for unknown authors could result in them being nominated for prizes or finding a better publisher. On the other hand, she could mobilize the forces of Andrew Wylie, Roger Straus, and their attorneys when she wanted to prevent the publication of something unpleasant about her. Sontag's close friends since the sixties, Richard Howard and Stephen Koch, both say that, by this time, Sontag had assembled a large entourage that protected her from many attacks but also deprived her of many influences. One commentator compared this entourage to the military wing of a political organization.[44] Sontag needed admirers, and many friends, assistants, and acquaintances were happy to oblige, not only because she was an influential woman but also because she could be an extremely charming, attentive, and generous friend who exuded a lively and youthful aura well into old age. Jeff Seroy, the publicity director of FSG, recalls how marvelous evenings with Sontag were. She was interested in so many things—theater, opera, Japanese food—and her capacity for enthusiasm was infectious. "With Susan you either sat in the passenger seat or you were road kill along the shoulder, but it was a wonderful thing to be in the passenger seat."[45]

A certain haughty bitterness at what she considered the decline of seriousness and idealism is also evident in the shorter essays Sontag was writing at the end of the 1990s. They were increasingly focused on what was for her the one bastion of high culture still standing, namely, literature. The tone of lament is clearest in "Thirty Years Later . . . ," her 1996 foreword for a new edition of the Spanish translation of *Against Interpretation*. Another author might have waxed nostalgic looking back on one of her most important books. Not Sontag. Instead, she declares herself highly ambivalent about her earlier work. One reason she gives is that cultural values, the defense of desire, sensuousness, and popular culture have in the meantime been revalued under the banner of triumphant consumer capitalism. When she advocated so vehemently for the abolishment of the hierarchy of elite and popular culture, she could not have known that the unbounded art she was promoting would some day facilitate the invasion of a frivolous consumer culture. The gap between the young cultural revolutionary Susan Sontag and the older Sontag who identifies herself as the conservative defender of high culture could not be greater: "Now the very idea of the serious (and of the honorable) seems quaint, unrealistic, to most people, and when allowed—as an arbitrary decision of temperament—probably unhealthy, too."[46]

Similar laments for serious and intelligent art and similar challenges to the forces of cultural leveling can be read in Sontag's other texts as well. In "A Century of Cinema," Sontag mourns the decline of difficult films that had set in after a hundred years of film history. She documents her pessimistic view especially with the dying out of the passion for film that compelled whole generations of movie lovers in the sixties and seventies to watch long retrospectives of challenging European filmmakers and subscribe to *Cahiers du Cinéma,* an influential French film magazine. In the eyes of cinephiles, she says, movies were magic, unrepeatable, and unique experiences—an attitude no longer possible in view of the current products of the film industry. When the piece appeared in the *New York Times* on February 25, 1996, under the title "The Decay of Cinema," it stirred up a controversy. Sontag had described a widespread feeling. But as if to prove that the author's complaint was right, the cultural editors at the *Times* deleted from the text the names of several directors whom they assumed readers would not recognize.[47]

But however justified the tone of lament was, it often sounded strained. It is absent from the most beautiful Sontag pieces of those years, her forewords to American translations of European and South American authors: Juan Rulfo's short 1955 novel *Pedro Páramo;* "A Mind in Mourning," about the German writer W. G. Sebald; "Afterlives: The Case of Machado de Assis"; and others collected in *Where the Stress Falls.* They reflect Sontag's practical engagement in promoting the arts in general, for example, as a member of the advisory board of the Mark Morris Dance Group or the New York branch of the Rainer Werner Fassbinder Foundation. She wrote a series of introductions to the works of authors almost totally unknown in America; in addition to Rulfo, Sebald, and Machado de Assis she introduced the postmodern Yugoslav Danilo Kiš, the Polish poet Adam Zagajewski, and the classic Polish avant-garde writer Witold Gombrowicz. With Sontag's encouragement, some of these authors acquired Andrew Wylie as their agent and were published by FSG.

In her forewords, Sontag breathes new life into an old-fashioned, elegant, and elevating devotion to world literature, becoming a passionate advocate for literary quality. Of course, her introductions always also inform us of her own self-definition as a writer and her own literary ambitions. But it is precisely her perspective on the writer's profession that produces fluid biographical sketches aptly characterizing her subjects and their works. With these essays, Sontag not only found a niche where she could pursue her intellectual interests but also helped expand in a practical way her "project for the great library." Some authors, such as Juan Rulfo, would never have been translated into English if Sontag had not brought her influence to bear. Others would never have found so many readers without her name on their dust jackets. She enjoyed playing the grande dame, the passionate and sometimes eccentric advocate of a *grande littérature.*

Life and Afterlife

(1998–2001)

I'm happy when I dance.

Susan Sontag, *I, etcetera* (1978)

For Susan Sontag, the nineties were primarily the years with Annie Leibovitz.[1] The two women went on many trips together— to Jordan, Egypt, Italy, Japan. Researching the life of Helena Modrzejewska for the novel *In America,* they visited the ruins of the Polish star's farm in Anaheim, California.[2] In 1996, Leibovitz purchased a picturesque property in Rhinebeck on the Hudson River in New York. The property, called Clifton Point, had once been the country estate of the Astor family, the most influential representatives of old New York's financial aristocracy and high society. It included several turn-of-the-century houses, a pond, and a stretch of Hudson riverbank. Leibovitz took great plea- sure in having the estate carefully restored, and she and Sontag moved into a small house on the pond. After completion of the restoration, it became Sontag's country house.[3]

After her bout with breast cancer, Sontag was very sensitive to the signals from her own body. When she began to feel increas- ingly ill in the summer of 1998, she had herself reexamined at the beginning of July.[4] The results were devastating: Sontag had cancer again, this time a rare kind of uterine sarcoma.[5] Although the prognosis was better than for her previous illness, there was only provisional hope for a sixty-five-year-old who had already had cancer once. As she had during her first confrontation with the illness, Sontag prepared herself psychologically for only one possibility: survival. David Rieff later described her attitude as "positive denial."[6] Sontag firmly believed she could beat the odds, just as she had twenty-three years earlier. "Susan didn't even mention the possibility that she could die," David said.[7]

Sontag spent the next year and a half in great pain. She underwent a radical hysterectomy and lengthy radiation and chemotherapy at Mount Sinai Hospital in New York.[8] In the first months of the illness, Annie Leibovitz was with her almost every day, and Sontag encouraged her to document the various stages of her illness. The small-format photographs Leibovitz published in 2006 in *A Photographer's Life* are among the most moving and controversial of her career. They show a groggy Sontag being washed by a nurse, getting chemotherapy supported by friends and assistants, and having her famous mane of hair cropped.

Sontag's agent Andrew Wylie visited her every day after his morning jog in Central Park. He recalls vividly how urgently Sontag connected her survival to her ongoing plans. Even when half dozing, she was thinking about the books she still planned to write. One morning when he entered her hospital room, the emaciated Sontag lay asleep in her bed. "I looked at her and thought, oh God, she's dead. I touched her arm and she woke up abruptly and said, 'I'm working!' 'What?' I asked. 'I'm working!' I hugged her and said, 'You're absolutely crazy.' It was typical Susan. She was literally in the jaws of death and yet she didn't want me to think she'd nodded off!"[9]

The chemotherapy had pushed back the sarcoma, but one of the side effects was a serious neuropathy in her feet. At the age of sixty-six, Sontag had to learn to walk again in a protracted course of physical therapy. The rehabilitation was harrowing, but she was a fighter—glad to be alive and determined to enjoy every minute.[10]

Meanwhile, with sheer boundless determination, she began to write again. The first work Sontag completed during her second bout with cancer was the introduction to a collection of photographs that she and Leibovitz had conceived together. *Women* appeared in the fall of 1999 and contained Leibovitz's portraits of two hundred American women—artists, politicians, housewives, farmers, and strippers—that amount to an anthropological compendium of women's lives in America at the turn of the millennium. In its conception, the collection owes a great deal to *Antlitz der Zeit* (*The Face of the Era*),[11] August Sander's 1929 collection of Germans in the Weimar Republic. Even more than Sander, Leibovitz's pictures juxtapose various social strata with the completely neutral eye of the camera. In her foreword, Sontag asks if there is something that connects all the women portrayed in the volume, but after reflections that sometimes strike one as anachronistic, she resists answering the question. In this essay, she continues a theme she had already addressed in the four monologues by women that end *The Volcano Lover* and in her play *Alice in Bed*: women's lives. The fact that, despite her interest, Sontag fails to get below the surface of the topic suggests that it was not really congenial to her. Her own life as a woman had run too contradictory a course for her to generalize about it. She neither takes up again the feminist discourses she had criticized in the sixties and seventies nor adopts the postfeminist gender discussion being carried on at American universities during the nineties. Instead, she reaches further back. In her interviews from the time, she declares her rediscovered passion for Virginia Woolf. In many ways, Sontag's anthropology-tinged reflections are reminiscent of Woolf's *A Room of One's Own* (1929). But unlike Woolf, Sontag fails to clarify basic questions of the everyday life of women or bring out universal aspects of the female human condition.

What emerged more positively from the glossy pages of *Women* was Sontag's triumphal return to the arena of public life after her serious illness, an affirmation of her image. At the end of the volume is one of the most beautiful of all the portraits in Susan Sontag's long love affair with the camera. Her closely cropped grayish-white hair, growing back densely after the chemotherapy, lends her dramatic features a sensual weight. Resting her chin in her hand and with keen eyes and dark turtleneck sweater, Sontag is more than ever an icon of self-contained critical authority.

In his essay "Illness as More than Metaphor," David Rieff says that although Sontag almost never talked about dying, the idea of her own death lurked like a "ghost at the banquet of many of her conversations." This was especially evident in Sontag's "single-minded focus on her own longevity" and "frequent voicing of the hope of living to be one hundred."[12] The main effect of this aggressive suppression of the thought of death was Sontag's sometimes seemingly superhuman hunger for life. She was still capable of spending the entire night talking, reading, and watching films rather than sleeping.[13] While she often remarked ironically that she felt she had already used up six of her nine lives, she also insisted that she was just getting started with her writing and her best works were yet to come. "I have a whole new life. It's going to be terrific," she declared in March 2000.[14] "There are just 24 hours in a day, though I try to treat it as though there were 48."[15] And that is exactly what she did. She even began to take piano lessons, something her mother had refused her as a child.[16] Sontag's enthusiasms were a life-affirming impulse her friends found infectious. When one of her assistants named Jeff Alexander set up an email account for her and taught her how to use the Internet, she plunged so eagerly into the new technology that within a month she knew more about it than he did. Sontag had several computers scattered around her penthouse so that she could write and use the Net wherever and whenever she wanted to.[17]

Sontag had finished *In America* while still undergoing chemotherapy. Like its predecessor *The Volcano Lover,* the novel based on the life of Helena Modrzejewska was a literary fictionalization of historical events. It too had a strong woman as its central character. Sontag combined a traditional, authorial narrative perspective with invented diary entries, letters, dialogues, and inner monologues.

Despite her efforts, however, the result was disappointing. Long stretches of the novel resemble a collection of clichés about actors, the cult of stardom, European immigrants, and the American dream. Many scenes are one-dimensional and stereotypical. The noble selflessness of the protagonist and her intoxication with art sometimes seem like a reflection of Sontag's own conception of her role as a public person, a conception she sometimes feigned naïveté about.

On the personal narrative level of the novel, there are indications that Sontag was also using her heroine to explore ideas about her own fame. Even more markedly than in *The Volcano Lover*, she inserted ironic references to her own biography, for instance, to her sojourns in Sarajevo, her marriage to Philip Rieff, and her Polish-Jewish grandparents. The introductory chapter of the novel is shot through with curious self-referential commentaries on her weakness for putting single words in quotation marks, a somewhat labored reference to her reputation as a serious intellectual.

Despite its tendency to experiment, long stretches of *In America* seem conventional. It is not just its obvious departure from the high modernist literature Sontag championed in the sixties. It also stands in sharp contrast to Sontag's authoritative pronouncements on world literature as high culture in her discussions of such authors as Joseph Brodsky, Anna Banti, Danilo Kiš, and Jorge Luis Borges. Even as she values her literary models' penchant for a complexity uninfluenced by fashion and attests to its subversive influence on mainstream culture, her own strategy of aiming for popularity with *In America* comes dangerously close to what the Swiss critic Andrea Köhler calls the "leisure-time readers' taste for content and story."[18]

After the success of *The Volcano Lover*, FSG put a similar effort into marketing *In America*. Although Sontag was still quite weakened by her treatments, she threw herself into promoting the book with great professionalism. When the novel was published in 2000, Jeff Seroy, the publicity director at FSG, had planned an extensive American reading tour, and he traveled with Sontag to Chicago, Seattle, Portland, San Francisco, Los Angeles, Berkeley, Denver, Iowa City, Houston, Miami, and Washington. Sontag enjoyed the trip despite the exertions of travel and was pleased by her audiences.[19]

In America garnered mixed reviews in the United States. Michiko Kakutani, who had so enthusiastically praised *The Volcano Lover,* described *In America* as "a thoroughly conventional imitation of a thoroughly conventional 19th-century novel."[20] Richard Lourie of the *Washington Post,* on the other hand, admitted there were weak sections but was charmed by the historical panorama and by the "élan, intelligence and delight" of Sontag's narration.[21]

Sontag received a particularly harsh response from Ellen Lee, an eighty-one-year-old amateur historian and cofounder of the California Helena Modjeska Foundation, who accused the writer of plagiarism in May 2000.[22] Lee found twelve passages in the novel that reproduced sentences—either word-for-word or with slight variations—from the performer's memoir *Memories and Impressions of Helena Modjeska* (1910); the letters of Modrzejewska's friend Henryk Sienkiewicz, collected in *Portrait of America* (1959); the obscure Modrzejewska biography *Fair Rosalind: The American Career of Helena Modjeska* (1969) by Marion Coleman; and Willa Cather's *My Mortal Enemy* (1926). Sontag reacted to these charges with a mixture of arrogance and evasive generalities. She referred to her note on the copyright page in which she emphasizes that the novel was "inspired by" the historical Modrzejewska and her entourage, "no less and no more. Most of the characters in the novel are invented, and those who are not depart in radical ways from their real-life models."[23] She defended herself to the *New York Times* with recourse to literary theory: "All of us who deal with real characters in history transcribe and adopt original sources . . . I've used these sources and I've completely transformed them . . . I've looked at these books. There's a larger argument to be made that all of literature is a series of references and allusions."[24]

A close examination of Sontag's text does not support the allegation of plagiarism. The passages in question occupy three pages of a 387-page novel. Jonathan Galassi and Jeff Seroy add that, as a purely legal matter, they could not have been plagiarized since Sontag's sources were no longer protected by copyright because of their age. Both agree, however, that such accusations could have been most easily avoided by listing the sources in detail.[25] On the other hand, the often-unacknowledged relationships between the texts of Sontag's literary works emerges clearly here, a technique that she also used in *The Volcano Lover* and *Alice in Bed* without it being particularly commented upon. The technique owes its presence partly to the historical material Sontag was using, and partly to the decades she spent writing essays that by definition demanded extensive research and the use of other texts. They have obviously influenced her fictional style.

Despite its critics, *In America* was nominated for a National Book Award. When Sontag stood on the stage of the Marriott Marquis in Manhattan to receive the $10,000 award, she could hardly conceal her surprise. "To say I'm astonished is an understatement . . . I am really more moved than I could say."[26] Commenting on the negative reviews in the subsequent press conference, Sontag said somewhat testily that she never read reviews. "I'm too squeamish. It's painful to be criticized."[27]

In the New York literary scene, where Sontag's imaginative works—in contrast to her essays—met with little favorable response, the book award was widely seen as an acknowledgment of her status as an intellectual icon.[28] In interviews she gave after the publication of the novel and the National Book Award, she remained undaunted by that widely held opinion and continued to insist that she was now primarily a novelist. She considered her fiction superior to her essays. Sometimes she even ventured the opinion that it would not bother her if her essays from the sixties were gradually forgotten and she was remembered for her novels.[29]

Although approaching seventy, Sontag did not act like an old woman. "Even at the end of her life," says Andrew Wylie, "she still seemed like a twenty-one-year-old. She was always interested in things she did not know. So many people later in life fall back on the things they know. But Susan always lived as if she were born yesterday and still had the whole world to explore."[30] She called her age "grotesque." She was still doing the things she had done all her life.[31] Even in her late sixties she lived unconventionally,[32] as shown by the intensity of her daily life, the openness with which she made new friends, and her capacity for excitement about new developments in art and politics.

Sontag now divided her time between New York and long trips to Berlin, Kyoto, the Bahamas, and Paris, where Annie Leibovitz had purchased an apartment on the Quai des Grands-Augustins with a view of the Seine and the Place Dauphine. Eugène Atget and Brassaï had both photographed the building in the nineteenth century, and Pablo Picasso had painted *Guernica* there in 1937.

Klaus Biesenbach, the curator of the Museum of Modern Art, recalls Sontag attending three or four events every evening, leaving for the next as soon as one lost her interest.[33] When one of her assistants mentioned a hip Bulgarian bar in Chinatown that had live rock and roll on Thursday nights, there was no question she was going to go. "Oscar Wilde said, 'I can resist everything except temptation,'" she explained, "and I thought, 'A Bulgarian bar! I have to go there!'"[34] Her capacity for enjoying certain aspects of pop culture remained strong to the end. She wrote a short piece for the booklet of Patti Smith's greatest hits collection *Land* (2002) and also composed a text for the anti-Bush song "We Need a War" for the album *Odyssey* (2005) by the Brooklyn electroclash duo Fischerspooner, whose music blended techno, punk, and synthesizer pop. Sontag nonchalantly recommended the movie *Toy Story 2* (1999), saying it had more to say about American suburban life than the highly praised *American Beauty* (1999).[35] When she found the Italian translation of *The Volcano Lover* unsatisfactory and demanded a different translator, the publisher sent her Paolo Dilonardo, who had already translated a number of her books. He told *The Guardian*, "We worked on the book together word by word . . . She loves language. She can discuss the meaning of just one word for hours."[36] Sontag and Dilonardo became close friends while working together on the translation. Many describe him as one of her closest companions in the last years of her life. They got along so well together that Dilonardo moved into her penthouse.[37]

According to Klaus Biesenbach, Sontag was especially interested in media artists such as Doug Aitken, Jeff Wall, and Douglas Gordon. They would look at new works together and then meet the artists.[38] Sontag introduced Biesenbach to colleagues from her generation, while he introduced her to such artists as Matthew Barney, Andreas Gursky, and Sasha Waltz in New York or Berlin. Sontag was always completely focused and spoke with great discrimination and seriousness. Her openness was a genuine part of her personality, whether she was talking to a cabbie on her way home from a party or with a trainee in the Kunst-Werke Institute for Contemporary Art in Berlin.[39]

Sontag met the performance artist Marina Abramović, originally from Yugoslavia, at a party with Klaus Biesenbach, Björk, and Matthew Barney. Abramović vividly recalls the writer's detailed knowledge of contemporary art, especially her enormous powers of perception. They often sat in Sontag's kitchen and talked until the wee hours about art and their experiences in the former Yugoslavia. "I always felt that I was too much for the other people around me," says Abramović, "and finally I had found someone who was too much for me!"[40]

When Bei Ling, the Chinese poet and editor, was arrested during a visit to China in August 2000 for his criticism of the regime, Susan pulled all the strings at her disposal to get him released. She spread the news of Ling's imprisonment to writers she knew all over the world, including the Nobel laureates Czesław Miłosz, Günter Grass, and Nadine Gordimer. She also initiated an open letter of protest from the American PEN

Center to the Chinese president, wrote a call to action for the editorial page of the *New York Times,* called up the office of Bill Clinton, and spoke personally with Secretary of State Madeleine Albright. In the face of public and political pressure, Ling was released after two weeks in prison.

Sontag's literary reputation had received a stamp of approval with the National Book Award for *In America.* In 2000 and 2001, Sontag proceeded to collect and revise articles and speeches from the previous two decades for the volume *Where the Stress Falls,* which appeared in the latter year. With her usual verve, she was also planning new projects such as a volume of her recent essays and speeches on literature, a new novel set in Japan, a collection of short stories, and a third autobiographical book about her illness.[41] But as she admitted herself, she still had too little discipline to write on a regular schedule. Instead she worked in intense bursts of activity. With an unconvincing breeziness she told *The Guardian* in January 2002, "I don't feel the need to write every day or even every week. But when I get started on something I just sit for 18 hours and suddenly realise that I have to pee. Many days I start in the morning and suddenly it's dark and I haven't gotten up. It's very bad for the knees."[42]

But these bursts of energy lasted only a short time. The difficulties Sontag encountered in trying to write were the source of a significant problem, since her need to ensure an ideal legacy had grown stronger after her second bout with cancer. As David Rieff writes in his foreword to the posthumous collection of her essays *At the Same Time* (2007), his mother was one of the authors "who assuage themselves about mortality . . . with at least the fantasy that their work would outlive them."[43] That this fantasy could also easily turn into frustration is audible in Sontag's frequent complaint that she had not succeeded in being as productive as other writers of her generation such as Philip Roth, John Updike, or Joyce Carol Oates. "I am not a full-time writer, I never have been, I never will be . . . I go months without writing, and then I'm just wandering around, or dreaming, or going someplace, or looking at something . . . I get restless, I want to go out."[44]

In the fall of 2000, Carl Rollyson and Lisa Paddock published an unauthorized and unsympathetic biography that represented an additional threat to the legacy Sontag hoped for. As Lucinda Childs and Terry Castle report, Sontag was furious at the two authors, who had been shadowing her for several years. Their neoconservative views compounded the personal and political animosity that pervades the biography.[45] Sontag persuaded most of her friends and acquaintances not to speak to Rollyson and Paddock, but despite help from lawyers working for Andrew Wylie and FSG, she was unable to prevent W. W. Norton and Company from publishing *Susan Sontag: The Making of an Icon*. In its press releases, she is described as the "Sibyl of Manhattan."

But Sontag had always had aspects of the enfant terrible and the diva. The biography hardly did any permanent damage to her reputation. On the contrary, that reputation continued to grow in the following years as the writer was awarded a series of important international literary prizes. In May 2001, she received the Jerusalem Prize at the Jerusalem International Book Fair. The prize committee lauded Sontag as one of the most important contemporary writers and compared her to Simone de Beauvoir, Jorge Luis Borges, J. M. Coetzee, and Jorge Semprún.

For Sontag, however, the pleasure at this recognition was not entirely unalloyed. The jury that awarded the prize was chaired by Israel's then foreign minister Shimon Peres, and Ehud Olmert, the mayor of Jerusalem, presented the prize. Both were aggressive advocates of Israel's settlement policy. American and Israeli leftists took Sontag's acceptance of the prize as indirect support for that policy.[46] With considerable tact, Sontag ventured onto this difficult political terrain in her speech "The Conscience of Words." She managed to take a firm stand on the Israeli-Palestinian conflict and criticize Israel while avoiding a direct affront to her hosts. To be sure, she based her critique not on her political convictions but on her role as a writer. For that role, she said, involved an ethics of responsibility that could not be more at odds with the predigested opinions of the mass media. "I . . . believe that there can be no peace here until the planting of Israeli communities in the Territories is halted . . . I say this . . . as a matter of honor. The honor of literature . . . The wisdom of literature is quite antithetical to having opinions . . . What writers do should free us up, shake us up. Open avenues of compassion and new interests. Remind us . . . that we can change."[47]

Many of those present agreed wholeheartedly with those sentiments. There was much applause, especially from the American contingent in the audience. Others left the hall or, like Ehud Olmert, sat in silence.[48]

In addition to working on her Jerusalem speech and preparing the essay collection *Where the Stress Falls,* Sontag devoted herself to other, smaller projects in 2000 and 2001, for instance, the largely forgotten Russian-Jewish writer Leonid Tsypkin (1926–1982). In the early nineties, Sontag had stumbled upon Tsypkin's novel *Summer in Baden-Baden* (1981) in an antiquarian bookstore in London and found it to be "among the most beautiful, exalting, and original achievements of a century's worth of fiction and para-fiction."[49] She began to research Tsypkin's life and became friends with his son Mikhail, who had immigrated to the United States from the Soviet Union in 1977. She also persuaded New Directions to issue a new edition of the novel, for which she wrote an enthusiastic foreword that also appeared in the *New Yorker.* It won Tsypkin a considerable number of readers in America and resulted in translations into several European languages.

Where the Stress Falls, Sontag's first essay collection in twenty years, appeared in the fall of 2001 and received mostly favorable reviews in America. One can sense in some of them a nostalgic relief at regaining an intellectual and writer who represented the American scene, writing again with her old passion and cultural engagement. At the same time, most reviewers harked back to her earlier, now legendary essays. For *Newsday,*

Sontag was one of those highly gifted authors "who is interested in everything."[50] The *Los Angeles Times* celebrated her as a fresh, mutable spirit that "creates arguments in progress, not holy writ. If she has written herself into a dead-end . . . she finds the energy to write herself back out."[51] The lack of any serious discussion of the essays in *Where the Stress Falls* is a result of the fact that most of them do not approach the dense complexity of her earlier work. From her articles on dance from the eighties through speeches, catalog entries, and afterwords (some written mainly out of financial need), to her forewords for Sebald, de Assis, and Rulfo from the late nineties, many of the pieces in the volume have a cursory character. The collection has little thematic unity and lacks the visionary dimension evident in Sontag's other volumes of essays. There were disparaging reviews in the *Washington Post* and the *New York Times*, critical of the book's pompous and missionary tone that often rose to "thundering announcements of the obvious or dubious . . . While *Where the Stress Falls* won't do much to enhance her stature as a thinker, never before has she made such large claims for her moral pre-eminence, her exemplary fulfillment of the intellectual's mission as society's conscience. In effect, she's the first person in a long while to nominate herself so publicly for sainthood."[52]

The Pain of Others

(2001–2004)

*All memory is individual,
unreproducible—it dies with each
person. What is called collective
memory is not a remembering but
a stipulating: that this is important,
and this is the story about how it
happened, with the pictures that
lock the story in our minds.*

Susan Sontag, *Regarding the Pain of
Others* (2003)

In January 2002, Susan Sontag signed a contract to sell her
10,000-volume library as well as her correspondence and manuscripts to the University of California at Los Angeles for $1.1
million.[1] It was the highest sum yet paid for the archives of an
author. Sontag stipulated that most of her unpublished manuscripts remain sealed for five years after her death. Originally she
had wanted to sell her papers to the New York Public Library,
but she was at least happy to also have a personal connection
to the place where her legacy would be housed and available
to the public.[2] The journey of her life seemed to be returning to
its starting point: Los Angeles, where Sontag's worship of high

culture had begun. The record sum paid by UCLA suggested that she herself had now entered the Olympus of the intellect.

Like a retrospective for a living visual artist, the sale of a writer's papers often marks the beginning of a gradual retreat from active production and withdrawal from the public eye. Not so for Sontag. The coming years would bring one more period of intense creativity and catapult the author again into the center of international media attention as a political provocateur.

On September 11, 2001, Susan Sontag was in Germany as a "distinguished visitor" at the American Academy in Berlin, a meeting place for German and American artists, writers, intellectuals, and politicians. She was there to give the first in a series of lectures by famous speakers. Thus, like most people all over the world, Sontag followed the events unfolding in her hometown on television, although she did not even possess a set back home. Now she sat transfixed before the screen in her room in the Hotel Adlon, watching replays of the attacks that killed almost 3,000 people and marked the beginning of the Bush administration's controversial War on Terror and the run-up to the war in Iraq. The telephone in her room rang almost continually with calls from journalists wanting her reaction. Harald Fricke reported in *Die Tageszeitung* how annoyed Sontag was by these attempts to exploit her "as an opinion machine." Nevertheless, she did not let annoyance stop her from writing a short piece for the *New Yorker* and sending it to the editor David Remnick.[3]

Almost a hundred people had gathered for her appearance at the American Academy, where she was to have read from her novel *In America*. Many now expected to hear Sontag's position on the September 11 attacks. "I'm not going to say anything," she declared at first, but then she took out the piece she had written for the *New Yorker* and proceeded to read it.[4] She seemed a bit uncomfortable as she stood at the lectern. The text, she conceded, "is not very polished linguistically. It moralizes. Perhaps it goes too far and exaggerates."[5] When she finished reading it, the audience sat in stunned silence.[6] The angry polemic "Feige waren die Mörder nicht" (The Murderers Were No Cowards) was published

in German translation in the *Frankfurter Allgemeine Zeitung*; a
shorter, untitled version appeared in the *New Yorker*'s "Talk of
the Town" section on September 24. Since its "monstrous dose
of reality" on September 11, America had "never been further
removed from reality."[7] She attacked the "self-righteous drivel and
outright deceptions" in the reactions of the press and politicians
and bemoaned the absence of discussion worthy of a democracy.
"The unanimity of the sanctimonious, reality-concealing rhetoric spouted by American officials and media commentators"
reminded her of "the unanimously applauded, self-congratulatory
bromides of a Soviet Party Congress."[8] She reserved her sharpest
criticism for the banal rhetoric concerning the cowardliness of
the terrorists that was a common thread through most American commentary. "Where is the acknowledgment that this was
not a 'cowardly' attack on 'civilization' or 'humanity' or 'the free
world' but an attack on the world's self-proclaimed superpower,
undertaken as a consequence of specific American alliances and
actions? . . . And if the word 'cowardly' is to be used, it might be
more aptly applied to those who kill from beyond the range of
retaliation, high in the sky, than to those willing to die themselves
in order to kill others."[9]

Moreover, Sontag demanded a reckoning with the failures of
American intelligence and policy in the Middle East and pleaded
for a serious discussion of the traumatic events. "Let's by all
means grieve together. But let's not be stupid together"[10] was one
of her much-quoted conclusions. The piece represents the credo
of an intellectual reflecting on America's imperialistic rhetoric,
from Pearl Harbor through the McCarthy era and the Cold War
to the Vietnam War and beyond, who discerns in the fundamen-
talist and conservative posture of the Bush administration an
echo of this ambivalent past.

Today, a decade after September 11 and the administration that employed exactly the kind of "cowboy rhetoric"[11] she
deplored, it is hard to imagine the worldwide scandal Sontag's
short text ignited when it appeared so soon after the events

in question. But in September 2001, her polemic stirred up an emotional reaction even among liberal Americans. The shorter version in the *New Yorker* made an even more condensed and furious impression than the longer version in the *Frankfurter Allgemeine Zeitung.* Significantly, the former left out the opening phrase in which Sontag declares herself an "appalled, sad American, and New Yorker."[12]

Many educated Americans took Sontag's suggestion of a connection between the terrorist attacks and American foreign policy as an grievous insult. That does not seem surprising in view of the fact that in the weeks after the attack, more than ninety percent of Americans stood behind the policy of the Bush administration Sontag so sharply attacked. Even most liberal New Yorkers, who actually sympathized with her position, could not suppress their indignation at Sontag's angry polemic, so great was their shock at the event and their pain and grief at the loss of friends and relatives. Sontag's geographic distance from the overwhelming reality of the terrible events was too inscribed in the text. Precisely the author who put so much stock in a politics of eyewitness testimony had, in her accidental distance from the event, made statements that did not sound like those of a longtime resident of the city. It is likely that Sontag would have written a different commentary had she heard the deafening sound of the Twin Towers collapsing, seen the masses of dust-covered, bewildered people fleeing through the streets, or smelled the pervasive stench that lingered for days.

The *New Yorker* received innumerable letters of protest against Sontag's commentary.[13] Sontag herself received hate mail and some death threats.[14] Even some people in Europe condemned Sontag's remarks as "shrill tones," "furious tirades," and "self-righteousness bordering on hysteria."[15] In America, such characterizations were among the milder reactions. Since her political engagement in the sixties, Sontag had lost nothing of her provocativeness for such neoconservative publications as the *Washington Times,* the *New York Post,* the *Weekly Standard,* and the *National Review,* and now they made her into a symbol of the "anti American Left" or the "leftist bombers" and branded her as a "traitor" and a "moral idiot." In several issues, the *Weekly Standard* awarded a "Susan Sontag Certificate [in] recognition of particular inanity by intellectuals and artists in the wake of the terrorist attacks."[16] The conservative blogger Andrew Sullivan founded a similar weekly Susan Sontag Award. Even moderate newspapers and magazines, including the *Washington Post* and the *New Republic*, accused Sontag of "moral obtuseness"[17] or began articles with the question, "What do Osama bin Laden, Saddam Hussein, and Susan Sontag have in common?" (The answer, according to the editor in chief of the *New Republic,* is the idea that the terrorist attacks can be traced back to America's foreign policy).[18]

Sontag was not the only critic of the administration who elicited such a fierce reaction. In the United States, a political and media climate had suddenly sprung up that would nearly smother the liberal democratic spirit. The Bush administration's press secretary Ari Fleischer issued an unmistakable warning at a White House press conference: "People have to watch what they say and watch what they do."[19] When Bill Maher made a similar remark on his talk show *Politically Incorrect* to the effect that you could not call the terrorists "cowards," he lost several sponsors and was dismissed from ABC despite apologies and clarifications. Newspaper editors in Texas and Oregon apologized that some of their columnists had criticized the president. One columnist was fired because of his anti-Bush statements.[20]

After catching the first flight back to New York from Berlin, Sontag had a taxi drive her as near as possible to the stinking and still smoldering mass grave that was the former World Trade Center, and she wandered around the neighborhood for half an hour.[21] Two weeks later, Annie Leibovitz, awaiting her first child at the age of fifty one, managed to get permission for herself and Sontag to enter the site of the catastrophe.[22] Much later, Sontag told an Italian journalist that only then did she grasp "the reality of the destruction and the enormous number of victims," which "fundamentally changed her view of the event."[23]

Although Sontag never explicitly distanced herself from her text about September 11,[24] in several interviews in American magazines and TV shows she did take the opportunity to comment on it. Even though she called her comments "clarifications," some of them were essentially self-corrections. In an interview on *Salon.com*, for example, she defended herself against the absurd demonization of her personally in the conservative media. "I am aware of what a radical point of view is," she explained. "Very occasionally I have espoused one. But I did not think for a moment my essay was radical or even particularly dissenting. It seemed very common sense."[25] She was particularly eager to clarify that she did not believe the terror attacks were "the pursuit of legitimate grievances by illegitimate means."[26] But she did not explain how this statement squared with her standpoint that they were "a consequence of specific American alliances and actions."[27] She elaborated her point of view with her accustomed straightforwardness. She would be happy if the "Islamic fascism" of the Taliban regime in Afghanistan were overthrown but wished this could be done without the usual American bombing of civilians. She also stated that a political about-face by America and Israel with regard to the occupied territories would do little to stop terror by Islamic fundamentalists. "If tomorrow Israel announced a unilateral withdrawal of its forces from the West Bank and the Gaza strip . . . followed by the proclamation of a Palestinian state, I don't believe it would make a dent in the forces that are supporting bin Laden's al-Qaida."[28]

These interviews show Sontag returning to her old political form. In numerous subsequent speeches, lectures, and interviews in both the United States and Europe, she establishes a profile as one of the smartest and best-informed critics of neoconservative America under the Bush administration. She mocked the Republicans' ideal of unquestioning patriotism,[29] agitated passionately for critical media, and advocated wide public availability of sources of information other than television, including foreign newspapers and Internet blogs.[30] At a time when much of the American public was behind Bush's war on terror, she pilloried the voluntary self-censorship of the media as a threat to American democracy and attacked the new concept of the war on terror as a "war with no foreseeable end," unmasking it as a metaphor "with powerful consequences."[31] She sharply opposed the diminution of civil rights introduced by the Patriot Act, such as the easing of restrictions on wiretaps and the loosening of bank confidentiality, and attacked the administration's break with the rules of diplomacy: "There are no endless wars. But there are declarations of the extension of power by a state that believes it cannot be challenged."[32]

As the United States invasion of Iraq became increasingly likely, Sontag argued vehemently against it, not only because she did not believe the Bush administration's claim about weapons of mass destruction but also to raise a warning that the Middle East could be plunged into a long civil war between Sunnis, Shiites, and Kurds.[33] These were the opinions not only of the majority of Europeans but also of a great number of East Coast intellectuals, but very few Americans espoused them as early and as openly as Susan Sontag. Even liberal newspapers such as the *New York Times* and the *Los Angeles Times* shrank from critical reporting on account of the state of war. Moreover, Sontag was coming much closer than she had in Jerusalem or right after September 11 to her self-proclaimed goal of not simply expressing opinions. Her arguments were on an ethical level far above the opinion-mongering on CNN, Fox News, or in the political columns of the daily papers. Not that her arguments were not partisan, but they raised basic questions supported by her deep knowledge of cultural history: Why does American foreign policy always assume that a foreign human life is worth less than an American one? In our concepts of war, why do we always have a blind spot for the civilians who are its real victims?[34] For many U.S. leftists, Sontag represented the conscience of America in those years.

One of the basic facts of contemporary life in the First World is that we experience war only by way of images. Every modern war

produces iconic photographs that become an inextinguishable
component of our cultural memory: the pictures of Auschwitz
and Bergen-Belsen taken by the Allies at the end of the Second
World War, the picture of the nine-year-old Kim Phúc fleeing
naked and screaming from a napalm attack during the Vietnam
War, the torture snapshots from Abu Ghraib. Sontag had given
an Amnesty International lecture at the University of Oxford in
February 2001, seven months before the attacks of September
11, in which she addressed the photographic representation of
war, a topic that had occupied her since, as a twelve-year-old
Jewish girl in California, she had first seen pictures of the victims
of Nazi concentration camps. Prompted by the media coverage
of the September 11 attacks and the subsequent war in Afghanistan, she now returned to this theme. Since the resulting book
Regarding the Pain of Others (a shorter version of which had
appeared in December 2002 in the *New Yorker*) was published
in March 2003, simultaneous with the start of the Iraq War, Sontag's thoughts were more relevant than ever.

Regarding the Pain of Others was Sontag's final return to
the essay, her signature genre. The central theme of the book is
the role war photography plays in the civilian understanding of
military force and its human "costs." In a certain sense, it can be
seen as the continuation and revision of her essay *On Photography,* written thirty years before. If then she was still stressing
the comprehensive logic of the world of images, in the new essay
she sets out to "return to the real," and it is no accident that
she includes recollections of, and commentaries on, her time in
Sarajevo. The essay is a treatise devoted equally to photography and war. Sontag discusses the catalog of famous war photos
that have entered our collective memory. She describes both the
history of their reception and their origins: some were posed,
thus violating the authenticity especially associated with war
photography. She analyzes notions of "good taste" that prohibit
the printing or display of American war dead, while the bodies of enemy dead, in an old colonial impulse, are present in all
the media. With reference to Virginia Woolf's 1938 book-length

essay *Three Guineas,* she thinks about the shock value of war photographs, to which the only possible answer for Woolf was pacifism. Sontag disagrees. For her, images have no unequivocal messages. They are not stories, so the way they are read depends on the context in which they occur and whether narratives about them already exist.

If the tone of Sontag's earlier essays was characterized by fondness for aphorisms and eruptions of passion, the voice in the new volume is that of a seasoned intellectual. Sontag raises questions, poses argument against argument, and is not in a hurry to give definitive answers. Especially the most fleeting and complicated ideas are approached calmly and examined from all sides, so that instead of confronting readers with grand assertions, she lets her thoughts seep into deeper levels of their consciousness.

Since the appearance of *On Photography,* some of Sontag's ideas about the medium had become commonplaces of journalism and academic discourse, and she uses *Regarding the Pain of Others* to revisit them. The earlier volume had asserted that, while events like wars are made more "real" by photos, the viewer becomes dulled by oversaturation. It was in this sense that her call for an "ecology of images" was to be understood. Now, a much more detached Sontag writes, "There isn't going to be an ecology of images. No Committee of Guardians is going to ration horror, to keep fresh its ability to shock. And the horrors themselves are not going to abate."[35] The horror of war really exists, she writes; it is not a simulation on a TV screen. And photographic representations of war are the only way most civilians in the West can imagine what it is like. Sontag undertakes a broad survey of graphic representations of war from the Crimean War through both world wars and the Spanish Civil War to the Vietnam War and points out that journalistic war photos have a different status than violent scenes in popular entertainment—the former are capable of eliciting compassion. For Sontag, it is this characteristic of war photos that makes them into witnesses. Although they cannot help us to understand the horror of war,

Sontag expresses the cautious hope that they enable us to think about war and act accordingly.

With the exception of the *New York Times*'s Michiko Kakutani, who criticized Sontag's revisionist tone of "Delphic wisdom,"[36] the reaction of the serious American press was almost unanimously favorable. *Newsday* celebrated *Regarding the Pain of Others* as a "genuine return to the source of the energy driving Sontag's critical prose from the 1960s and '70s."[37] For the *Washington Post,* the book provided a welcome guide to the pictures that were to be expected from the war in Iraq.[38] The *Los Angeles Times* noted Sontag's strength in "firing devastating questions and providing no answers for shelter."[39]

Susan Sontag's return to cultural criticism was also the cause of her increasing popularity in Europe. France, Germany, and Russia had already expressed clear reservations about the military plans of the Bush administration in the run-up to the Iraq War. Once the intervention began, their criticism grew into the most serious transatlantic disagreement since the Second World War. Even in America's official coalition partners, including Great Britain, Spain, and Poland, the almost universal opposition to the war in the media ran the gamut from pure incomprehension of U.S. policy to outright anti-Americanism. Against that background, Sontag seemed more than ever like the most European of American writers. During sojourns in Berlin, Paris, and London in those years, she was often called upon to comment as a critical intellectual who could clarify American opinion. If her stance against the Iraq War was a minority view in America, it was the majority view in Europe. "A figure that had begun to disappear with the fall of the Soviet Union and the Eastern Bloc," wrote the influential Munich daily *Süddeutsche Zeitung,* "seemed to have returned in the person of the American Susan Sontag: the intellectual as dissident."[40]

When Sontag was awarded one of Germany's most prestigious literary prizes in October 2003, the Peace Prize of the German Book Trade, it was therefore taken primarily as a political signal in both Germany and America. In its statement, the foundation council for the prize (which included influential publishers, writers, jurists, and politicians) confirmed that impression. Sontag, they declared, had "never lost sight of the European legacy" and had become "one of the most prominent intellectual ambassadors between our two continents." With a subtle and very German sideswipe at the American administration's unilateral policy, they continued, "In a world of falsified images and mutilated truths, she is a voice for the dignity of free thought."[41]

Despite the objections of conservative German politicians and the absence of the American ambassador Dan Coats, the German chancellor Gerhard Schröder, and the foreign minister Joschka Fischer, there was no scandal at the awards ceremony in October 2003 in Frankfurt.[42] Ivan Nagel, a close friend of Sontag's, made impressive laudatory remarks highlighting aspects of her work in which she reflects on war. Her contradictory, neither purely pacifist nor strongly bellicose judgments of the wars in Vietnam, Israel, Bosnia, and Iraq seemed to Nagel in retrospect "sober and clear, even prophetic." Nagel summarized his observations on the contradictions in Sontag's work by saying, "To be complete . . . is to have often changed." Even his remark that "the dominion over peoples, armies, and companies has been transferred into the hands of men who have never known war," and for whom it is therefore easy "to unleash atrocities,"[43] did not lend itself easily to the reflex critique of America among European intellectuals at the time.

Nor did Sontag's speech of thanks contain any anti-American forays. On the contrary, her wise, rhetorically polished performance was supported "by the basic vocabulary of reconciliation," according to Christoph Schröder in the *Frankfurter Rundschau*.[44] Titled "Literature Is Freedom," her talk submits the "latent antagonism between Europe and America"[45] to a critical reading in which, with reference to Alexis de Tocqueville and D. H. Lawrence, she makes it clear that transatlantic irritations were always more the rule than the exception. Popular stereotypes about the differences between the continents were not only leitmotifs of nineteenth-century American literature but also the general observations of European travelers in America. For Sontag, these stereotypes come down to a fundamental opposition between "old" Europe and "new" America. Referring to Donald Rumsfeld's mocking distinction between "Old" and "New" Europe, she noted that America reserved to itself the right to decide what is "new" in its choice of allies. Even if Sontag can see no solution for this antagonism "in the immediate future,"[46] she does see a chance for reconciliation. And here is where she sees literature playing a part. After all, it is capable of developing countermyths. Writers, says Sontag, can counter the clichés of difference by providing experiences "that confound what you thought you thought, or felt, or believed."[47] She ended the speech with a lovely anecdote about her girlhood in Arizona. She said that reading the classics of German literature saved her, even while at night she had nightmares about Nazi soldiers coming to get her. Only a few hundred miles away, her future German editor Fritz Arnold sat in a prisoner-of-war camp and got through his imprisonment by reading the classics of American and English literature. For both of them, literature meant an escape from the "prison of national vanity, of philistinism, of compulsory provincialism."[48] For both, she said, literature meant freedom.

The Peace Prize of the German Book Trade was by no means the last honor accorded to Susan Sontag. Only two weeks later, she received the Prince of Asturias Award for Literature in the Spanish provincial capital of Oviedo, and she entertained hopes of winning the Nobel Prize as well. Shortly before her death, she told her agent Andrew Wylie that she consoled herself that Borges did not get the Nobel Prize either.[49] The prizes she received in her final years were supplemented by honorary doctorates and invitations to give prestigious lectures. She gave the speech honoring Ishai Menuchin, executive director of the human rights organization Public Committee Against Torture in Israel, in the

Rothko Chapel in Houston when he received the Oscar Romero Award for Human Rights in May 2003. Sontag also delivered the St. Jerome Lecture on Literary Translation (since renamed the Sebald Lecture) in Queen Elizabeth Hall in London in June 2003, and the first Nadine Gordimer Lecture in Cape Town and Johannesburg, South Africa, in March 2004.

Sontag used these prize speeches and lectures above all to articulate her understanding of literature and the task of the writer as a critical intellect. Her numerous forewords—which had become a Sontag tradition—fulfilled the same function. She wrote the introductions for the American editions or republications of the letters of Boris Pasternak, Marina Tsvetaeva, and Rainer Maria Rilke; for the novels *Artemisia* (1947) by the Italian writer Anna Banti; *The Case of Comrade Tulayev* (1967) by the nearly forgotten Russian-French author Victor Serge; and *Under the Glacier* (1968) by the Icelandic Nobel laureate Haldór Laxness. In these texts, Sontag's understanding of literature took on almost religious overtones. For her, Rilke, Tsvetaeva, and Pasternak were "a god and two worshippers, who are also worshippers of each other (and who we, the readers of their letters, know to be future gods)."[50] She describes Banti's *Artemisia* as "a phoenix of a book, written out of the ashes of another book."[51] And in the revolutionary Communist and anti-Stalinist Serge, she finds "the truth of fiction" that displaces historic contradictions and everyday cruelties "with a healing openness to everything finite and cosmic,"[52] while Laxness's *Under the Glacier* is an example of "mystifying wisdom."[53] In her St. Jerome Lecture, Sontag even speaks of an "evangelical incentive" for translating world literature.[54] In unconcealed hope of salvation, she argues that "one function of literature—of important literature, of necessary literature—is to be prophetic."[55] After all, "the chief glory of every people arises from its authors."[56]

Such unfashionable declarations of literature's promise of salvation reflect the original desire Sontag associated with reading from earliest childhood. To be a good writer, she said in 2004, you should have been born in a time "when it was likely that you would be definitively exalted and influenced by Dostoyevsky, and Tolstoy, and Turgenev, and Chekhov."[57] It is the prophetic character of these literary elective affinities that Sontag discerns in all the narratives of world literature and that she aims to marshal against the interchangeable, recyclable narratives of the age of television. For Sontag in her final years and months, literature is not only a space of fundamental freedom but also a prophetic space for radical social responsibility. This quasi-religious impulse would also become the principal theme of the last volume of essays she was planning during 2003 and 2004. *At the Same Time* appeared posthumously in March 2007 and is a sometimes desperate-sounding plea for the kind of social engagement on the part of the writer that had almost completely fallen from fashion. In addition to the already mentioned forewords and lectures, this final collection also contains her acceptance speeches for the German Peace Prize and the Jerusalem Prize, as well as her controversial article on September 11. The book is the culmination of the original impulse toward high culture with which she was able to survive a chaotic childhood and which she now wanted to rescue from its threatened loss of social relevance.

In early March 2004, Nadine Gordimer persuaded Susan Sontag to come with her on a short vacation to a country house in the South African bush. Shortly after Sontag returned to New York, she noticed she had a number of mysterious bruises. She knew right away that it was a bad sign.[58] By the time she met Jeff Seroy at the Brooklyn Academy of Music for a production of Shakespeare's *Midsummer Night's Dream,* she already had the diagnosis in hand. She had myelodysplastic syndrome, a precursor of acute leukemia, probably caused by the radiation therapy she had received during her first bout with cancer. Sontag needed tranquilizers to control her panic attacks. She was devastated and told Seroy, "This is Armageddon."[59]

Sontag's final journey lasted nine and a half months. Presented with the alternatives of a treatment that would enable her to spend her last months in relative comfort versus a bone marrow transplant that was her only chance for survival, Sontag chose the latter despite a small likelihood of success. "I am not interested in quality of life!" she declared to Dr. Stephen Nimer, who was treating her at the Memorial Sloan-Kettering Cancer Center in Manhattan.[60] In tears, she told Andrew Wylie that she had no other choice: "There are still so many things I have to do, I'll never be able to forgive myself if I don't do them."[61]

David Rieff remembers how hopeful his mother was after she had decided to undergo the bone marrow transplant; her panic attacks grew less frequent.[62] She even began to work again and in May wrote an impressively cogent essay on the torture photographs from Abu Ghraib for the *New York Times Magazine*. "The photographs are us," she wrote, as if it were self-evident.[63]

But the hopeful interval proved to be relatively short. After Sontag had recovered from a serious infection that almost cost her life, she set off for the Fred Hutchinson Cancer Research Center in Seattle, the best address for transplantation therapy. Annie Leibovitz borrowed a private plane from a friend to fly Sontag to Seattle.[64]

Susan Sontag did not foresee how brutal the aftermath of the failed transplant therapy would be. In his essay on his mother's final illness, David Rieff describes in depressing detail how shocked Sontag was at her body's rejection of the transplant and the return of the leukemia. She was badly shaken and screamed out that this meant she was going to die for sure.[65] With a picturesque view of Lake Union and Mount Rainier outside her window, Susan Sontag was racked with pain. In the last photos Annie Leibovitz took of her friend, Sontag—unconscious and bloated from the medications—is no longer recognizable. The long hair she had continued to dye black until the end of her life has been replaced by a white, closely cropped hospital cut. Surrounded by medical apparatus, she seems to be inhabiting the narrow borderland between total exhaustion and death. With her camera, Leibovitz documented Sontag's private war against cancer, a war she lost. The result was photographs that many of Sontag's friends and acquaintances found shocking since it was obvious that Sontag herself was no longer capable of giving her approval for them. Their eventual publication in *A Photographer's Life* was a complicated question of conscience for Leibovitz. In the end, the feeling that the enlightened and aesthetically demanding Sontag "would be championing this work" outweighed her doubts.[66]

Annie Leibovitz saw to it that Sontag was flown back to Sloan-Kettering in Manhattan. Dr. Stephen Nimer attempted a final experimental treatment that had helped a few leukemia patients. But Sontag's case was hopeless. She spent her final weeks in semiconsciousness, hardly able to communicate. On the morning of December 28, 2004, Susan Sontag died, surrounded by her son and her closest friends. "And her death was easy, as deaths go, in the sense that she was in little pain and little visible anguish," wrote her son, David Rieff. "She simply went."[67]

Prologue

1. Marina Abramović, interview with the author on March 8, 2007; Michael Krüger, "Ah, Susan! Toujours fidèle" [Ah, Susan! Faithful as Always], *Frankfurter Allgemeine Sonntagszeitung* (January 1, 2006); Joseph Hanimann, "Verpasstes Rendezvous; Pariser Gedenktopographie" [Missed Rendezvous: Paris Memorial Topography], *Frankfurter Allgemeine Zeitung* (January 19, 2005).

2. Lothar Müller, "An den Abgründen der Oberfläche" [At the Depths of the Surface], *Süddeutsche Zeitung* (December 30, 2004).

3. Henning Ritter, "Sie kam, sah und schrieb . . . Zum Tode von Susan Sontag" [She Came, Saw, and Wrote . . . On the Death of Susan Sontag], *Frankfurter Allgemeine Zeitung* (December 20, 2004).

4. Margalit Fox, "Susan Sontag, Social Critic with Verve, Dies at 71." *New York Times* (December 28, 2004).

5. Ibid.

Memories of a So-Called Childhood

1. Chapter epigraph is from a 1987 interview with Marithelma Costa and Adelaida López first published in Spanish as "Susan Sontag o la pasion por las palabras" and translated by Kathy Leonard as "Susan Sontag: The Passion for Words," in *Conversations with Susan Sontag*, edited by Leland Poague (Jackson: University Press of Mississippi, 1995), 222–36.

2. David Rieff, interview with the author. In "Pilgrimage" Sontag portrays her visit to Thomas Mann as having taken place while she was still a high-school student. In fact, her journal entry of December 29, 1949 (published after the German-language original of the present biography) makes clear that she visited the German novelist after having spent the 1949 spring semester at Berkeley and the fall semester at the University of Chicago. Cf. Susan Sontag, *Reborn: Journals and Notebooks, 1947–1963*, ed. by David Rieff (New York: Farrar, Straus and Giroux, 2008), 57–61.

3. Sontag, *I, etcetera* (New York: Farrar, Straus and Giroux, 1978), 13. In an interview with Geoffrey Movius, Sontag declared, "Some recent stories, such as 'Project for a Trip to China' in the April 1973 *Atlantic Monthly*, do draw on my own life" (Poague, *Conversations with Susan Sontag*, 49–50).

4. Sontag, "Pilgrimage," *New Yorker* (December 21, 1987), 38.

5. Edward Hirsch, "Susan Sontag: The Art of Fiction No. 143," *Paris Review*, no. 137 (Winter 1995).

6. Lucinda Childs, interview with the author on April 13, 2007.

7. Ellen Hopkins, "Susan Sontag Lightens Up," *Los Angeles Times Magazine* (August 16, 1992).

8. See Carl Rollyson and Lisa Paddock, *Susan Sontag: The Making of an Icon* (New York: Norton, 2000), 4.

9. Hopkins, "Susan Sontag Lightens Up."

10. Rollyson and Paddock, *Susan Sontag: The Making of an Icon,* 4. Rollyson and Paddock have consulted the official documents but do not point out the obvious contradiction between them and Sontag's later statements.

11. Sontag, *I, etcetera,* 17.

12. Joan Acocella, "The Hunger Artist," *New Yorker* (March 6, 2000), 72.

13. Poague, *Conversations with Susan Sontag,* 53.

14. Marta Kijowska, "Die Wohltäterin" [The Benefactor], *Frankfurter Allgemeine Zeitung* (January 4, 2004).

15. David Rieff, *Going to Miami: Exiles, Tourists, and Refugees in the New America,* (Boston: Little, Brown, 1987), 4.

16. Poague, *Conversations with Susan Sontag,* 134.

17. Andrew Wylie, interview with the author on March 20, 2007.

18. Hirsch, "Susan Sontag: The Art of Fiction," 182.

19. Eve Curie, *Madame Curie: A Biography,* trans. by Vincent Sheean (Cambridge, Mass.: Da Capo, 2001).

20. "In Depth with Susan Sontag," interview on C-SPAN, March 2, 2003.

21. Zoë Heller, "The Life of a Head Girl," *The Independent* (London) (September 20, 1992): 10ff.

22. Sontag, "Pilgrimage," 39.

23. Hirsch, "Susan Sontag: The Art of Fiction," 182.

24. Ron Grossman, "At the C Shop with Susan Sontag," *Chicago Tribune* (December 1, 1992): S1–2.

25. Hirsch, "Susan Sontag: The Art of Fiction," 183.

26. Sontag, *I, etcetera,* 6.

27. Sontag, "Pilgrimage," 38.

28. Annie Leibovitz, *A Photographer's Life, 1990–2005* (New York: Random House, 2006).

29. Ibid.

30. Sontag, *Where the Stress Falls* (New York: Farrar, Straus and Giroux, 2001), 256.

31. Ibid, 255.

32. Hirsch, "Susan Sontag: The Art of Fiction," 179.

33. Poague, *Conversations with Susan Sontag,* 121.

34. Ibid., 215.

35. Ibid., 222.

36. Leslie Garis, "Susan Sontag Finds Romance," *New York Times Magazine* (August 2, 1992).

37. Ibid.

38. Sontag, "Pilgrimage," 41.

39. Nadine Gordimer, interview with the author March 6, 2007.

40. Ibid.

The Invention of Susan Sontag

1. Chapter epigraph is from Elizabeth Farnsworth, "Conversation: Interview with Susan Sontag," *NewsHour with Jim Lehrer*, PBS, February 2, 2001.

2. Acocella, "The Hunger Artist," 72.

3. Richard Howard (American poet), interview with the author on December 2, 2006; Stephen Koch (American writer), interview with the author on March 28, 2007; Steve Wasserman (American editor), interview with the author on March 6, 2007.

4. Sontag, "Pilgrimage," 43.

5. Ibid.

6. Ibid, 38.

7. Ibid.

8. Zoë Heller, "The Life of a Head Girl."

9. Rollyson and Paddock, *Susan Sontag: The Making of an Icon*, 19.

10. Ibid., 19–20.

11. Sontag, "Pilgrimage," 39.

12. Poague, *Conversations with Susan Sontag*, 173.

13. Sontag, "Pilgrimage," 39.

14. Ibid., 40.

15. Ibid.

16. Poague, *Conversations with Susan Sontag*, 191.

17. Wasserman, interview with the author.

18. Sontag, "Pilgrimage," 41; also see Acocella, "The Hunger Artist," 72.

19. Philip Fisher, "Susan Sontag and Philip Fisher: A Conversation," *Salmagundi*, no. 139–40 (Summer–Fall 2003): 177–78.

20. Poague, *Conversations with Susan Sontag*, 233.

21. Sontag, "Pilgrimage," 42.

22. Ibid., 46.

23. Ibid., 53.

Intellectual Delirium

1. Chapter epigraph is from Sontag, "The Letter Scene," in *Telling Tales*, edited by Nadine Gordimer (New York: Picador/Farrar, Straus and Giroux, 2004): 225.

2. Grossman, "At the C Shop with Susan Sontag."

3. See Mary Ann Dzuback, *Robert M. Hutchins: Portrait of an Educator* (Chicago: University of Chicago Press, 1991): 5–45.

4. Poague, *Conversations with Susan Sontag*, 271.

5. Ibid., 75.

6. Grossman, "At the C Shop with Susan Sontag," S1–2; Poague, *Conversations with Susan Sontag*, 272.

7. See Sharon Cohen, "The Nobel-ist of All. University of Chicago Celebrates 100th," *ATP-Press* (September 29, 1991).

8. Poague, *Conversations with Susan Sontag,* 272.

9. Zoë Heller, "The Life of a Head Girl."

10. Grossman, "At the C Shop with Susan Sontag."

11. Ibid.

12. Poague, *Conversations with Susan Sontag,* 274.

13. See Gerhard Spörl, "Die Leo-Konservativen" [The Leo-Conservatives], *Der Spiegel* (August 4, 2003), 42–45.

14. Hirsch, "Susan Sontag: The Art of Fiction."

15. Ibid.

16. See Christine Stansell, *American Moderns: Bohemian New York and the Creation of a New Century* (New York: Henry Holt/Metropolitan Books, 2000): 147ff.

17. See Jack Selzer, *Kenneth Burke in Greenwich Village: Conversing with the Moderns, 1915–1931* (Madison: University of Wisconsin Press, 1996).

18. Hirsch, "Susan Sontag: The Art of Fiction."

19. Suzie Mackenzie, "Finding Fact from Fiction," *The Guardian* (London) (May 27, 2000): 31.

20. Garis, "Susan Sontag Finds Romance."

21. See Brett Harvey, *The Fifties: A Woman's Oral History* (New York: Harper Collins, 1993).

22. Mackenzie, "Finding Fact from Fiction."

23. Acocella, "The Hunger Artist," 73.

24. Sontag, "The Letter Scene," 225.

25. Zoë Heller, "The Life of a Head Girl."

26. Acocella, "The Hunger Artist," 72.

27. Ibid.

28. Poague, *Conversations with Susan Sontag,* 277.

29. Ibid., xxvi.

30. Jeff Alexander (Sontag's assistant), interview with the author on March 2, 2007.

31. Michael D'Antonio, "Little David, Happy at Last," *Esquire* 113, no. 3 (March 1990): 137.

32. Poague, *Conversations with Susan Sontag,* 31.

33. Suzy Hansen, "Rieff Encounter," *New York Observer* (May 2, 2005).

34. Sontag, *In America* (New York: Farrar, Straus and Giroux, 2000): 24.

35. Rollyson and Paddock, *Susan Sontag: The Making of an Icon,* 41.

36. Mackenzie, "Finding Fact from Fiction."

37. Acocella, "The Hunger Artist," 72–73.

38. See David Halberstam, *The Fifties* (New York: Random House, 1993): 3–24.

39. Poague, *Conversations with Susan Sontag,* 115.

40. Ibid., xxvi.

41. Sontag, "The Letter Scene," 225.

Paris, a Romance

1. Sigrid Löffler, "Eine europäische Amerikanerin, Kantianerin und Vordenkerin ihrer Epoche im Gespräch in Edinburgh" [A European American, Kantian, and Pioneer Intellectual of Her Epoch in Conversation in Edinburgh], *Literaturen* (October 2003). The chapter epigraph is from Sontag's presentation at the French Institute/Alliance Française's Trophée des Arts Gala honoring Isabelle Huppert in New York on November 5, 2003. It is quoted in "For Isabelle," in *Isabelle Huppert: Woman of Many Faces,* edited by Elfriede Jelinek and Serge Toubina (New York: Abrams, 2005): 41.

2. Sontag, "The Letter Scene," 225.

3. Ibid, 252.

4. Zoë Heller, "The Life of a Head Girl."

5. Sontag, "The Letter Scene," 233.

6. Stanley Karnow, *Paris in the Fifties* (New York: Times Books/Random House, 1997): 3.

7. Sontag, *Reborn: Journals and Notebooks, 1947–1963,* edited by David Rieff (New York: Farrar, Straus and Giroux, 2008): 160–61.

8. Poague, *Conversations with Susan Sontag,* 134.

9. Susan Sontag, foreword to *A Place in the World Called Paris,* edited by Steven Barclay, xviii (San Francisco: Chronicle Books, 1994).

10. Sontag, *Reborn,* 166.

11. Edward Field, *The Man Who Would Marry Susan Sontag* (Madison: University of Wisconsin Press, 2005): 161.

12. Sontag, *Reborn,* 165.

13. Ibid., 167.

14. Ibid., 162.

15. Ibid., 189.

16. Ibid., 188–89.

17. Koch, interview with the author.

18. Elliott Stein, interview with the author on December 7, 2006.

19. See Tony Judt, *Past Imperfect: French Intellectuals, 1944–1956* (Berkeley: University of California Press, 1992).

20. Poague, *Conversations with Susan Sontag,* 129.

21. Sontag, "The Letter Scene," 233.

The New York Nexus

1. Chapter epigraph is from Hopkins, "Susan Sontag Lightens Up."

2. Howard, interview with the author.

3. Barbara Rowes, "Bio—Susan Sontag," *People Magazine* (March 20, 1978): 74–76, 79–80.

4. Hansen, "Rieff Encounter."

5. Sontag, "The Third World of Women," *Partisan Review,* no. 40 (Spring 1973): 205.

6. Annette Michelson (American film scholar), interview with the author on January 15, 2007.

7. Poague, *Conversations with Susan Sontag,* xxvi–xxvii; Richard Howard, "Remembering Susan Sontag," *Los Angeles Times* (January 2, 2005).

8. D'Antonio, "Little David, Happy at Last," 132.

9. Acocella, "The Hunger Artist," 73.

10. Ibid.

11. Hansen, "Rieff Encounter."

12. Sontag, *Reborn,* 248.

13. Howard, interview with the author.

14. Field, *The Man Who Would Marry Susan Sontag,* 161.

15. Ibid., 160–64.

16. Stein, interview with the author.

17. Acocella, "The Hunger Artist," 74.

18. Field, *The Man Who Would Marry Susan Sontag,* 162.

19. Howard, interview with the author.

20. See Acocella, "The Hunger Artist," 74; Rollyson and Paddock, *Susan Sontag: The Making of an Icon,* 56.

21. Sontag, *Reborn,* 218.

22. Maria M. Delgado and Caridad Svich, eds., *Conducting a Life: Reflections on the Theatre of María Irene Fornés* (Lyme, N.H.: Smith and Kraus, 1999): 255. Sontag told the same story with minor variations in Poague, *Conversations with Susan Sontag,* 227.

23. Poague, *Conversations with Susan Sontag,* 227; Field, *The Man Who Would Marry Susan Sontag,* 163.

24. Sontag, *Reborn,* 221.

25. Howard, interview with the author.

26. Field, *The Man Who Would Marry Susan Sontag,* 162.

27. D'Antonio, "Little David, Happy at Last," 137.

28. Ibid., 132.

29. Hirsch, "Susan Sontag: The Art of Fiction."

30. Ibid.

31. Letter of July 1, 1981, from Robert Giroux to Susan Sontag, Farrar, Straus and Giroux files, Box 346.

32. Hopkins, "Susan Sontag Lightens Up"; see also Miriam Berkley, *Publisher's Weekly* (October 22, 1982).

33. See Christopher Lehmann-Haupt, "Roger W. Straus Jr., Book Publisher from the Age of Independents, Dies at 87," *New York Times* (May 27, 2004); James Atlas, "Roger Straus: Charismatic Co-Founder of Farrar," *The Independent* (May 31, 2004); "Writers Pay Tribute to Roger Straus," *Los Angeles Times Book Review* (June 6, 2004).

34. Michael Krüger, interview with the author on March 19, 2007.

35. Jonathan Galassi, interview with the author on March 26, 2007.

36. Sigrid Nunez, interview with the author on March 21, 2007.

37. Letters of April 30, 1962, and January 14, 1963, from Roger Straus to Susan Sontag, Farrar, Straus and Giroux files, Box 344.

38. Various letters in Farrar, Straus and Giroux files, Box 344.

39. Adam Zagajewski, John McPhee, and Robert McCrum, "Writers Pay Tribute to Roger W. Straus Jr.," *Los Angeles Times Book Review* (June 6, 2004).

40. Koch, interview with the author.

41. Howard, interview with the author.

42. Ned Rorem, interview with the author on December 7, 2006.

43. Koch, interview with the author.

44. Ned Rorem, *The Later Diaries of Ned Rorem, 1961–1972* (San Francisco: Da Capo, 1983): 143.

45. Richard Howard and Elliott Stein, interviews with the author.

46. William Phillips, *A Partisan View: Five Decades of the Literary Life* (New York: Stein and Day, 1983).

47. Elizabeth Hardwick, interview with the author on April 6, 2007.

48. See Arthur Marwick, *The Sixties: Cultural Revolution in Britain, France, Italy, and the United States, c. 1958–c. 1974* (Oxford: Oxford University Press, 1998): 2–41, 288–359; David Denby, "The Moviegoer: Susan Sontag's Life in Film," *New Yorker* (September 12, 2005): 102ff.

49. Farrar, Straus and Giroux files, original draft for the dust jacket, Box 344.

50. Daniel Stern, "Life Becomes a Dream." *New York Times Book Review* (September 8, 1963).

51. Carolyn G. Heilbrun, "Speaking of Susan Sontag," *New York Times Book Review* (August 27, 1967): 2, 30.

52. Deborah Solomon, *Utopia Parkway: The Life and Works of Joseph Cornell* (New York: Farrar, Straus and Giroux, 1997): 317.

Camp

1. Chapter epigraph is from Sontag, *Where the Stress Falls*, 270–71.

2. See Steven Watson, *Factory Made: Warhol and the Sixties* (New York: Pantheon Books, 2003) and Jon Margolis, *The Last Innocent Year—America in 1964, the Beginning of the "Sixties"* (New York: William Morrow, 1999): 3–36.

3. Sontag, *As Consciousness Is Harnessed to Flesh: Journals & Notebooks, 1964–1980*, edited by David Rieff (New York: Farrar, Straus and Giroux, 2012), 3–5.

4. Letter of June 4, 1964, from Roger Straus to Harry Ford, Farrar, Straus and Giroux files, Box 344.

5. Michelson, interview with the author.

6. Heilbrun, "Speaking of Susan Sontag."

7. Hirsch, "Susan Sontag: The Art of Fiction."

8. See Anna Fels, *Necessary Dreams: Ambition in Women's Changing Lives* (New York: Pantheon Books, 2004): 99–106.

9. Sontag, *As Consciousness Is Harnessed to Flesh*, 29.

10. Sontag, "On Self," *New York Times Magazine* (September 10, 2006), entry of July 27, 1964.

11. Hirsch, "Susan Sontag: The Art of Fiction."

12. "In Depth with Susan Sontag," C-SPAN interview.

13. Judith Thurman in a panel discussion during the Susan Sontag Tribute at the 92nd Street Y in Manhattan on February 5, 2007.

14. Acocella, "The Hunger Artist."

15. Hirsch, "Susan Sontag: The Art of Fiction."

16. Ibid.

17. Sontag, "On Self," entry of July 27, 1964.

18. Howard, "Remembering Susan Sontag."

19. Susan Sontag letter of November 18, 1965, about a symposium where she spoke on avant-garde films by Jonas Mekas, Kenneth Anger, and Mike Kuchar, Farrar, Straus and Giroux files, Box 342A.

20. See the detailed description of events in Steven Watson, *Factory Made*, 143–47.

21. Sontag, *Against Interpretation and Other Essays* (New York: Farrar, Straus and Giroux, 1967): 231.

22. Hopkins, "Susan Sontag Lightens Up."

23. Rollyson and Paddock, *Susan Sontag: The Making of an Icon*, 76.

24. Hopkins, "Susan Sontag Lightens Up."

25. Letter of April 9, 1964, from Roger Straus to Maurice Temple Smith, Farrar, Straus and Giroux files, Box 343.

26. See Victor Navasky, "Notes on Cult: or, How to Join the Intellectual Establishment," *New York Times Magazine* (March 27, 1966): 128.

27. Poague, *Conversations with Susan Sontag*, 57.

28. Letter of April 9, 1964, from Roger Straus to Maurice Temple Smith, Farrar, Straus and Giroux files, Box 343.

29. Letter of May 7, 1965, from Lila Karpf to Gerard Pollinger (London), Alexander Gans (Amsterdam), and Herbert Lottman (Paris), Farrar, Straus and Giroux files, Box 343.

30. Navasky, "Notes on Cult."

31. Sontag, *Against Interpretation*, 231.

32. See William Phillips, letter to the *New York Times* (under the heading "Susan Sontag Finds Romance"), August 23, 1992.

33. Howard, "Remembering Susan Sontag."

34. Stein, interview with the author.

35. Sontag, *Against Interpretation*, 287.

36. Ibid., 286.

37. Ibid., 281.

38. Denby, "The Moviegoer," 90.

39. See Navasky, "Notes on Cult."

40. Thomas Meehan, "Not Good Taste, Not Bad Taste—It's 'Camp.' " *New York Times Magazine* (March 21, 1965): 30–31, 113–15.

41. Poague, *Conversations with Susan Sontag*, xxvii.

42. Fremont-Smith.

43. Callie Angell, *Andy Warhol Screen Tests: The Films of Andy Warhol Catalogue raisonné*, Vol. 2 (New York: Abrams, 2006): 190.

44. Ibid.

Styles of the Avant-Garde

1. Chapter epigraph is from Maxine Bernstein and Robert Boyers, "Women, the Arts, & the Politics of Culture: An Interview with Susan Sontag," *Salmagundi*, no. 31–32 (Fall 1975–Winter 1976): 29–48.

2. Koch, interview with the author.

3. Sontag, *Against Interpretation,* 7.

4. Ibid.

5. Ibid., 9.

6. Ibid., 13.

7. "In Depth with Susan Sontag," C-SPAN interview.

8. Stein, interview with the author.

9. Sontag, *Against Interpretation*, 13.

10. Ibid., 14.

11. Eliot Weinberger, "Notes on Susan," *New York Review of Books* (August 16, 2007).

12. Sontag, *Against Interpretation*, 303.

13. Ibid.

14. Benjamin DeMott, "Lady on the Scene," *New York Times Book Review* (January 23, 1966): 5, 32.

15. Robert Mazzocco, "Swingtime," *New York Review of Books* (June 9, 1966).

16. See Elizabeth W. Bruss, *Beautiful Theories: The Spectacle of Discourse in Contemporary Criticism* (Baltimore, Md: Johns Hopkins University Press, 1982): 224–37.

17. Norman Podhoretz, *Making It* (New York: Random House, 1968): 154.

18. Harvey Teres, *Renewing the Left: Politics, Imagination, and the New York Intellectuals* (New York: Oxford University Press, 1996): 173–203.

19. See Fremont-Smith; Herbert Mitgang, "Victory in the Ashes of Vietnam?" *New York Times* (February 4, 1969).

20. See Irving Howe, *Decline of the New* (New York: Harcourt, Brace, 1970): 260.

21. Liam Kennedy, *Susan Sontag: Mind as Passion* (Manchester, U.K.: Manchester University Press, 1995): 16–46.

22. Navasky, "Notes on Cult."

23. Koch, interview with the author.

24. Ibid.

25. Edmund Wilson, *The Sixties: The Last Journal, 1960–1972* (New York: Farrar, Straus and Giroux, 1993): 569, 748.

26. Hopkins, "Susan Sontag Lightens Up."

27. Howe, *Decline of the New,* 260.

28. Hardwick, interview with the author.

29. Howard, "Remembering Susan Sontag"; Nunez, interview with the author.

30. Howard, "Remembering Susan Sontag"; Koch, interview with the author.

31. BBC 2, November 17, 1964. See also the November 17, 1964, letter from Laurence Pollinger to Roger Straus, Farrar, Straus and Giroux files, Box 343.

32. Zoë Heller, "The Life of a Head Girl."

33. Terry Castle, interview with the author on March 4, 2007.

34. Castle, interview with the author; Wendy Lesser, interview with the author on March 7, 2007.

35. See Sontag, "On Self," undated entry from February 1960 and entry of November 8, 1965.

36. Sontag, *As Consciousness Is Harnessed to Flesh,* 138.

37. Sontag, "On Self," entry of July 4, 1965.

38. Letter of July 5, 1972, from Susan Sontag to Roger Straus, Farrar, Straus and Giroux files, Box 344.

39. Poague, *Conversations with Susan Sontag,* 146.

40. Kennedy, *Susan Sontag,* 1.

41. Heilbrun, "Speaking of Susan Sontag."

42. See "On Self," entry of November 17, 1964.

43. Letter of November 23, 1966, from Lila Karpf to Susan Sontag, Farrar, Straus and Giroux files, Box 343.

44. Howard, "Remembering Susan Sontag."

45. See Henry Luhrman, "A Bored Susan Sontag: 'I Think Camp Should Be Retired,' " *Columbia Owl* (March 23, 1966); Charles Poore, "Against Joan of Arc of the Cocktail Party," *New York Times* (April 28, 1966).

46. Letter of August 11, 1966, from Susan Sontag to Roger Straus, Farrar, Straus and Giroux files, Box 342A.

47. Letter of August 8, 1966, from Susan Sontag to Roger Straus, Farrar, Straus and Giroux files, Box 342A.

48. Koch, interview with the author.

49. Carlin Romano, "Desperately Seeking Sontag," *FAME Magazine* (April 1989).

50. Stephen Koch and Elliott Stein, interviews with the author.

51. "On Self," entry of November 24, 1965.

52. Ibid., entry of October 8, 1966.

53. Sontag, *As Consciousness Is Harnessed to Flesh,* 168.

54. Koch, interview with the author.

55. Rorem, interview with the author.

56. See Joseph Cornell, *Joseph Cornell's Theater of the Mind: Selected Diaries, Letters, and Files,* ed. and with an introduction by Mary Ann Caws (New York: Thames and Hudson, 1993): 327–38.

57. Robert Wilson, conversation with the author on April 7, 2007.

58. Sontag, "On Self," entry of August 9, 1966.

Radical Chic

1. Chapter epigraph is from a March 1978 interview in *High Times* conducted by Victor Bockris and quoted in "The Dark Lady of Pop Philosophy," in *Beat Punks* by Victor Bockris (New York: Da Capo, 2000): 85.

2. "In Depth with Susan Sontag," C-SPAN interview.

3. Stephen Koch and Elliott Stein, interviews with the author; Howard, "Remembering Susan Sontag."

4. Poague, *Conversations with Susan Sontag,* 15.

5. James Baldwin et al., "Police Shooting of Oakland Negro," *New York Times* (May 6, 1968): 46.

6. Letter of January 17, 1968, from Lila Karpf to Fritz Raddatz, Farrar, Straus and Giroux files, Box 342A.

7. Koch, interview with the author.

8. Hardwick, interview with the author.

9. See Tom Wolfe, *Radical Chic & Mau-Mauing the Flak Catchers* (New York: Farrar, Straus and Giroux, 1970).

10. Hardwick, interview with the author.

11. See Weinberger, "Notes on Susan."

12. See Scott McLemee, "The Mind as Passion," *American Prospect* 16, no. 2 (February 2005).

13. Sontag, *Styles of Radical Will* (New York: Farrar, Straus and Giroux, 1969): 194.

14. Ibid.

15. Ibid., 198.

16. Ibid., 195.

17. Ibid., 203.

18. Letter of April 8, 1968, from Hall D. Vursell to the graphic designer Milton Glaser, Farrar, Straus and Giroux files, Box 347.

19. Undated memorandum from Robert Giroux to Susan Sontag, Farrar, Straus and Giroux files, Box 347.

20. Sontag, *Styles of Radical Will,* 74–99.

21. Andrew Kopkind, "Communism and the Left," *The Nation* (February 27, 1982).

22. See the letter of November 8, 1968, from Lila Karpf to Giuliana Broggi, Farrar, Straus and Giroux files, Box 347.

23. Ibid.

24. Letter of August 26, 1968, from Susan Sontag to Roger Straus, Farrar, Straus and Giroux files, Box 347.

25. See also Kennedy, *Susan Sontag,* 61–73.

26. Sontag, *Styles of Radical Will,* 271.

27. Charles Ruas, "Susan Sontag: Past, Present and Future," *New York Times* (October 24, 1982).

28. Evans Chan, "Against Postmodernism, Etcetera—A Conversation with Susan Sontag," *Postmodern Culture (PMC)* (January 12, 2001).

29. Sontag, *Styles of Radical Will,* 214.

30. Ibid., 259.

31. Koch, interview with the author.

32. Letter of March 17, 1967, from Roger Straus to the Italian publisher Alberto Mondadori and letter of August 11, 1966, from Susan Sontag to Roger Straus, Farrar, Straus and Giroux files, Box 342A.

33. Letter of March 17, 1967, from Roger Straus to Alberto Mondadori, Farrar, Straus and Giroux files, Box 342A.

34. Hirsch, "Susan Sontag: The Art of Fiction."

35. Eliot Fremont-Smith, "Diddy Did It—Or Did He?" *New York Times* (August 18, 1967): 31.
36. Benjamin DeMott, "Diddy or Didn't He?" *New York Times Book Review* (August 27, 1967): 1–2, 30.
37. Poague, *Conversations with Susan Sontag*, 43.
38. Alfred Kazin, *Bright Book of Life: American Novelists and Storytellers from Hemingway to Mailer* (Boston: Little, Brown, 1973): 180, 184.
39. Susan Sontag, *Todesstation* [Death Station] (Munich: Fischer, 1985): 373.
40. Rieff, interview with the author, May 29, 2006.
41. Koch, interview with the author.

Behind the Camera

1. Chapter epigraph is from Sontag, *Against Interpretation*, 237.
2. See Poague, *Conversations with Susan Sontag*, 97–105, 143–164, 113ff.
3. Ibid.
4. Hopkins, "Susan Sontag Lightens Up."
5. See Denby, "The Moviegoer."
6. Ibid., 95.
7. "In Depth with Susan Sontag," C-SPAN interview.
8. Mel Gussow, "Susan Sontag Talks About Filmmaking," *New York Times* (October 3, 1969): 36.
9. See Victoria Schultz, "Susan Sontag on Film," *Changes* (May 1, 1972): 3–5; Sue Johnston, "Duet for Cannibals: Interview with Susan Sontag," *Cinema Papers* (July–August 1975).
10. Stephen Koch and Sigrid Nunez, interviews with the author.
11. Schultz, "Susan Sontag on Film," 4; Leticia Kent, "What Makes Susan Sontag Make Movies?" *New York Times* (October 11, 1970): sec. 2, 13.
12. Gussow, "Susan Sontag Talks About Filmmaking."
13. Letter to Roger Straus, November 9, 1968, Farrar, Straus and Giroux files, Box 342A.
14. H. Michael Levenson, "The Avant-Garde and the Avant-Guardian," *Harvard Crimson* (July 27, 1973).
15. See numerous letters and bills in the Farrar, Straus and Giroux files, especially in boxes 342B and 344.
16. Ibid.
17. Sontag, "Posters: Advertisement, Art, Political Artifact, Commodity," in *The Art of Revolution: Castro's Cuba, 1959–1970,* by Dugald Stermer (New York: McGraw-Hill, 1970): xvii.
18. See letter to Roger Straus, March 4, 1969, Farrar, Straus and Giroux files, Box 342A.
19. Sontag, "Some Thoughts on the Right Way (for Us) to Love the Cuban Revolution," *Ramparts* magazine (April 1969): 10.
20. *New York Times* (May 21, 1971).
21. See Mary Breasted, "Discipline for a Wayward Writer," *Village Voice* (November 4, 1971): 1.
22. See Poague, *Conversations with Susan Sontag*, 114.

23. Ibid., 63, 65.

24. Ibid., 86.

25. Hugh Kenner, "The Harold Robbins Bit Styled to Make It with the Literati," *New York Times Book Review* (November 2, 1969).

26. "Suicide off L.I. Is Identified as Woman Writer," *New York Times* (November 9, 1969).

27. Koch, interview with the author.

28. Letter of January 19, 1971, from Susan Sontag to Roger Straus, Farrar, Straus and Giroux files, Box 342B.

29. Letter of March 9, 1969, from Susan Sontag to Roger Straus, Farrar, Straus and Giroux files, Box 342A.

30. Schultz, "Susan Sontag on Film," 4.

31. Dennis V. Paoli, "Child Admitted Only with College Graduate," *Village Voice* (August 24, 1972): 55.

In Semi-Exile

1. Chapter epigraph is from Sontag, *I, etcetera*, 38.

2. Poague, *Conversations with Susan Sontag*, 122.

3. Kent, "What Makes Susan Sontag Make Movies?"

4. Howard, interview with the author.

5. Helen Benedict, *Portraits in Print: A Collection of Profiles and the Stories Behind Them* (New York: Columbia University Press, 1991): 23.

6. Poague, *Conversations with Susan Sontag*, 10.

7. Robert Brustein, "If an Artist Wants to Be Serious, and Respected and Rich, Famous and Popular, He Is Suffering from Cultural Schizophrenia," *New York Times Magazine* (September 26, 1971).

8. See Ronald Bergan, "Nicole Stéphane: Renowned for Her Acting Debut She Later Struggled to Bring Proust to the Screen," *The Guardian* (London) (March 23, 2007): 42; "Kommentar: Jede Menge verlorener Zeit" [Comment: A Lot of Wasted Time], *Frankfurter Allgemeine Zeitung* (March 29, 2007): 37.

9. See Schultz, "Susan Sontag on Film," 5.

10. Letter of July 11, 1972, from Susan Sontag to Roger Straus, Farrar, Straus and Giroux files, Box 344.

11. Jonathan Rosenbaum, "Goodbye, Susan, Goodbye: Sontag and Movies," *Synoptique* 7 (February 14, 2005), http://www.synoptique.ca/core/en/articles/rosenbaum/.

12. Howard, interview with the author.

13. Sontag, *Under the Sign of Saturn* (New York: Farrar, Straus and Giroux, 1980): 176.

14. Poague, *Conversations with Susan Sontag*, 175.

15. Ibid., 109.

16. Letter of April 25, 1973, from Tom Rosenthal to Deborah Rogers, Farrar, Straus and Giroux files, Box 342B.

17. Sontag to Straus, May 13, 1973. See also the legal correspondence between Henri Carter Carnegie and Straus, Farrar, Straus and Giroux files, Box 342B.

18. Sigrid Nunez, "Sontag Laughs," *Salmagundi* 152 (Fall 2006): 11–21.

19. Poague, *Conversations with Susan Sontag,* 189.

20. Nunez, "Sontag Laughs," 16.

21. Letter of June 2, 1973, from Susan Sontag to Roger Straus, Farrar, Straus and Giroux files, Box 342B.

22. See Leo Lerman, *The Grand Surprise: The Journals of Leo Lerman,* ed. Stephen Pascal (New York: Knopf, 2007): 413.

23. Poague, *Conversations with Susan Sontag,* 175.

24. Several letters from Straus to Sontag in Paris, Farrar, Straus and Giroux files, Box 342A and 342B.

25. See Philip Nobile, *Intellectual Skywriting: Literary Politics and the New York Review of Books* (New York: Charterhouse, 1974): 211ff.

26. Nunez, interview with the author. Sigrid Nunez was an assistant at the *New York Review of Books* at the time.

27. Letter of July 5, 1972, from Susan Sontag to Roger Straus, Farrar, Straus and Giroux files, Box 344.

28. Letter of May 21, 1973, from Susan Sontag to Roger Straus, Farrar, Straus and Giroux files, Box 342B.

29. Sontag, *Under the Sign of Saturn,* 10.

30. Ibid., 9.

31. Poague, *Conversations with Susan Sontag,* 176.

32. See Bruss, *Beautiful Theories,* 208–16.

33. Poague, *Conversations with Susan Sontag,* 60.

34. Letter of August 1, 1973, from Susan Sontag to Roger Straus, Farrar, Straus and Giroux files, Box 342B.

35. Sontag, *I, etcetera,* 51.

36. Rollyson and Paddock, *Susan Sontag: The Making of an Icon,* 146.

37. Schultz, "Susan Sontag on Film," 3.

38. Quotations from the film booklet for the screening in the New Yorker Theater in the summer of 1974, now in the archive of the Museum of Modern Art, Box "Sontag."

39. Farrar, Straus and Giroux bill to the *New Yorker,* Farrar, Straus and Giroux files, Box 342B.

40. Letter of February 7, 1974, from Susan Sontag to Roger Straus, Farrar, Straus and Giroux files, Box 342B.

41. Koch, interview with the author.

42. Wendy Perron, "Susan Sontag on Writing, Art, Feminism, Life and Death," *SoHo Weekly News* (December 1, 1977): 23–24, 45.

43. Ibid, 45.

44. Schultz, "Susan Sontag on Film," 4.

45. Koch, interview with the author.

46. Sontag, *Against Interpretation,* 25–26.

47. See letter of January 19, 1975, from Susan Sontag to Roger Straus, Farrar, Straus and Giroux files, Box 342B.

48. The German original had appeared in 1973.

49. See Sontag, *Under the Sign of Saturn,* 73–105.

50. Adrienne Rich and Susan Sontag, "Feminism and Fascism: An Exchange," *New York Review of Books* (March 20, 1975): 65ff.

51. Ibid., 66.

52. Howard, interview with the author.

53. Gordimer, interview with the author.

54. Poague, *Conversations with Susan Sontag*, 63.

55. Wasserman, interview with the author.

The Kingdom of the Sick

1. Chapter epigraph is from Sontag, *Illness as Metaphor* (New York: Farrar, Straus and Giroux, 1978): 3.

2. Sontag to Straus, February 7, 1974, Farrar, Straus and Giroux files, Box 344.

3. Acocella, "The Hunger Artist," 68ff.

4. Garis, "Susan Sontag Finds Romance," 21ff.

5. Perron, "Susan Sontag on Writing, Art, Feminism, Life and Death."

6. Ruas, "Susan Sontag Found Crisis of Cancer Added a Fierce Intensity to Life," *New York Times* (January 30, 1978).

7. Koch, interview with the author; Sontag, Introduction to Peter Hujar, *Portraits in Life and Death,* (New York: Da Capo, 1976).

8. Garis, "Susan Sontag Finds Romance."

9. Benedict, *Portraits in Print,* 25.

10. Koch, interview with the author.

11. Ibid.

12. Undated appeals in the Farrar, Straus and Giroux files, Box 342B.

13. Benedict, *Portraits in Print,* 25.

14. Poague, *Conversations with Susan Sontag*, 109.

15. Nunez, interview with the author.

16. Wasserman, interview with the author.

17. See Acocella, "The Hunger Artist," 68ff.; Howard, interview with the author.

18. Howard, interview with the author.

19. Ibid.

20. Sontag, *On Photography* (New York: Farrar, Straus and Giroux, 1977): 3.

21. Ibid., 179–80.

22. William H. Gass, "A Different Kind of Art," *New York Times Book Review* (December 19, 1977).

23. Lerman, *The Grand Surprise,* 415.

24. Koch, interview with the author.

25. Poague, *Conversations with Susan Sontag*, 116.

26. Gary Indiana, "Susan Sontag (1933–2004)," *Village Voice* (December 28, 2004).

27. Poague, *Conversations with Susan Sontag*, 109.

28. Sontag, *Illness as Metaphor.*

29. Poague, *Conversations with Susan Sontag*, 230.

30. Howard, interview with the author.

31. Poague, *Conversations with Susan Sontag,* 230.

32. Email from Darryl Pinckney to the author, April 14, 2007.

33. Nunez, interview with the author.

34. Ibid.

35. Bockris, "The Dark Lady of Pop Philosophy," 77.

36. Ibid, 78.

37. See Lerman, *The Grand Surprise,* 413.

38. Koch, interview with the author.

39. Anatole Broyard, "Styles of Radical Sensibility," *New York Times* (November 11, 1978): 21.

40. Krüger, interview with the author.

The Last Intellectual

1. Chapter epigraph is from an interview with Monika Beyer, *Polityka,* no. 22 (May 31, 1980).

2. See James Atlas, "The Changing World of New York Intellectuals," *New York Times Magazine* (August 25, 1985).

3. See Kennedy, *Susan Sontag,* 106–9.

4. Poague, *Conversations with Susan Sontag,* 167.

5. Hal Foster, "A Reader's Guide," *Artforum* 7 (March 2005): 188.

6. Ibid.

7. Richard Sennett (American sociologist), interview with the author on March 22, 2007.

8. See Kennedy, *Susan Sontag,* 106–9.

9. Sennett, interview with the author; Edmund White (American writer), interview with the author on February 27, 2007.

10. Sontag, *Where the Stress Falls,* 283.

11. Edmund White, interview with the author.

12. Sennett, interview with the author.

13. Sontag, *Where the Stress Falls,* 332.

14. Richard Howard, Sigrid Nunez, Edmund White, and Stephen Koch, interviews with the author.

15. Koch, interview with the author.

16. Herbert Mitgang, "Publishing the Eclectic Susan Sontag," *New York Times* (October 10, 1980).

17. Sontag, *Where the Stress Falls,* 331.

18. David Rieff, foreword to *At the Same Time: Essays and Speeches*, by Susan Sontag, edited by Paolo Dilonardo and Anne Jump (New York: Farrar, Straus and Giroux, 2007): xiv.

19. Ruas, "Susan Sontag: Past, Present and Future."

20. John Leonard, "On Barthes and Goodman, Irony and Eclecticism," *New York Times* (October 13, 1980).

21. Sontag, *Under the Sign of Saturn,* 202.

22. Ibid., 175.

23. Ibid., 121.

24. Ibid., 131.

25. Ibid., 117.

26. Ibid., 134.

27. Garis, "Susan Sontag Finds Romance."

28. Richard Lacayo, "Stand Aside, Sisyphus." *Time* (October 24, 1988): 86–88.

29. Hirsch, "Susan Sontag: The Art of Fiction."

30. "Susan Sontag Provokes Debate on Communism," *New York Times* (February 27, 1982).

31. Ibid.

32. Christopher Hitchens, "Poland and Other Questions," *The Nation* (February 27, 1982): 237.

33. Diana Trilling, "Susan Sontag's God That Failed," *SoHo Weekly News* (February 24, 1982).

34. Alexander Cockburn, untitled, *The Nation* (February 27, 1982).

35. Benedict, *Portraits in Print*, 33.

36. Ruas, "Susan Sontag: Past, Present and Future."

37. Edmund White, interview with the author.

38. Alexander Cockburn, "Susan Sontag," *Village Voice* (October 11, 1983).

39. Galassi, interview with the author.

40. Walter Kendrick, "In a Gulf of Her Own," *The Nation* (October 23, 1982): 404–6.

Small-Scale Politics

1. Chapter epigraph is from Sontag, "When Writers Talk Among Themselves," *New York Times Book Review* (January 5, 1986): 1, 22–23.

2. Koch, interview with the author.

3. Edmund White, interview with the author.

4. Darryl Pinckney, interview with the author on April 14, 2007.

5. Karen Kennerley, interview with the author on March 24, 2007.

6. All of Susan Sontag's articles discussed hereafter were collected in *Where the Stress Falls* (New York: Farrar, Straus and Giroux, 2001).

7. See Benedict, *Portraits in Print*, 25.

8. Howard, interview with the author.

9. See "In Depth with Susan Sontag," C-SPAN interview.

10. Howard, interview with the author.

11. Childs, interview with the author.

12. Ibid.

13. See Jack Rosenberger, "Susan Sontag." *Splash Magazine* (April 1989).

14. Robert Wilson, conversation with the author.

15. Frank Rich, "Stage—Milan Kundera's 'Jacques and His Master,'" *New York Times* (January 24, 1985): C19.

16. Mackenzie, "Finding Fact from Fiction," 31ff.

17. Childs, interview with the author.

18. Poague, *Conversations with Susan Sontag*, 258.

19. Howard, interview with the author.

20. Email from Robert Hass to the author, February 27, 2007.

21. Sontag, "When Writers Talk Among Themselves."

22. Ibid.

23. Anon., "PEN Plans a Forbidden Reading of 'Forbidden Reading,'" *New York Times* (November 11, 1986).

24. See Sontag's letters to the *New York Review of Books* on March 13, 1983; March 28, 1985; August 14, 1986; and November 24, 1988.

25. Gordimer, interview with the author.

26. Francis King, *Visiting Cards* (London: Constable, 1990).

27. Kennerley.

28. See Walter Goodman, "U.S. PEN Unit Fights for Eastern Bloc Victims," *New York Times* (May 30, 1988).

29. Since no other German house dared to publish the book either, a working group that included Günter Grass and Hans Magnus Enzensberger founded the "Artikel 19" publishing company to issue the embattled novel.

30. Kennerley.

31. Sontag, *AIDS and Its Metaphors,* 25.

32. Lehmann-Haupt.

33. Rosenberger, "Susan Sontag."

34. Poague, *Conversations with Susan Sontag,* 260.

35. Mackenzie, "Finding Fact from Fiction."

36. Romano, "Desperately Seeking Sontag."

Return to the Magic Mountain

1. Hopkins, "Susan Sontag Lightens Up."

2. Wasserman, interview with the author.

3. Bob Thompson, "A Complete Picture: Annie Leibovitz Is Ready for An Intimate View of Her Life," *Washington Post* (October 19, 2006): C1.

4. Author's interview with two of Leibovitz's assistants who wish to remain anonymous.

5. Richard Howard and Stephen Koch, interviews with the author.

6. Howard, interview with the author.

7. Nunez, interview with the author.

8. Castle, interview with the author.

9. Acocella, "The Hunger Artist"; Mackenzie, "Finding Fact from Fiction."

10. Edmund White, interview with the author.

11. Terry Castle, Richard Howard, Sigrid Nunez, Edmund White, and Stephen Koch, interviews with the author.

12. Guthmann.

13. "In Depth with Susan Sontag," C-SPAN interview.

14. Benedict, *Portraits in Print,* 28.

15. Sontag, "On Self," entry of January 4, 1966.

16. Rosenberger, "Susan Sontag."

17. See Margaret Fichtner, "Susan Sontag's Train of Thought Rolls into Town," *Miami Herald* (February 19, 1989); Galassi, interview with the author.

18. Paula Span, "Susan Sontag: Hot at Last," *Washington Post* (September 17, 1992): C1–2.
19. Wylie, interview with the author.
20. Frank Bruni, "The Literary Agent as Zelig," *New York Times Magazine* (August 11, 1996).
21. Wylie, interview with the author.
22. See, for example, Fichtner, "Susan Sontag's Train of Thought Rolls into Town."
23. Andrew Wylie and Jonathan Galassi, interviews with the author.
24. Wasserman, interview with the author.
25. Ibid.
26. Galassi, interview with the author.
27. Hopkins, "Susan Sontag Lightens Up."
28. Garis, "Susan Sontag Finds Romance."
29. Ibid.; Wendy Lesser and Jonathan Galassi, interviews with the author.
30. Hirsch, "Susan Sontag: The Art of Fiction."
31. Sara Mosle, "Magnificent Obsessions—Talking with Susan Sontag," *Newsday* (August 30, 1992).
32. Hirsch, "Susan Sontag: The Art of Fiction."
33. Ibid.
34. Span, "Susan Sontag: Hot at Last."
35. Hopkins, "Susan Sontag Lightens Up."
36. Michiko Kakutani, "Historical Novel Flavored with Passion and Ideas," *New York Times* (August 4, 1992).
37. Gordimer, interview with the author.

Theater at the Spiritual Front

1. Chapter epigraph is from Tony Kushner, "On Art and Politics: Susan Sontag," in *Tony Kushner in Conversation*, edited by Robert Vorlicky (Ann Arbor: University of Michigan Press, 1998): 179.
2. Rieff, interview with the author.
3. Castle, interview with the author.
4. Ariel Dorfman, interview with the author on February 22, 2007.
5. Sontag, *Alice in Bed* (New York: Farrar, Straus and Giroux, 1993): 117.
6. Ibid.
7. Ibid., 116.
8. Pinckney, interview with the author.
9. Hirsch, "Susan Sontag: The Art of Fiction."
10. Rüdiger Schaper, "Schwestern von gestern, Brüder von morgen" [Yesterday's Sisters, Tomorrow's Brothers], *Süddeutsche Zeitung* (September 17, 1993).
11. Gerhard Stadelmaier, "Schlafschmock: Bühne und Bett—Bob Wilson inszeniert Susan Sontag." [Hack in a Nightgown: Stage and Bed—Bob Wilson Stages Susan Sontag], *Frankfurter Allgemeine Zeitung* (September 17, 1993).
12. John Simon, "One Singular Sensation," *New York* magazine (November 20, 2000).

13. Robert Wilson, conversation with the author.

14. Ibid.

15. See Acocella, "The Hunger Artist," 68ff.

16. Dorfman, interview with the author.

17. Robert Wilson, conversation with the author.

18. David Rieff, *Slaughterhouse: Bosnia and the Failure of the West* (New York: Simon and Schuster, 1995).

19. Ed Vulliamy, "This Time It's Not Personal," *The Observer* (May 20, 2000).

20. Carolin Emcke, interview with the author on March 19, 2007.

21. Alfonso Armada, "Sarajevo," *The Guardian* (July 29, 1993): 8–9.

22. Ibid.

23. Noah Richler, "The Listener: Reflections on Darkness," *The Independent* (November 21, 1999).

24. Mark Danner (American journalist), interview with the author on April 11, 2007.

25. Ibid.

26. Paul Berman, "On Susan Sontag," *Dissent* 52, no. 2 (Spring 2005): 110.

27. John Pomfret, "'Godot' amid the Gunfire," *Washington Post* (August 19, 1993): C1, C6.

28. Ibid.

29. Danner, interview with the author.

30. See Sontag, "Godot Comes to Sarajevo," *New York Review of Books* (October 21, 1993): 52–60; Pomfret, "'Godot' amid the Gunfire."

31. Davor Koric, "Warten auf das Endspiel" [Waiting for the Endgame], *Frankfurter Allgemeine Zeitung* (August 20, 1993).

32. JR (pseud.), "Susan in den Ruinen" [Susan in the Ruins], *Süddeutsche Zeitung* (October 19, 1993).

33. Armada, "Sarajevo."

34. Sontag, *Where the Stress Falls,* 285–89.

35. Kushner, "On Art and Politics: Susan Sontag," 179.

36. Berman, "On Susan Sontag."

37. Lesser, interview with the author.

38. Ibid.

39. Wylie, interview with the author.

40. Castle, interview with the author.

41. See Dana Heller, "Desperately Seeking Susan," *Common Review* 5, no. 1 (Summer 2006): 10–16.

42. Franklin Foer, "Susan Superstar: How Susan Sontag Became Seduced by Her Own Persona." *New York* magazine 38, no. 3 (January 14, 2005): 34–42.

43. Stephen Koch and Sigrid Nunez, interviews with the author.

44. Gary Younge, "Susan Sontag, the Risk Taker," *The Guardian* (January 19, 2002): 6.

45. Terry Castle, Richard Howard, Stephen Koch, and Sigrid Nunez, interviews with the author; Jeff Seroy, interview with the author on March 21, 2007; Edmund White, interview with the author.

46. Sontag, *Where the Stress Falls*, 273.

47. Denby, "The Moviegoer."

Life and Afterlife

1. Chapter epigraph is from Sontag, *I, etcetera*, 45.

2. See Leibovitz, *A Photographer's Life*.

3. Ibid.

4. Ibid.

5. David Rieff, "Illness as More Than Metaphor," in *The Best American Essays 2006*, edited by Lauren Slater (Boston: Houghton Mifflin, 2006): 161.

6. Ibid., 160.

7. Childs, interview with the author.

8. Andrew Wylie, Stephen Koch, and Jeff Seroy, interviews with the author; Mackenzie, "Finding Fact from Fiction," 31ff.; Kevin Jackson, "Susan Sontag—In the Line of Fire," *The Independent* (August 9, 2003): 6, 9–11.

9. Wylie, interview with the author.

10. Howard, interview with the author; Acocella, "The Hunger Artist," 68ff.; Mackenzie, "Finding Fact from Fiction," 31ff.

11. August Sander, *Antlitz der Zeit: Sechzig Aufnahmen deutscher Menschen des 20. Jahrhunderts* [The Face of the Era: Sixty Photographs of 20th-Century Germans], with foreword by Alfred Döblin (Munich: Transmarc/Wolff, 1929).

12. Rieff, "Illness as More Than Metaphor," 161.

13. Steve Wasserman and Marina Abramović, interviews with the author; Klaus Biesenbach, interview with the author on April 4, 2007.

14. Jackson, "Susan Sontag—In the Line of Fire," 6; Acocella, "The Hunger Artist," 68.

15. Liam Lacey, "Waiting for Sontag," *Globe and Mail* (November 23, 2002): R5.

16. Acocella, "The Hunger Artist," 68.

17. Alexander, interview with the author.

18. Andrea Köhler, "Das Mal der Subjektivität" [The Stigma of Subjectivity], *Neue Zürcher Zeitung* (July 9, 2005), 47.

19. Seroy, interview with the author.

20. Michiko Kakutani, "Love as Distraction that Gets in the Way of Art," *New York Times* (February 29, 2000)

21. Richard Lourie, "Stages of Her Life," *Washington Post* (March 5, 2000).

22. See Doreen Carvajal, "So Whose Words Are They, Anyway?" *New York Times* (May 27, 2000): B9, B11.

23. Sontag, *In America*.

24. Carvajal, "So Whose Words Are They, Anyway?"

25. Jonathan Galassi and Jeff Seroy, interviews with the author.

26. Linton Weeks, "Susan Sontag Wins National Book Award for Fiction," *Washington Post* (November 16, 2000).

27. Ibid.

28. Laura Miller, "National Book Award Winner Announced," *Salon.com* (November 16, 2000).

29. See "In Depth with Susan Sontag," her C-SPAN interview, for instance.

30. Wylie, interview with the author.

31. "In Depth with Susan Sontag," C-SPAN interview.

32. Emcke, interview with the author.

33. Biesenbach, interview with the author.

34. Ibid.

35. Simon Houpt, "Goodbye Essays, Hello Fiction, Says Sontag," *Globe and Mail* (Canada) (October 23, 2000): 3.

36. Younge, "Susan Sontag, the Risk Taker."

37. Wendy Lesser, Terry Castle, Marina Abramović, and Darryl Pinckney, interviews with the author.

38. Biesenbach, interview with the author.

39. Ibid.

40. Abramović, interview with the author.

41. Rieff, foreword to *At the Same Time,* vii.

42. Younge, "Susan Sontag, the Risk Taker."

43. Rieff, foreword to *At the Same Time,* xii.

44. Jackson, "Susan Sontag—In the Line of Fire."

45. Lucinda Childs and Terry Castle, interviews with the author.

46. Alexander Cockburn, "What Sontag Said in Jerusalem," *The Nation* (June 4, 2001).

47. Sontag, *At the Same Time,* 152–54.

48. Cockburn, "What Sontag Said in Jerusalem"; Herbert R. Lottman, "For Jerusalem, a Bustling 20th Fair," *Publishers Weekly* 248, no. 22 (May 28, 2001).

49. Susan Sontag, Introduction to Leonid Tsypkin, *Summer in Baden-Baden,* trans. Roger and Angela Keys (New York: New Directions, 2003): ix.

50. Hitchens, "An Internationalist Mind."

51. Hilary Mantel, "Not Either/Or But Both/And," *Los Angeles Times Book Review* (October 7, 2001).

52. William Deresiewicz, "The Radical Imagination," *New York Times Book Review* (November 4, 2001): 7.

The Pain of Others

1. Chapter epigraph is from Sontag, *Regarding the Pain of Others* (New York: Farrar, Straus and Giroux, 2003): 86.

2. Mimi Avins, "UCLA Buys Sontag's Archive," *Los Angeles Times* (January 26, 2002).

3. Harald Fricke, "Meinung und nichts als die Meinung" [Opinion and Nothing But Opinion], *Die Tageszeitung* (September 15, 2001).

4. breb (pseud.), "Monströse Realität" [Monstrous Reality], *Frankfurter Allgemeine Zeitung* (September 15, 2001).

5. Fricke, "Meinung und nichts als die Meinung."

6. Ibid.

7. Sontag, "Feige waren die Mörder nicht" [The Murderers Were No Cowards], *Frankfurter Allgemeine Zeitung* (September 15, 2001); Sontag, untitled (abbreviated version of "Feige waren die Mörder nicht"), *New Yorker* (September 24, 2001): 32.

8. Sontag, untitled.

9. Ibid.

10. Ibid.

11. Sontag, *At the Same Time*, 110.

12. Sontag, "Feige waren die Mörder nicht," published posthumously in its original English version as "9.11.01." in *At the Same Time*, 105–7.

13. Celestine Bohlen, "In New War on Terrorism, Words Are Weapons, Too," *New York Times* (September 29, 2001).

14. David Talbot, "The 'Traitor' Fires Back," *Salon.com* (October 16, 2001).

15. Susanne Ostwald, "Besonnenheit und schrille Töne" [Prudence and Shrill Tones], *Neue Zürcher Zeitung* (September 17, 2001).

16. Anonymous, "Sontagged," editorial in *Weekly Standard* (October 15, 2001): 42–43.

17. Charles Krauthammer, "Voices of Moral Obtuseness," *Washington Post* (September 21, 2001).

18. Lawrence Kaplan, "No Choice," *New Republic* 225 (October 1, 2001).

19. Bohlen, "In New War on Terrorism, Words Are Weapons, Too"; Tim Rutten and Lynn Smith, "When the Ayes Have It, Is There Room for Naysayers?" *Los Angeles Times* (Southern California Living section) (September 28, 2001).

20. See Bohlen, "In New War on Terrorism, Words Are Weapons, Too"; Rutten and Smith, "When the Ayes Have It, Is There Room for Naysayers?"

21. Sontag, *At the Same Time*, 109.

22. Leibovitz, *A Photographer's Life.*

23. "In Depth with Susan Sontag," C-SPAN interview.

24. Rieff, interview with the author.

25. Talbot, "The 'Traitor' Fires Back."

26. Ibid.

27. Sontag, untitled, 32; *At the Same Time*, 105.

28. Talbot, "The 'Traitor' Fires Back."

29. Sontag, *At the Same Time*, 108–17.

30. Talbot, "The 'Traitor' Fires Back."

31. Sontag, *At the Same Time*, 118–19.

32. Ibid., 122.

33. "In Depth with Susan Sontag," C-SPAN interview.

34. Ibid.

35. Sontag, *Regarding the Pain of Others*, 108.

36. Michiko Kakutani, "A Writer Who Begs to Differ . . . with Herself," *New York Times* (March 11, 2003).

37. Scott McLemee, "Understanding War Through Photos," *Newsday* (March 30, 2003).

38. Lorraine Adams, "Picturing the Worst," *Washington Post* (April 13, 2003).

39. Neal Ascherson, "How Images Fail to Convey War's Horrors," *Los Angeles Times Book Review* (March 16, 2003): R8.

40. Müller, "An den Abgründen der Oberfläche."

41. http://www.friedenspreis-des-deutschen-buchhandels.de/445722/?aid=44 5968.

42. See Hubert Spiegel, "Europas Kind: Susan Sontags Dankesrede in der Paulskirche" [Europe's Child: Susan Sontag's Acceptance Speech in St. Paul's Church], *Frankfurter Allgemeine Zeitung* (October 13, 2003).

43. Ivan Nagel, "Nur wer sich wandelt, ist vollkommen: Krieg und Frieden im Jahr 2003" [Only the Person Who Changes Is Perfect: War and Peace in the Year 2003], *Frankfurter Allgemeine Zeitung* (October 14, 2003).

44. Christoph Schröder, "Ein ganz gewöhnlicher Sontag-Vormittag" [An Ordinary Sontag Morning], *Frankfurter Rundschau* (October 13, 2003).

45. Sontag, *At the Same Time*, 194.

46. Ibid., 202.

47. Ibid., 204.

48. Ibid., 209.

49. Wylie, interview with the author.

50. Sontag, *At the Same Time*, 16.

51. Ibid., 39.

52. Ibid., 88.

53. Ibid., 89.

54. Ibid., 157.

55. Ibid., 195.

56. Ibid., 210.

57. Ibid., 211.

58. Gordimer, interview with the author.

59. Seroy, interview with the author. On the diagnosis see Rieff, "Illness as More Than Metaphor," 159, and Leibovitz, *A Photographer's Life.*

60. Rieff, "Illness as More Than Metaphor," 163.

61. Wylie, interview with the author.

62. Rieff, "Illness as More Than Metaphor," 160.

63. Sontag, "Regarding the Torture of Others," *New York Times Magazine* (May 23, 2004): 24–29.

64. Leibovitz, *A Photographer's Life.*

65. Rieff, "Illness as More Than Metaphor," 161.

66. Emma Brockes, "My Time with Susan," interview with Annie Leibovitz, *The Guardian* (October 7, 2006): 18–33.

67. Rieff, "Illness as More Than Metaphor," 171.

Works by Susan Sontag

BOOKS

Against Interpretation and Other Essays. New York: Farrar, Straus and Giroux, 1966.

AIDS and Its Metaphors. New York: Farrar, Straus and Giroux, 1989.

Alice in Bed. New York: Farrar, Straus and Giroux, 1993.

As Consciousness Is Harnessed to Flesh: Journals & Notebooks, 1964–1980. Edited by David Rieff. New York: Farrar, Straus and Giroux, 2012.

At the Same Time: Essays and Speeches. Edited by Paolo Dilonardo and Anne Jump. Foreword by David Rieff. New York: Farrar, Straus and Giroux, 2007.

The Benefactor. New York: Farrar, Straus and Co., 1963.

Death Kit. New York: Farrar, Straus and Giroux, 1967.

I, etcetera. New York: Farrar, Straus and Giroux, 1978.

Illness as Metaphor. New York: Farrar, Straus and Giroux, 1978.

In America. New York: Farrar, Straus and Giroux, 2000.

On Photography. New York: Farrar, Straus and Giroux, 1977.

Reborn: Journals & Notebooks, 1947–1963. Edited by David Rieff. New York: Farrar, Straus and Giroux, 2008.

Regarding the Pain of Others. New York: Farrar, Straus and Giroux, 2003.

Styles of Radical Will. New York: Farrar, Straus and Giroux, 1969.

Under the Sign of Saturn. New York: Farrar, Straus and Giroux, 1980.

The Way We Live Now. New York: Noonday Press/Farrar, Straus and Giroux, 1991.

Where the Stress Falls. New York: Farrar, Straus and Giroux, 2001.

ARTICLES, ESSAYS, STORIES, INTRODUCTIONS, AND FOREWORDS

"The Decay of Cinema." *New York Times Magazine* (February 25, 1996): 60–61.

"Feige waren die Mörder nicht" [The Murderers Were No Cowards]. *Frankfurter Allgemeine Zeitung* (September 15, 2001).

"For Isabelle." In *Isabelle Huppert: Woman of Many Faces,* edited by Elfriede Jelinek and Serge Toubina, 4–43. New York: Abrams, 2005.

"Godot Comes to Sarajevo." *New York Review of Books* (October 21, 1993): 52–60.

Introduction to *Portraits in Life and Death* by Peter Hujar. New York: Da Capo, 1976.

"The Letter Scene." In *Telling Tales,* edited by Nadine Gordimer, 215–37. New York: Picador/Farrar, Straus and Giroux, 2004.

"On Self." *New York Times Magazine* (September 10, 2006): 52–58.

"Pilgrimage." *New Yorker* (December 21, 1987): 38–54.

"Posters: Advertisement, Art, Political Artifact, Commodity." In *The Art of Revolution: Castro's Cuba, 1959–1970,* by Dugald Stermer, vii–xxiii. New York: McGraw-Hill, 1970.

"Regarding the Torture of Others." *New York Times Magazine* (May 23, 2004): 24–29.

"Some Thoughts on the Right Way (for Us) to Love the Cuban Revolution." *Ramparts* magazine (April 1969): 6–19.

"The Third World of Women." *Partisan Review,* no. 40 (Spring 1973): 180–206.

Untitled (abbreviated version of "Feige waren die Mörder nicht"). *New Yorker* (September 24, 2001): 32.

"When Writers Talk Among Themselves." *New York Times Book Review* (January 5, 1986): 1, 22–23.

Secondary Literature and Interviews

Abramović, Marina. Interview with the author on March 8, 2007.

Acocella, Joan. "The Hunger Artist." *New Yorker* (March 6, 2000): 68–77.

Adams, Lorraine. "Picturing the Worst." *Washington Post* (April 13, 2003).

Alexander, Jeff. Interview with the author on March 2, 2007.

Anonymous. "Sontagged." Editorial in *Weekly Standard* (October 15, 2001): 42–43.

———. "Susan Sontag Provokes Debate on Communism." *New York Times* (February 27, 1982).

Armada, Alfonso. "Sarajevo." *The Guardian* (July 29, 1993): 8–9.

Ascherson, Neal. "How Images Fail to Convey War's Horrors." *Los Angeles Times Book Review* (March 16, 2003): R8.

Avins, Mimi. "UCLA Buys Sontag's Archive." *Los Angeles Times* (January 26, 2002).

Benedict, Helen. *Portraits in Print: A Collection of Profiles and the Stories Behind Them.* New York: Columbia University Press, 1991.

Berman, Paul. "On Susan Sontag." *Dissent* 52, no. 2 (Spring 2005): 109–12.

Bernstein, Richard. "Susan Sontag, as Image and as Herself." *New York Times* (January 26, 1989): C17.

Biesenbach, Klaus. Interview with the author on April 4, 2007.

Bockris, Victor. "The Dark Lady of Pop Philosophy." In *Beat Punks* by Victor Bockris, 73–86. New York: Da Capo, 2000.

Bohlen, Celestine. "In New War on Terrorism, Words Are Weapons, Too." *New York Times* (September 29, 2001).

Breasted, Mary. "Discipline for a Wayward Writer." *Village Voice* (November 4, 1971).

breb (pseud.). "Monströse Realität" [Monstrous Reality]. *Frankfurter Allgemeine Zeitung* (September 15, 2001).

Brockes, Emma. "My Time with Susan," interview with Annie Leibovitz. *The Guardian* (October 7, 2006): 18–33.

Broyard, Anatole. "Styles of Radical Sensibility." *New York Times* (November 11, 1978): 21.

Bruss, Elizabeth W. *Beautiful Theories: The Spectacle of Discourse in Contemporary Criticism.* Baltimore: Johns Hopkins University Press, 1982.

Carvajal, Doreen. "So Whose Words Are They, Anyway?" *New York Times* (May 27, 2000): B9, B11.

Castle, Terry. Interview with the author on March 4, 2007.

Chan, Evans. "Against Postmodernism, Etcetera—A Conversation with Susan Sontag." *Postmodern Culture (PMC)* (January 12, 2001).

Childs, Lucinda. Interview with the author on April 13, 2007.

Cockburn, Alexander. Untitled. *The Nation* (February 27, 1982).

———. "What Sontag Said in Jerusalem." *The Nation* (June 4, 2001).

Danner, Mark. Interview with the author on April 11, 2007.

D'Antonio, Michael. "Little David, Happy at Last." *Esquire* 113, no. 3 (March 1990): 128–35.

DeMott, Benjamin. "Diddy or Didn't He?" *New York Times Book Review* (August 27, 1967): 1–2, 30.

———. "Lady on the Scene." *New York Times Book Review* (January 23, 1966): 5, 32.

Denby, David. "The Moviegoer: Susan Sontag's Life in Film." *New Yorker* (September 12, 2005): 90–97, 102ff.

Deresiewicz, William. "The Radical Imagination." *New York Times Book Review* (November 4, 2001): 7.

Dorfman, Ariel. Interview with the author on February 22, 2007.

Emcke, Carolin. Interview with the author on March 19, 2007.

Farnsworth, Elizabeth. "Conversation: Interview with Susan Sontag." *NewsHour with Jim Lehrer.* PBS, February 2, 2001.

Farrar, Straus and Giroux (FSG) files, New York Public Library.

Fichtner, Margaret. "Susan Sontag's Train of Thought Rolls into Town." *Miami Herald* (February 19, 1989).

Field, Edward. *The Man Who Would Marry Susan Sontag.* Madison: University of Wisconsin Press, 2005.

Fisher, Philip. "Susan Sontag and Philip Fisher: A Conversation." *Salmagundi,* no. 139–40 (Summer–Fall 2003): 174–88.

Foer, Franklin. "Susan Superstar: How Susan Sontag Became Seduced by Her Own Persona." *New York* magazine 38, no. 3 (January 14, 2005): 34–42.

Fox, Margalit. "Susan Sontag, Social Critic with Verve, Dies at 71." *New York Times* (December 28, 2004).

Fremont-Smith, Eliot. "After the Ticker Tape Parade." *New York Times* (January 31, 1966).

——. "Diddy Did It—Or Did He?" *New York Times* (August 18, 1967): 31.

Fricke, Harald. "Meinung und nichts als die Meinung" [Opinion and Nothing But Opinion]. *Die Tageszeitung* (September 15, 2001).

Galassi, Jonathan. Interview with the author on March 26, 2007.

Garis, Leslie. "Susan Sontag Finds Romance." *New York Times Magazine* (August 2, 1992): 20–23, 31, 43.

Gass, William H. "A Different Kind of Art." *New York Times Book Review* (December 19, 1977).

Gordimer, Nadine. Interview with the author on March 6, 2007.

Grossman, Ron. "At the C Shop with Susan Sontag." *Chicago Tribune* (December 1, 1992): S1–2.

Gussow, Mel. "Susan Sontag Talks About Filmmaking." *New York Times* (October 3, 1969): 36.

Guthmann, Edward. "Love, Family, Celebrity, Grief—Leibovitz Puts Her Life on Display in Photo Memoir." *San Francisco Chronicle* (November 1, 2006): E1.

Hanimann, Joseph. "Verpasstes Rendezvous; Pariser Gedenktopographie" [Missed Rendezvous: Paris Memorial Topography]. *Frankfurter Allgemeine Zeitung* (January 19, 2005).

Hansen, Suzy. "Rieff Encounter." *New York Observer* (May 2, 2005).

Hardwick, Elizabeth. Interview with the author on April 6, 2007.

Heilbrun, Carolyn G. "Speaking of Susan Sontag." *New York Times Book Review* (August 27, 1967): 2, 30.

Heller, Dana. "Desperately Seeking Susan." *Common Review* 5, no. 1 (Summer 2006): 10–16.

Heller, Zoë. "The Life of a Head Girl." *The Independent* (London) (September 20, 1992): 10ff.

Hirsch, Edward. "Susan Sontag: The Art of Fiction No. 143." *Paris Review*, no. 137 (Winter 1995), http://www.theparisreview.org/interviews/1505/the -art-of-fiction-no-143-susan-sontag.

Hitchens, Christopher. "An Internationalist Mind." *Newsday* (September 9, 2001).

——. "Poland and Other Questions." *The Nation* (February 27, 1982): 237.

Hopkins, Ellen. "Susan Sontag Lightens Up." *Los Angeles Times Magazine* (August 16, 1992): 22–24, 26, 40.

Houpt, Simon. "Goodbye Essays, Hello Fiction, Says Sontag." *Globe and Mail* (Canada) (October 23, 2000): 3

Howard, Richard. Interview with the author on December 2, 2006.

——. "Remembering Susan Sontag." *Los Angeles Times* (January 2, 2005).

Howe, Irving. *Decline of the New.* New York: Harcourt, Brace, 1970.

"In Depth with Susan Sontag." Interview on C-SPAN, March 2, 2003.

Indiana, Gary. "Susan Sontag (1933–2004)." *Village Voice* (December 28, 2004).

Jackson, Kevin. "Susan Sontag—In the Line of Fire." *The Independent* (August 9, 2003): 6, 9–11.

Johnston, Sue. "Duet for Cannibals: Interview with Susan Sontag." *Cinema Papers* (July–August 1975).

JR (pseud.). "Susan in den Ruinen" [Susan in the Ruins]. *Süddeutsche Zeitung* (October 19, 1993).

Kakutani, Michiko. "Historical Novel Flavored with Passion and Ideas." *New York Times* (August 4, 1992).

———. "Love as Distraction That Gets in the Way of Art." *New York Times* (February 29, 2000).

———. "A Writer Who Begs to Differ . . . with Herself." *New York Times* (March 11, 2003).

Kaplan, Lawrence. "No Choice." *New Republic* 225 (October 1, 2001).

Kazin, Alfred. *Bright Book of Life: American Novelists and Storytellers from Hemingway to Mailer.* Boston: Little, Brown, 1973.

Kendrick, Walter. "In a Gulf of Her Own." *The Nation* (October 23, 1982): 404–6.

Kennedy, Liam. *Susan Sontag: Mind as Passion.* Manchester, U.K.: Manchester University Press, 1995.

Kenner, Hugh. "The Harold Robbins Bit Styled to Make It with the Literati." *New York Times Book Review* (November 2, 1969).

Kennerley, Karen. Interview with the author on March 24, 2007.

Kent, Leticia. "What Makes Susan Sontag Make Movies?" *New York Times* (October 11, 1970): sec. 2, 13.

Kijowska, Marta. "Die Wohltäterin" [The Benefactor]. *Frankfurter Allgemeine Zeitung* (January 4, 2004).

Koch, Stephen. Interview with the author on March 28, 2007.

Köhler, Andrea. "Das Mal der Subjektivität" [The Stigma of Subjectivity]. *Neue Zürcher Zeitung* (July 9, 2005).

Koric, Davor. "Warten auf das Endspiel" [Waiting for the Endgame]. *Frankfurter Allgemeine Zeitung* (August 20, 1993).

Krauthammer, Charles. "Voices of Moral Obtuseness." *Washington Post* (September 21, 2001).

Krüger, Michael. "Ah, Susan! Toujours fidèle" [Ah, Susan! Faithful as Always]. *Frankfurter Allgemeine Sonntagszeitung* (January 1, 2006).

———. Interview with the author via email on March 19, 2007.

Kushner, Tony. "On Art and Politics: Susan Sontag." In *Tony Kushner in Conversation*, edited by Robert Vorlicky, 170–87. Ann Arbor: University of Michigan Press, 1998.

Lacayo, Richard. "Stand Aside, Sisyphus." *Time* (October 24, 1988): 86–88.

Lacey, Liam. "Waiting for Sontag." *Globe and Mail* (November 23, 2002): R5.

Lehmann-Haupt, Christopher. "Shaping the Reality of AIDS Through Language." *New York Times* (January 16, 1989): C18.

Leibovitz, Annie. *A Photographer's Life, 1990–2005.* New York: Random House, 2006.

Leonard, John. "On Barthes and Goodman, Irony and Eclecticism." *New York Times* (October 13, 1980).

Lerman, Leo. *The Grand Surprise: The Journals of Leo Lerman.* Edited by Stephen Pascal. New York: Knopf, 2007.

Lesser, Wendy. Interview with the author on March 7, 2007.

Levenson, H. Michael. "The Avant-Garde and the Avant-Guardian." *Harvard Crimson* (July 27, 1973).

Löffler, Sigrid. "Eine europäische Amerikanerin, Kantianerin und Vordenkerin ihrer Epoche im Gespräch in Edinburgh" [A European American, Kantian, and Pioneer Intellectual of Her Epoch in Conversation in Edinburgh]. *Literaturen* (October 2003).

Lottman, Herbert R. "For Jerusalem, a Bustling 20th Fair." *Publishers Weekly* 248, no. 22 (May 28, 2001).

Lourie, Richard. "Stages of Her Life." *Washington Post* (March 5, 2000).

Luhrman, Henry. "A Bored Susan Sontag: 'I Think Camp Should Be Retired.' " *Columbia Owl* (March 23, 1966).

Mackenzie, Suzie. "Finding Fact from Fiction." *The Guardian* (London) (May 27, 2000): 31.

Mantel, Hilary. "Not Either/Or But Both/And." *Los Angeles Times Book Review* (October 7, 2001).

Marwick, Arthur. *The Sixties: Cultural Revolution in Britain, France, Italy, and the United States, c. 1958–c. 1974.* Oxford: Oxford University Press, 1998.

Mazzocco, Robert. "Swingtime." *New York Review of Books* (June 9, 1966).

McLemee, Scott. "The Mind as Passion." *American Prospect* 16, no. 2 (February 2005).

———. "Understanding War Through Photos." *Newsday* (March 30, 2003).

Meehan, Thomas. "Not Good Taste, Not Bad Taste—It's 'Camp.' " *New York Times Magazine* (March 21, 1965): 30–31, 113–15.

Michelson, Annette. Interview with the author on January 15, 2007.

Miller, Laura. "National Book Award Winner Announced." *Salon.com* (November 16, 2000).

Mitgang, Herbert. "Publishing the Eclectic Susan Sontag." *New York Times* (October 10, 1980).

———. "Victory in the Ashes of Vietnam?" *New York Times* (February 4, 1969).

Mosle, Sara. "Magnificent Obsessions—Talking with Susan Sontag." *Newsday* (August 30, 1992).

Müller, Lothar. "An den Abgründen der Oberfläche" [At the Depths of the Surface]. *Süddeutsche Zeitung* (December 30, 2004).

Nagel, Ivan. "Nur wer sich wandelt, ist vollkommen: Krieg und Frieden im Jahr 2003" [Only the Person Who Changes Is Perfect: War and Peace in the Year 2003]. *Frankfurter Allgemeine Zeitung* (October 14, 2003).

Navasky, Victor. "Notes on Cult: or, How to Join the Intellectual Establishment." *New York Times Magazine* (March 27, 1966): 128.

Nunez, Sigrid. Interview with the author on March 21, 2007.

———. "Sontag Laughs." *Salmagundi* 152 (Fall 2006): 11–21.

Ostwald, Susanne. "Besonnenheit und schrille Töne" [Prudence and Shrill Tones]. *Neue Zürcher Zeitung* (September 17, 2001).

Perron, Wendy. "Susan Sontag on Writing, Art, Feminism, Life and Death." *SoHo Weekly News* (December 1, 1977): 23–24, 45.

Pinckney, Darryl. Interview with the author on April 14, 2007.

Poague, Leland, ed. *Conversations with Susan Sontag.* Jackson: University Press of Mississippi, 1995.

Podhoretz, Norman. *Making It.* New York: Random House, 1968.

Pomfret, John. "'Godot' amid the Gunfire." *Washington Post* (August 19, 1993): C1, C6.

Poore, Charles. "Against Joan of Arc of the Cocktail Party." *New York Times* (April 28, 1966).

Rich, Frank. "Stage—Milan Kundera's 'Jacques and His Master.'" *New York Times* (January 24, 1985): C19.

Richler, Noah. "The Listener: Reflections on Darkness." *The Independent* (November 21, 1999).

Rieff, David. Foreword to *At the Same Time: Essays and Speeches*, by Susan Sontag, edited by Paolo Dilonardo and Anne Jump, xi–xvii. New York: Farrar, Straus and Giroux, 2007.

———. *Going to Miami: Exiles, Tourists, and Refugees in the New America.* Boston: Little, Brown, 1987.

———. "Illness as More Than Metaphor." In *The Best American Essays 2006*, edited by Lauren Slater, 159–71. Boston: Houghton Mifflin, 2006.

———. Interview with the author on May 29, 2006.

Ritter, Henning. "Sie kam, sah und schrieb . . . Zum Tode von Susan Sontag" [She Came, Saw, and Wrote . . . On the Death of Susan Sontag]. *Frankfurter Allgemeine Zeitung* (December 20, 2004).

Rollyson, Carl, and Lisa Paddock. *Susan Sontag: The Making of an Icon.* New York: Norton, 2000.

Romano, Carlin. "Desperately Seeking Sontag." *FAME Magazine* (April 1989).

Rorem, Ned. Interview with the author on December 7, 2006.

Rosenbaum, Jonathan. "Goodbye, Susan, Goodbye: Sontag and Movies." *Synoptique* 7 (February 14, 2005), http://www.synoptique.ca/core/en/articles/rosenbaum/.

Rosenberger, Jack. "Susan Sontag." *Splash Magazine* (April 1989).

Rowes, Barbara. "Bio—Susan Sontag." *People Magazine* (March 20, 1978): 74–76, 79–80.

Ruas, Charles. "Susan Sontag Found Crisis of Cancer Added a Fierce Intensity to Life." *New York Times* (January 30, 1978).

———. "Susan Sontag: Past, Present and Future." *New York Times* (October 24, 1982).

Rutten, Tim, and Lynn Smith. "When the Ayes Have It, Is There Room for Naysayers?" *Los Angeles Times* (Southern California Living section) (September 28, 2001).

Schaper, Rüdiger. "Schwestern von gestern, Brüder von morgen" [Yesterday's Sisters, Tomorrow's Brothers]. *Süddeutsche Zeitung* (September 17, 1993).

Schröder, Christoph. "Ein ganz gewöhnlicher Sontag-Vormittag" [An Ordinary Sontag Morning]. *Frankfurter Rundschau* (October 13, 2003).

Schultz, Victoria. "Susan Sontag on Film." *Changes* (May 1, 1972): 3–5.

Sennett, Richard. Interview with the author on March 22, 2007.

Seroy, Jeff. Interview with the author on March 21, 2007.

Simon, John. "One Singular Sensation." *New York* magazine (November 20, 2000).

Span, Paula. "Susan Sontag: Hot at Last." *Washington Post* (September 17, 1992): C1–2.

Spiegel, Hubert. "Europas Kind: Susan Sontag's Dankesrede in der Paulskirche" [Europe's Child: Susan Sontag's Acceptance Speech in St. Paul's Church]. *Frankfurter Allgemeine Zeitung* (October 13, 2003).

Stadelmaier, Gerhard. "Schlafschmock: Bühne und Bett—Bob Wilson inszeniert Susan Sontag" [Hack in a Nightgown: Stage and Bed—Bob Wilson Stages Susan Sontag]. *Frankfurter Allgemeine Zeitung* (September 17, 1993).

Stein, Elliott. Interview with the author on December 7, 2006.

Stern, Daniel. "Life Becomes a Dream." *New York Times Book Review* (September 8, 1963).

Talbot, David. "The 'Traitor' Fires Back." *Salon.com* (October 16, 2001).

Trilling, Diana. "Susan Sontag's God That Failed." *SoHo Weekly News* (February 24, 1982).

Vulliamy, Ed. "This Time It's Not Personal." *The Observer* (May 20, 2000).

Wasserman, Steve. Interview with the author on March 6, 2007.

Weeks, Linton. "Susan Sontag Wins National Book Award for Fiction." *Washington Post* (November 16, 2000).

Weinberger, Eliot. "Notes on Susan." *New York Review of Books* (August 16, 2007).

White, Edmund. Interview with the author on February 27, 2007.

Willms, Johannes. "Die weltberühmte Dreiecksgeschichte" [The World-Famous Love Triangle]. *Süddeutsche Zeitung* (March 31, 1993).

Wilson, Robert. Conversation with the author on April 7, 2007.

Wylie, Andrew. Interview with the author on March 20, 2007.

Younge, Gary. "Susan Sontag, the Risk Taker." *The Guardian* (January 19, 2002): 6.

Zagajewski, Adam, John McPhee, and Robert McCrum. "Writers Pay Tribute to Roger W. Straus Jr." *Los Angeles Times Book Review* (June 6, 2004).

Daniel Schreiber is a Berlin-based writer. An art and literary critic, he contributes to numerous German and Swiss magazines and newspapers, including *Die Zeit, DU— das Kulturmagazin, Philosophie Magazin, Literaturen,* and *Weltkunst,* as well as the radio station *Deutschlandradio Kultur.* He is a columnist for the daily *taz—Die Tageszeitung,* and his essays on art and culture appear in a number of anthologies. He was previously contributing editor to *Monopol* and headed the culture section of the magazine *Cicero.*

David Dollenmayer is emeritus professor of German at Worcester Polytechnic Institute and is the winner of the 2008 Helen and Kurt Wolff Prize for his translation of Moses Rosenkranz's *Childhood: An Autobiographical Fragment.*